Advance Praise

'Are Indian companies and start-ups missing something important by ignoring local language viewers and users of digital content? Are women entrepreneurs too shy of boasting about their achievements? What kind of eco-system will make the life of start-ups in digital age smoother and more meaningful are some of the questions this books addresses, rather well. Those who wish to enter and shake up the inertia in digital markets may find this book useful. But those who wish to support them may find it even more useful.'

Prof Anil K. Gupta
Professor at IIM Ahmedabad and founder of Honey Bee Network

'The Internet has transformed business and society. Today to very many of us, life without the web is unimaginable. In business a new breed of entrepreneurs have sprung up whose whole life is the web, creating new business models, reaching new markets and becoming the new normal. These stories are inspiring examples of such successes!'

T.V. Mohandas Pai
Chairman, Aarin Capital Partners

'Nobody knows what the world of business will look like in 20 years' time. But the digital entrepreneurs of today are the ones who will create it.'

Paul Sloane
Author and public speaker

'Anuradha Goyal's *The Mouse Charmers* is a fascinating account of India's trailblazing digital entrepreneurs, innovators who are taking technology and applying it to meet the unique needs of Indian customers across traditional sectors like jewellery, grocery, travel, matchmaking, real estate, eating out and books as well as new sectors such as online images, blogs, games, talk shows and peer to peer finance. Well researched and with deep insights into how these businesses work, *The Mouse Charmers* will inspire others to both study Indian entrepreneurs like Goyal has done or take up the challenge of entrepreneurship like those she writes about have done. Either way this is an important, timely and inspiring book that showcases the opportunities that India offers and the challenges that have to be overcome along the way.'

Jaideep Prabhu
Professor at Judge Business School, University of Cambridge and co-author of the bestselling *Jugaad Innovation*

THE MOUSE CHARMERS

DIGITAL PIONEERS OF INDIA

ANURADHA GOYAL

PORTFOLIO
PENGUIN

An imprint of Penguin Random House

PORTFOLIO

USA | Canada | UK | Ireland | Australia
New Zealand | India | South Africa | China | Singapore

Portfolio is part of the Penguin Random House group of companies
whose addresses can be found at global.penguinrandomhouse.com

Published by Penguin Random House India Pvt. Ltd
4th Floor, Capital Tower 1, MG Road,
Gurugram 122 002, Haryana, India

Penguin
Random House
India

Published by Random House India in 2014
Second impression in 2014
This edition published in Portfolio by Penguin Random House 2020

10 9 8 7 6 5 4 3 2

ISBN 9788184004922

Typeset in Electra LT Std by R. Ajith Kumar

Printed at Repro India Limited

www.penguin.co.in

To my Dadi—Smt. Leelawati Agarwal,
who passed on a bit of her curiosity to me

CONTENTS

FOREWORD

Entrepreneurship is increasingly emerging as an exciting new career choice for many young people across the globe. Inspirational names such as Bill Gates, Richard Branson, and Eric Schmidt have encouraged many young students to chase their dreams and start business ventures of their own—not only with the aim of commercial success, but for a unique and creatively fulfilling experience. In India, especially, entrepreneurship and the job creation it entails is the key to a prosperous future to ensure the right opportunities for our demographic dividend. The advent of Internet has escalated this to an entirely new level, with unforeseen opportunities in the digital space. With Web 2.0, the ever-increasing user base of the Internet has transformed traditional services like groceries and medicines through the click of a button.

Digital entrepreneurs are mushrooming at an astonishing speed in India. They are venturing into hitherto uncharted territory like jewellery and groceries—one a high-value product and the other highly perishable. These digital startups are permeating into every recess of the economy and are challenging the very idea of a physical store. Mentorship and financial support as well as the ecosystem in cities such as Bangalore are giving further fillip to this emerging wave.

In *The Mouse Charmers*, Anuradha profiles the stories of 12 such companies, categorized as: commerce, content entrepreneurs, and connectors. Each company is a pioneer in its field. The author studies the business model, innovation, differentiating factors, and the journey so far of these digital businesses. The companies range from *MakeMyTrip*, *Zomato* to *BigBasket* and *Rang De*. The book aims to showcase a spectrum of businesses across verticals and categories, and present insights into potential new opportunities.

As the Internet is still such a recent phenomenon, all the entrepreneurs profiled are first generation. The book is an excellent guide for aspiring entrepreneurs looking to start their very own digital company with extremely helpful suggestions and pointers. It discusses what has worked and not worked for these entrepreneurs and how they have managed to overcome challenges and seized opportunities that have come their way. The book also focusses on the burgeoning online business, and finding the key differentiator to set one's business apart from these multitude platforms.

I do wish that this book inspires many more young entrepreneurs to take the plunge into the world of digital startups. The rest as they say is a click of a button away!

Sam Pitroda
Advisor to the Prime Minister of India on Public
Information, Infrastructure, and Innovation;
Chairman, National Innovation Council

INTRODUCTION

IN THE HISTORY OF mankind there have been few times when the ways of the world have transitioned in an irreversible way. Some of the earlier transitions happened when man discovered agriculture that led to permanent settlements, when wheel was discovered that enabled long journeys, when printing press was discovered and education and learning changed forever, and of course the industrial revolution that made mass production a norm and customization a luxury. In our generation, the advent of Internet has brought in a similar transition. It has irreversibly changed the way we do many things. My generation—born in 1970s and grown up in 1980s—never thought that that of our life would be very different from that of our parents. We started working sometime in 1990s, a lot of us in professions that did not exist while we were in school, and by the turn of the millennium, we were not only using cutting-edge technology products but also contributing to creating them for the rest of the world. What is more relevant is the quantum of change we saw from having countable number of phones in the neighbourhood to juggling multiple communication devices in our bags, from running to libraries in search of answers to carrying multiple library sources on our gadgets, and from having limited career options to celebrating entrepreneurship. As a nation, our image in the world changed from that of Snake Charmers to Mouse Charmers.

Mouse Charmers are a new breed of entrepreneurs in emerging India powered by Internet and the opportunities that it offers to create new markets and to cater to old markets in a new way. Some of them have already achieved success where they can be called iconic and inspiring while others have powerful ideas that put them on the same path. Looking at the spectrum of entrepreneurs I got to study and interact with during the writing of this book, it may not be wrong to say that these entrepreneurs are on their way to create a complete parallel economy, offering us solutions literally at our fingertips. Today, most of what we can go out and buy in the market is available online and can be brought from the comfort of our Internet-enabled devices—everyday groceries, jewellery, entertainment, alternate education, and various services that we consume. If there is anything that we cannot buy as yet, rest assured, someone out there is working on getting it on our online shopping kart. This book is my journey to explore how some of the pioneers in various categories and verticals of digital enterprises have created new markets and irreversibly changed the way we shop, connect, and create.

Personally, I have been an early adaptor of technology, but I still get jittery when I have to use my credit card on a website for the first time. I was sceptical of certain categories making it to the online medium but to my surprise, or should

I say delight, they are not only being accepted by the users but also being explored to their fullest potential by innovative digital entrepreneurs. For example, I never thought people would buy garments or shoes online. They may browse to see what is available but they would want to try them on before making the purchase. After all a shoe must fit properly and a garment must accentuate your natural shape, both of which are not standard. However, fashion retailers came up with the 'try before you buy' offer for their online buyers. Till few year back, gold was always bought from trusted family jewellers. But companies like Tanishq broke that notion and organized this highly fragmented market. After that, online retailers took it to the next level with money back guarantees and options to customize the selections. And, this may just be the beginning.

Arenas of Mouse Charmers

Internet-based businesses have existed in the west for some time now. A lot of Indian entrepreneurs started by picking up established business models from there and then went ahead and customized them for local needs. E-tailing would fall in this category where the base model was picked up from other markets and features were built in to cater to the local market. Then there are concepts that are quintessentially Indian and our entrepreneurs have ported them online and broadened the horizons for their users beyond what they could have ever imagined. For example, we have a tuition culture in India that is supposed to complement and supplement our school education. It provides support to students with varying grasping powers. Till recently, a teacher always meant a neighbour or a coaching centre next door. Online ventures like TutorVista connect students and teachers globally and besides helping students, these companies leverage the latent talent present in many Indian homes like highly educated housewives who are unable to take up full-time jobs for multiple reasons.

While shopping and education existed in the world even before the arrival of Internet, global communities of people sharing common interests and passions have flourished online. These special interest groups create their own little world in their communities. Their earliest genesis may lie in Yahoo Groups—which are still popular and in use by early communities. Then came networking portals like Ryze. It was meant to be a business network but managed to create offline communities in cities of the people who first met online. This gave way to Orkut, Facebook, LinkedIn, Twitter and others in due course of time. Most of these are generic communities of family, friends, colleagues, and followers. Then, there are small niche communities that may choose any of the platforms or tools available to interact, communicate, and co-ordinate, but their main objective is to connect for a common purpose like bird photography or supporting a cause. Who would have thought we would interact with our neighbours through electronic devices; but it is all happening just like we could not have foreseen that we'd be able to instantly share pictures with friends across the globe one day or instantly find required talent available on freelancing platforms for our workplace.

Google has changed the way we use our memory. We no

longer need to remember any kind of data. Google or for that matter any other search engine is limited to providing generic information that we seek. To get specific searches, for say looking for a house to buy or rent in a particular locality within a certain budget, we need portals that are repository of moving inventories of what we are looking for. Let's call them niche searches and this is another space that the Internet took to another level and helped us look at options far and wide. In their offline avatar they used to be called classifieds. Take the case of matrimonial searches, where you search for a potential life partner based on different criteria. There is need for privacy and security while engaging with people you meet through search results. An ecosystem needs to be developed to make people comfortable being a part of the database and making them communicate in limited privacy.

Till the advent of free for all Internet, creative professions were limited to those who could find space in the limited pages of newspapers, magazines, books or in the time bound slots of radio and television. Cinema was freer but then the number of screens to show still limited it. Internet brought in unlimited space for creative people who could now have their own weblog or a website that is a personal version of a newspaper or a magazine or an album or even a book. As digital entrepreneurs kept giving us tools, we started creating or creatively expressing ourselves through written word, images, videos, games and a combination of all this. In the process, we created a generation of digital entrepreneurs who create new content.

Making Sense of Digital Space

When I started researching for this book, I had a long list of about 50 odd companies that I looked at and as I kept researching, this list grew to more than 100 companies across various categories and in various domains and verticals. I tried to synthesize the information into various categories to understand the various categories that exist in the digital space. There are multiple ways to categorize companies. You can divide them by verticals they serve, by size based on revenues or employees, on business models they use like B2B (Business to Business), B2C (Business to Consumer), C2C (Consumer to Consumer), or on the basis of their offline predecessors. All these categorizations have their own merits and serve their own purpose. I chose to classify them into three categories based on the similarities in the way they operate as digital businesses:

- Commerce
- Content
- Connectors

Through these categories I have attempted to highlight the various business segments that are emerging in the digital space. As a corollary, we get to see potential gaps and white spaces that the next generation of entrepreneurs can explore. Each of these categories has different characteristics in terms of capital requirement, technology focus, revenue models, and ways to reach the market. They have their own challenges which the aspiring entrepreneurs must be aware of. They are also creating new types of jobs and careers within categories.

For example, logistics which is emerging as a major ancillary industry for e-commerce companies along with agencies that provide services like payment processing or cash collection. There are generic career options that are being created across categories like Social Media Management, which is becoming a field in itself, or designers who are needed by all kinds of digital companies.

Businesses featured in this book have been structured roughly on few parameters like the business model they use, technology focus they have, how they engage their customers, how they create or convert markets, the challenges they face and the innovations they adopt. Of course, each story takes its own flow.

Business Model

All the three categories—Commerce, Content, and Connectors—have different business models. E-commerce space is primarily driven by the transactions that happen on the website. Like offline traders and retailers, these companies procure products at a price and sell them at a higher price with the differential being their profit. Building a supplier base, logistics for order fulfilment, secure transactions, and payment processing are the key operational components of an e-commerce venture. Of course each vertical within it brings its own nuanced challenges to deal with. The advertising-based revenue model dominates the content space, just like it does in the print and electronic media. The game depends on how many visitors consume your content and how much of your content is shared by them across their networks, in other words—what is the traffic to your site. Traffic in turn dictates how attractive your site is for other businesses to advertise. Some B2B ventures in content space drive value by selling their content to other businesses that in turn still use the content for advertising most of the times. Connector space is interesting as it encompasses niche searches, directory services, classified, and communities all of which exist for the purpose of connecting two unknown people who are looking for each other for some purpose. Through advanced search tools and matching algorithms, these businesses make the choices wider and search easy for the users. The revenue model here is a mix of subscription and advertising. For these portals, advertising goes beyond advertising networks and moves into a space where complimenting businesses pay for access to their users or want to run campaigns on their networks.

Technology

Technology platforms are the equivalents of brick and mortar in the physical world. How your portal looks, how inviting it is for customers online, how well it interacts with them, how well it protects them from potential malicious activities, and how easy it is for them to navigate and get what they want to making them wish to come back—everything depends on the technology architecture and design. Entrepreneurs usually do not talk much about these technological advances because the customer need not know what goes on behind the scene. I found that the simpler the portal, the more sophisticated and robust the technology has to be at the back-end. So, as we explore the entrepreneurs' journeys we will also look at how they play with the technology.

We intuitively understand that a technology platform is required to host the website and run an e-commerce engine. We also understand the robustness expected from these technology platforms as they operate 24X7. Now, what is not obvious is that more often than not, successful digital entrepreneurs are technology innovators as well. They build a unique back-end that is the key to their front-end success. Despite so many off the shelf solutions available, most of them have custom build their technology platforms. Let us take the example of redBus—while the customer would assume that all the software does is display options and allow you to buy a bus ticket, a lot goes on behind the scenes. A look at their back-end operations show that they have a custom-built software application for the small bus operators, using which the operators upload the inventory and get connected with the redBus system. The licensing of this software is an independent source of income for them that also enables the variety of options on the front-end platform.

Technology is a very democratic tool. Core technology is equally available to everyone. Open source technologies are available at near-zero cost. Successful technology-based companies differentiate themselves by making intelligent use of technology for their own and their customer's advantage. This reminds me of a doha by 16th-century poet Rahim where he says:

Lohe ki na lohar ki, Rahiman kahe vichar
Jo hani maare sees pe, taahi ki talwar

A sword does not belong to either the iron that it is made of or the ironsmith who makes it, but to the warrior who uses it to hack off the enemy's head.

Almost all the businesses studied here have in-house technology teams that work on building the core engine, the new layers around the core system, and maintain it to support operations. Since a lot of these companies do not have established models to follow, they experiment with features and, based on the response, either build upon them or let them go. Companies like Flipkart have evolved their technologies in a way that they can experiment new features with a small set of users by having the multiple live versions of the portal. This helps them test the technology both technically and in terms of its customer response. Digital companies need to keep pace with the velocity of change in technology along with the emerging channels to reach out to customers. For example with the adoption of data services on mobile, it is fast emerging as a preferred interface to access Internet. All the companies have to respond to this by catering to the specific needs of the small screen and make available key features of their portals on mobile.

Most companies started with technology as a base and always had it in-house. A few companies like MakeMyTrip and CaratLane experimented with outsourcing its technology to begin with, but eventually had to bring the controls in-house. Technology is the key pillar of any digital company, a key differentiator which needs both internal control and high level of agility. Today, the architecture, design, and operation of technology are tightly held in-house in all the companies, though small parts of application development are outsourced as and when required.

Engaging Customers

Anyone who has access to Internet is a potential customer for digital companies. The interesting bit is that there is only one place for all the competing businesses to reach out to the customers—their computer or laptop screens. We can add mobile screens to this, but primarily it's a screen that you look at—typically a space of about 14 inches or so. To be on your screen is what everyone is vying for. Even when the online businesses are engaging the mainstream media and traditional media spaces for promoting themselves, they are essentially luring the customers to see them on that small screen.

The attention span of online users is extremely short with multiple things vying for their attention simultaneously and one can switch to another site with a click of a button. So the biggest challenge of web portals is to be inviting enough and then be able to engage the attention till customers have made a purchase or at least registered on their website as a user. The portal needs to be extremely user-friendly, easy-to-use, interactive, educative, and intuitive at the same time. Design plays a big role in making the customer experience enriching. Driving traffic thus becomes a key function for all kinds of digital businesses. In this book, we will explore the different approaches these companies adopt for reaching out to their users and customers.

Interaction between the enterprise and consumers is, almost always, routed through a machine. We will try to explore how these companies are impacting the way Indians are changing their buying habits and how they are making better informed choices compared to offline buying. We will see how they are engaging through special interest groups, how they are coming together as communities for a common purpose, and how the networks are becoming a sum total of all the people one can ever know.

Challenges and Innovations

Some of the challenges faced by digital companies are common like the limited Internet penetration in the country, even more limited credit card penetration, and the limiting broadband speed. Some challenges are specific to categories like logistics for e-tailing companies, piracy for content companies, and better matchmaking for connectors. We will look at these challenges and the solutions that these entrepreneurs have discovered or invented to meet these challenges or work around them. In every company that I studied, there were key innovations that changed the game for the business. Sometimes it is a small feature that builds customer confidence, but what is not very obvious is that it is based on deep customer insights that companies get from the customer behaviour that they observe with every click on their portals.

THE ENVIRONMENTAL FACTOR

Businesses cannot exist in isolation. They impact the environment that they inhabit. The nature of online businesses has altered the way products reach customers. Instead of buyers going to a retail outlet, now the product has to reach the customer where he is—usually at his home or his workplace. This requires logistics or supply chains to work differently for this scenario compared to when a customer walks to a store and picks the products. Recently a leading logistics company announced a separate line of operations for online businesses. Similarly other support businesses have cropped up to offer services to digital companies like payment processors, cash collectors, security services, and industry associations. For content-based businesses, individual contributors become a source of content. For communities based companies, the number of users are their strength and power, and while businesses impact how their members interact with each other, the users demand and hence define the next versions of the product.

Competition for online ventures comes from both the other similar online ventures as well as the offline ventures that offer similar products and services. In fact, the first generation entrepreneurs chronicled in this book had the tough task of first converting offline customers into online customers by giving them impeccable service and building customer confidence in online shopping. As much as they focussed on building their brand and customer base, they had to focus on converting a traditional customer into a digital customer. Social media platforms are the places where potential customers are roaming and networking, and it is automatically assumed that this is where they are influencing and getting influenced. We would explore how social media is being used by different businesses and how much it actually impacts a category of business.

An Internet business is something that you can run from anywhere; all you need is a reliable Internet connection. It's apparent that doing business from bigger cities is far costlier than doing it from smaller cities, then why are most digital businesses concentrated in bigger cities like Bangalore, Delhi, and Mumbai? Ram NK of Rang De, based at Bangalore, feels that it is the ecosystem of mentors, advisors, talent, and informal meetups that makes Bangalore a very viable option for startups, especially technology-based ones. He is essentially saying that the collective intellectual capital of the city is available to a new entrepreneur to provide the required support system that an infant organization needs. This leads into insights of what other cities need to do to encourage digital entreprenueurs in their cities. In my endeavour to find digital entrepreneurs in smaller cities, I came upon some examples like Edewcate in Vishakhapatnam that is mentioned in the content section and iTokri in Gwalior that is a niche e-commerce portal.

Picking Needles from the Hay Stack

As I set out for a structured study of digital entrepreneurs in India, I realized that it is nearly impossible to put a structure to something that is so vast and dynamic. The Sanskrit word *anant* can sufficiently describe the limitless world of Internet and the accompanying world of entrepreneurs. New businesses are sprouting up all the time and becoming popular in no time; old ones change guards or add new features that make them look different. The variety ranges from solopreneurs to full-fledged organizations, from just giving you information to taking all your information, but all of them give you something that would not have been possible without the wired world. I have not looked at pure play technology companies that are a whole world in themselves. I have focussed on the enterprises that use technology as their key tool to run their businesses. Most of these companies are established names in India and even a casual reader would have heard or read about them somewhere. Incidentally when you search for these companies online, more often than not you find out the rounds of venture funds they have received. I wanted to explore what makes these organizations attractive for the venture funds. What are they doing right that VCs are investing in these ventures that are not always backed by a marquee name—personally or as part of a business house.

I used some basic criterion to choose the companies featured in this book:

- Only Indian companies were considered.
- Only first generation startups were considered.
- Online ventures of existing companies or brands were not considered as they are extensions of their existing businesses rather than fresh businesses and honestly none of them have really cracked the digital code.

- Pure technology companies or B2B companies were not considered, as I was looking at the impact of direct customer interactions.
- An attempt was made to choose companies that cover the major domains where online ventures have made an impact while also covering the categories of businesses.
- An attempt was made to look at companies from across India but it met with little success here as most companies tended to be huddled in few hubs.

My knowledge and reach limit the small part of a big universe covered in this book. There must be many more stories that deserved a mention here but have been missed because I never heard of them or because they operated in their own small niches. Some were axed due to space constraint, but I have tried to at least mention them so that curious readers can explore it themselves.

So go ahead and dive into the fascinating world of the digital pioneers of India.

PART 1

COMMERCE

E-COMMERCE

Commerce a Click Away

AT THE TURN OF the millennium, e-commerce was a buzzword. Everyone wanted a piece of the pie, but there were no customers online. A decade later it is a reality—and by the looks of it, a reality that is here to stay and grow. E-commerce or electronic commerce is nothing but buying and selling of products over electronic networks enabled by computers and the Internet. It began with users buying airline and railway tickets online but has extended to include almost everything that we consume—both products and services. Today, you can buy anything online—from custom-made solitaire rings to everyday groceries to movie tickets and everything in between. With every new Internet connection, the horizon for e-commerce widens. Given the Internet penetration that we are yet to get in the country, the future certainly looks bright for e-commerce companies. Even today when Internet penetration, that is the availability of Internet to

Components of Digital Commerce Markets, 2012
(₹ 47,395 Crores)

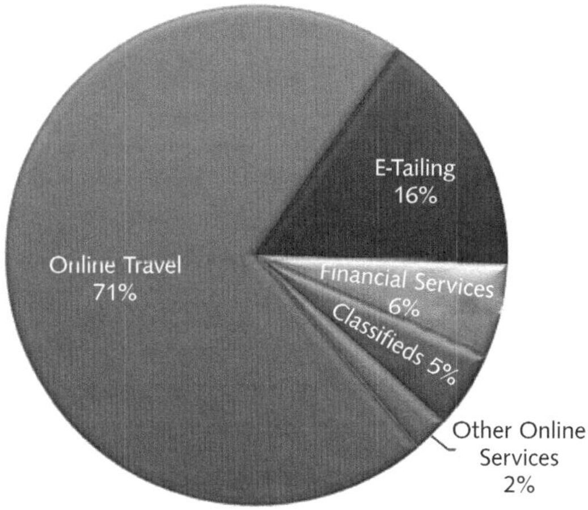

Most Popular categories: Online Travel, Apparels and Footwear, Books, and Mobile Phones and Mobile Accessories

Fig 1: E-Commerce Landscape

the percentage of population, stands at less than 15 percent, the absolute numbers are still very large and present a huge market in themselves. An encouraging trend is that lot of online users seeking information about products are now converting into buyers.

E-commerce or online commerce makes the biggest direct impact on our lives as it alters the way we have been making purchases right from our daily groceries to luxury items. E-commerce companies, especially e-tailers or online retailers, are biggest players in terms of numbers of products that they sell and the number of customers they have. They also touch our lives on a day-to-day basis as we tend to go back for other needs once we have began purchasing online. Travel gets the lion's share of online business with a major chunk of air, train, and bus tickets being sold online along with hotels and holiday packages. These services are easy to sell online as there is no physical delivery involved and physical tickets have smoothly given way to e-tickets. This is also a segment in which many dominant Indian players exist indicating the maturity this vertical has gained over a period of time. Next come the financial products like various types of insurance that we can buy online primarily from the online platform of banks and insurance companies. Retail products including books, electronic and electrical gadgets, white goods, garments, and groceries form the third strong segment of online commerce. Geographically, south India is leading the e-commerce movement and this is evident from the fact that even the smallest businesses in and around the three anchor cities of south India—Bangalore, Chennai, and Hyderabad—has a web presence. In fact, a lot of e-ventures are based out of Bangalore.

Interest from various venture capital firms and private equity firms in e-commerce is another indication of the potential it holds in terms of sheer business opportunity. In the last couple of years, we have seen major investments by investment funds in e-commerce companies. However, we will not focus on the investment part of the businesses in this book; we will rather look at the business models, opportunities, challenges, and the impact these companies have had so far.

At this point in time, many e-commerce companies are floating across various categories—general as well as niche. Eventually there will be consolidation and we would see some mature players in horizontal portals and few defined verticals. Niche players will keep catering to their intended audience and this would include boutique offerings. We have already started witnessing some consolidation as the mature players acquire smaller players to add categories of products or a segment of customers to their portfolio. For example, Flipkart acquired LetsBuy, a company that sold consumer electronic goods online and added it as a category on their portal. This should accelerate in future as big players further strengthen their position and establish themselves as clear leaders. At the same time, startups will keep emerging to give competition to the existing players like in any other industry. Though the e-commerce market is still in its early days in India as compared to developed markets

Table 1: Digital-commerce market size from 2009 to 2013
(Figures in crores. Percentages indicate share of the overall market size)

Year	Dec 2009	Dec 2010	Dec 2011	Dec 2012	Dec 2013 (estimated)
Total Market Size	19,249	26,263	35,142	47,349	62,967
Online Travel Industry	14,953 (78%)	20,440 (78%)	26,572 (76%)	34,544 (73%)	44,907 (71%)
Online Non-travel Industry	4,296 (22%)	5,823 (22%)	8,570 (24%)	12,805 (27%)	18,060 (29%)
• E-tailing	1,550	2,372	3,842	6,454	10,004
• Financial Services	1,540	1,848	2,255	2,886	3,607
• Classifieds	775	1,085	1,682	2,354	3,061
• Other Online Services	431	518	792	1,110	1,388

in the west, nonetheless quite a few players have established their roots well in the system in last 3–4 years and can now scale and flourish with ease. Vipul Parekh of BigBasket gives a score of 2 out of 10 to Indian e-commerce at the moment, where he himself expects to be a leading player.

In June 2013, India had 190 million Internet users of which 130 million were urban users and 60 million were rural. By October 2013, the number of Internet users had reached 205 million and was expected to be around 213 million by end of 2013. There were about 91 million users accessing Internet via mobile of which 70 million were urban users. Any user who uses Internet at least once a month is classified as active user and about 85% of Internet users in India are active. More than 50% users access Internet at least once a day. Growth in Internet users is coming from smaller towns and college going students form the largest set of Internet users.*

* IAMAI Report—Internet in India 2013

BRIDGING RURAL URBAN DIVIDE

E-commerce is fast emerging as a strong channel for brands to reach the semi-urban, rural and remote locations where it may not be feasible or commercially viable to have a physical presence. As of now, more than 50 percent e-commerce transactions happen in non-metro cities both for products and services. This segment is bound to grow faster as people in these cities attain access to products and services that were not so easily accessible to them so far. In a way, e-commerce is acting as a great leveller for consumers across geographies by giving them access to similar facilities. Companies, however, need to do more to cater to these non-metro customers by making their content available in multiple local languages and enabling their logistics capabilities to include the remotest corners of the country. In fact logistics players like DTDC have launched their specialized line of e-businesses that help them reach out to the nooks and corners of the country without the need to establish their own logistics arm. Most large players have setup their own logistics arms, and the smaller players need support of a pure play logistics company to reach out to its wide customer base. We will look at this in detail in the Ecosystem section.

Trends that Favour e-commerce

Internet penetration on rise.
Mobile data services usage on rise.
Young population with disposable income.
Acceptability of e-commerce as an alternative to traditional shopping.
High-value transactions on rise.
Multiple payments options including Cash on Delivery.
Return policies/ free home delivery.
Limited offline presence in rural/ semi-urban areas.

Lauching e-commerce in India

First generation e-commerce players have established their business models through trial and error. Though the base business models were well-established in the western markets, they needed serious localizations for the Indian markets. The first task they had on hand was to dispel customer doubts about shopping from a store that is only on their screen, and then work on selling them the value proposition that they offer as a company. They had to inspire confidence that the products they order will be delivered at the right time and in the right condition. They had to make sure that the prices were competitive with respect to their real world counterparts. For some categories, this barrier has been crossed and customers do not think before buying online. Pioneers in the new verticals, say jewellery e-tailers, continue to work as much on converting a non-online customer into an online customer as they work on selling the products from their inventory. Once these players set the ground, the second-generation entrepreneurs will just have to build on top of it. So, most of the players mentioned in this section are not only building their businesses but also creating a foundation for the industry, moving the markets from physical stores to the computer screens, and then further on to mobile stores.

From a customer's perspective, the three things that determine the success of an online e-commerce portal are: range or variety of products offered, convenience of buying online, and price. Wide variety is a direct advantage online stores have over brick and mortar stores as there is no limit to the available physical space. Online storess can virtually have unlimited range of products on offer especially when they are in marketplace model that allows multiple sellers to sell their products on their portal like eBay. Convenience is a relative concept. It can be interpreted in terms of the ease of finding the product a customer is looking for, speed with which she can have it, or all the questions she can get answered about the product before buying it. It obviously includes the convenience of buying from the comfort of your home or office without having to move across the city traffic. As users get comfortable with online shopping and as portals keep tuning their systems to make it as comfortable as possible for its customers, this factor will keep tilting in favour of online shopping. Online stores can usually offer prices lower than offline counterparts because of the economies of scale and the lack of cost required for physical infrastructure at multiple and premium locations. This advantage offsets to an extent the additional logistics cost for delivering the orders. Logistics cost very high for rural and semi-urban areas compared to the cost of delivering in big cities. Given the fact that online companies have to provide same service levels to both their urban and non-urban customers, one segment may be offsetting the cost of other. How this cost element will play in the future will depend upon the mix of order source and how logistics industry gears up to capture the new territories.

Cash on Delivery (CoD) is an innovative offering that Indian e-commerce companies have not only pioneered but also mastered to an extent. It has provided the biggest boost to Indian e-commerce as various reports put the percentage of CoD business done by e-commerce companies anywhere between 50–80 percent. It allows two sets of customers to transact online—those who are sceptical of using their credit cards online and those who do not have access to credit cards or net banking and still want to buy online. It is possible that CoD has moved some credit or debit cardholders also to use CoD as customers feel safer paying after the product is in their hands. In CoD transactions, customers do not get the benefit of credit that credit cards offer but merchants save on the transaction fee that banks charge for credit card usage. Not many players are putting a minimum order value for free shipping at the moment, but as they go on, they will have to do it and we can see that happening in some of the companies discussed in this section. This ensures that per order value is high enough for the company to bear the logistics cost or the customer pays for it. Payment Gateways enable electronic payments for the digital portals. So far, credit card frauds on e-commerce sites have been few and far between, but you can never rule them out given the increasing security threats online. Bigger challenge for payment gateways is the high transaction failure rates that lead to customer dissatisfaction and needs additional processes to clear these held up transactions. We will look at this in detail in the Ecosystem chapter.

The Untapped Potential

Of the Internet user base only 1 percent or just about 10 million users are engaged in e-commerce indicating the magnitude of untapped opportunity both as Internet penetration increases and as e-commerce companies become more commonplace, trusted, and mature. Add to it 300 million data services users on mobile that is growing faster. Mobile will become a major consumer of e-commerce on the go. Indian e-commerce is expected to grow at CSGR of 40 percent between 2010–20, fastest in the Asia Pacific region.

Number of people accessing the Internet to get information are gradually converting into buyers. In 2012, the number stood at 73 percent, up from 55 percent in the previous year.

* IAMAI Report

Technology is at the core of an Internet-based business. Technology is the engine that drives the whole machine of e-commerce, right from being an interface for its users to managing transactions and back-end operations. While the base engine is pretty standard, the differentiator lies in the detail and we will see how these pioneers have managed the details to their and their customer's advantage. There are many open source e-commerce platforms available for the new entrepreneurs that can be used off the shelf or customized as per the specific needs of the venture. Some companies have used these off the shelf solutions while others have designed

ONLINE SHOPPING BEHAVIOUR AMONG INTERNET USERS

(Base: 33.8 million Active Internet Users in 35 cities surveyed in I-Cube 2012)

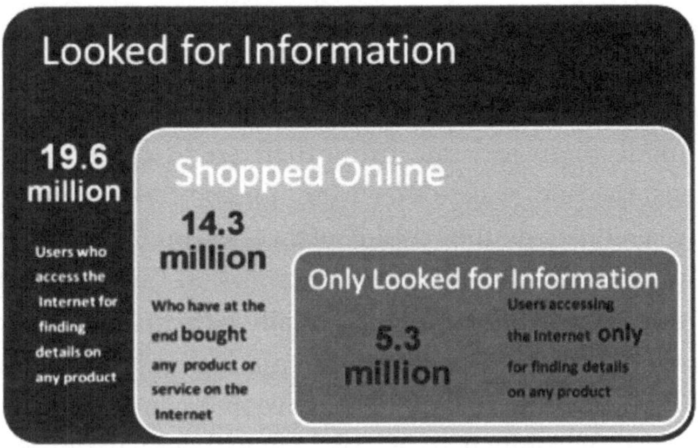

Fig 2: Information Seekers Become Buyers

their own architecture for their specific needs. Agility or the nimbleness with which business can respond to market needs is the key requirement for e-commerce companies as they have high number of transactions, are available 24X7, and have to deal with ever evolving technology platforms. The technology architecture has to be such that new features can be added, tested, experimented, and modified on the go without disturbing the on-going operations.

There are innumerable e-commerce and e-tail ventures in the Indian digital space today and selecting a few of them was a tough task. So I stuck to the pioneers in two major categories i.e. travel and retail. In retail I picked up a horizontal player and two categories at two different ends of the spectrum, both of which by their very nature were not easy to move online.

Flipkart is the poster boy of Indian retail, the biggest brand in the digital world in India even if sheer numbers tell different stories at different points in time. To me, Flipkart is the brand that made many Indians comfortable with online shopping. It made them feel safe using their credit cards for online purchases and in case they were not comfortable or did not have credit cards, they could opt for Cash on Delivery. It must have been a big risk to experiment with CoD as there is no way to ensure that the customer actually pays up, the collecting agent does not run away with the money, and that the model will be accepted. Today CoD has become a de-facto feature for all e-tailing companies, one without which they cannot think of existing, forget being successful. Another factor that Flipkart worked hard on was on-time delivery to build the trust around their brand, and gain credibility with customers. Most of its customers will vouch for its delivery commitment and most of its competition is still struggling to catch up. In this book, they represent the horizontal general retailers online—i.e they retail products across multiple general verticals like books, electronics, garments, personal care, music etc.

MakeMyTrip is in the book for multiple reasons—they are the biggest player in the travel segment, a segment that clearly dominates the online spend. They are one of the very few listed companies in the digital world and, most importantly, they are the true pioneers of Indian e-commerce across all categories. They started way before the dotcom bubble burst and are surviving through it. They are a strong brand. What has consistently kept them on top is their understanding of the customer and their constant endeavour to innovate to cater to their needs. They have also re-adjusted their business focus with the times like in the recent past it moved from airline and ticketing to hotels and holiday packages. They have been pioneers in launching a mobile application and are one of the few companies that are already generating substantial revenue from the mobile transactions. They represent the travel vertical and the services segment.

I studied some niche e-tailers who are breaking the set norms. These include high-end diamond and gold jewellery being sold by online portals like CaratLane, BlueStone, and VelvetBox. Incidentally they all have very similar looking websites and are experimenting with more or less similar products and markets. I chose CaratLane to study in detail because at the time of writing this book, they were ahead of the curve vis-à-vis their competitors. Moreover, they have also been around for the longest time, while the others have come and gone. They are looking at a mass market and their products are not too costly despite the fact that they are dealing in precious metals and stones. They are moving into the arena of online shopping by delighting the customers through Try at Home services, and launching their own collections to suit the needs of a modern day independent woman creating a whole new market for contemporary jewellery. CaratLane is a good combination of two entrepreneurs—one with a legacy of domain expertise and understanding of the jewellery business and the other a hardcore technocrat who brings in the understanding of the world of technology. The two make a unique team as put together they can have the core ingredients in place for an online venture in a niche or specialty domain.

Besides jewellery, I also looked at niche retailers in apparel, shoes, electronics, and handicrafts. I picked up a grocery retail chain because it is a tough business to do online, as the number of items to deal with is very large with a good percentage of them being perishable. It involves a complex supply chain especially if the inventory is to be maintained locally. I chose BigBasket from the few players who are operating at the moment because although the portal was launched in its current avatar in 2011, the management team comes with a strong background of successfully running the groceries retailing business both online and offline. They are also the only chain that operates successfully, across three cities and I must admit that they got the benefit of my being a very loyal and happy customer. BigBasket may be one of the first companies to bring out a sustainable online groceries model in India. Worldwide, experiments have been done with online placements of orders coupled with store pick ups or some companies even setting up multiple pick up points where you just swipe your order code and take your car in a particular bay and pick up the order. Given that in India we have multiple modes of travel, it would not work. Home delivery has failed in western world to some extent because people are not comfortable with time slots as they do not have somebody at home at all times or do not want to have restricted movement just because groceries are expected. In India that is not much of a problem as families still spend most of their leisure time at home and there are a lot of joint families or families with domestic helps where someone is always there to receive the order at home. The bigger challenge for BigBasket is to ensure quality of fresh produce every time to build and sustain the customer interest and give competition to the neighbourhood sabziwallah.

There are some other e-commerce portals that deserve to be here but cannot be for want of space. Snapdeal is an excellent example of marketplace model to study general retail. What also stands out is Snapdeal's agility. They started as a deals platform à la Groupon, but were very quick in realizing that it was not working and they used the network and infrastructure to quickly re-vamp themselves into an online marketplace. Their rapid growth is unprecedented among digital companies. RedBus is my all time favourite online venture not only because they made booking bus tickets easier for us, but also for the fact that they have made running buses a viable business option for many small time entrepreneurs. Their software product for bus operators allows them to manage their seat inventory easily. I also looked at some boutique portals that may remain boutique in nature but are creating their own niche space. iTokri is a small portal based out of Gwalior in Madhya Pradesh which sells Indian fabrics and fabric-based products sourced from small handicraft units from across the country. With a designer label on the offering, they may be an online answer to offline chains like Fabindia and Anokhi.

When multiple players in the same categories compete against each other, the need for price comparison websites or aggregators arises and they appear on the scene. They aggregate data across websites and tell you which website is offering the best price on what items. Inspite of their online presence, they are yet to reach a level where they can be the first point of contact for customers. They follow the maturity curve of the e-commerce sites themselves. For example, a mere price comparison may not serve your purpose if the vendor offering the lowest price has not included the shipping cost in its pricing or if the delivery time is much longer all factors that go into the customers' decision-making process.

On a lighter note, the one pleasure that e-commerce merchants are taking away from us is that of haggling with the shopkeepers. The joy of shopping in India also includes bargaining for the best price and some freebies for a promise of more business. Online, it is limited to one way as vendors can put offers and promotional schemes but customers only have an option to choose between what the various vendors offer or wait for their wish-list items to come down to the price they are willing to pay. You never know when our Mouse Charmers may come out with a feature that lets you practice your negotiation skills online too.

FLIPKART

First Chapter of Indian E-commerce

FLIPKART IS UNDOUBTEDLY INDIA'S poster boy of e-commerce. Most of us started our e-spending habits with them and they won our confidence with their impeccable service delivery, every time. They took risks by bringing the products to our homes with just a promise that we would pay once we have the product in our hands and today this is the de-facto mode of payment for any online shopping. By doing all this they built a formidable brand that has set many a benchmark and ensured a place in history for introducing online shopping to Indians. With constant innovation, they have managed to stay ahead of the curve so far and, given their DNA, would hopefully be able to maintain it in the longer run too.

Flipkart has often been called the big daddy of Indian e-commerce, but they are still a very young company, only about 6 years old. Flipkart's journey started in 2007 by selling books through a simple portal that resembled its inspiration—Amazon. Another category, consumer electronics, was added in 2010 and since then they have been adding them quicker than ever and have more than 15 categories like books, music, electronics, white goods, and lifestyle products. They have stepped into the emerging digital content market with Flyte, their proprietary digital music store.

Interestingly, founders Sachin Bansal and Binny Bansal wanted to start a comparison shopping website to begin with, but in 2007, they realized there were not enough websites operating in India to compare products or prices. This led to the idea of starting an e-commerce site and the rest, as they say, is history. To me, Flipkart's story showcases what smart, young Indians can achieve with the right focus. I am not too worried about the small ups and downs that they see as a business as they grow across categories or spread across geographies. My inherent faith in them comes from having been their customer and affiliate and the ease with which I transact on both accounts. Having said that, you never know what the future holds, but what has already been written is that Flipkart will always be the first chapter in the history of Indian e-commerce. No one can take that away from them.

Journey so far

On the face of it, Flipkart's business model is very simple like that of a general trader. You buy from the suppliers at a cost and you sell it to your customers at the cost plus profits. The channel to interact and transact with customers is a web portal where the customers have access to all the details of the available products. The devil lies in the detail. Do you buy products from the suppliers and store them in your warehouse or do you pass on the order to the suppliers and hope that they will deliver it as per your commitment to the customer? Do you tie up with a logistics company or create your own logistics arm to handle the kind of volumes you expect to generate? Do you remain a store that sells or do you become a marketplace and allow others to sell through your channel? Once you have answered these questions, the next level of details look you in the face—how much of what product to buy, where to store, how big and where should the warehouse be, what customers can my logistics partners serve, and how dependable are they; which suppliers should I tie up with and on what terms? You need to orchestrate an eco-system comprising of vendors, suppliers, employees, and customers to create a company that delivers to each of the stakeholders and is inviting enough for the investors.

Flipkart started with a model where they would procure on demand from the suppliers but switched to their own warehouses where they store products based on their sales forecast. Once they reached a level of sales volumes through their supplier base, they decided to introduce the marketplace model also on their portal, that allows other sellers to sell to their users. I must add that they are doing this in a very cautious and integrated fashion, conscious of the value that their brand carries in their customers' minds.

In its early days, Flipkart's biggest selling point was their lowest prices and it played a big role in bringing the first customers to them. The customer loyalty though depended on Flipkart's delightful customer service. They made sure that orders were delivered within the promised time, every time. Lowest price model is not sustainable in the long run and of late we have seen Flipkart moving into the realistic price point range. However, as the e-commerce industry is still opening up, every other day we see new entrants who are ready to offer lowest prices. Customers are having fun till it lasts but eventually, when the industry consolidates and matures, the prices will be comparable across platforms with occasional gimmicks to poach customers from one another.

Organic growth for Flipkart came from adding new product categories on a regular basis. The current portfolio of product categories has been built over a period of time, mostly organically but at times by acquiring companies that had complimentary offerings. Sachin Bansal talks about learning the nuances of each product category, building its base with suppliers and customers, and moving on to the new one. When I asked them about their considerations before introducing a new product, they said there is a typical business case analysis done for each category and the two parameters that play major roles in decision-making are:

- Customer's adoption capability of the new category.
- Supply chain capability to deliver the new category.

At times they have filled in the gaps in the product space quickly with buyouts like LetsBuy.com, an established player in the electronics space, and now a key category on Flipkart. It had an established supply chain with warehousing, cataloguing, supplier base, and an on-going customer base that was integrated into the Flipkart system. This added one of the fastest moving categories to their portfolio and also brought in a customer base that is savvy and used to online shopping.

WHAT THEY DID DIFFERENTLY

Having no predecessors to look at, there are many things that Flipkart experimented with, as that was the only way to invent the future. Here I look at some of the things which have made the maximum impact on Flipkart as well as the industry.

Cash on Delivery

In the developed markets, e-commerce sites run on the basic premise of plastic-enabled money. Almost everyone there has access to credit cards and more importantly they are as comfortable using them online as they are for offline transactions. In India, credit cards are still a luxury for most people and large sections of society have no access to credit cards. Those who have cards are sceptical to use them online—you never know whom you are paying to and every other day you read about credit card frauds. This puts a large section of potential customers out of reach for e-commerce portals. Flipkart came out with the concept of Cash on Delivery (CoD) which means that you can place an order and pay in cash when the product is delivered at your doorstep. Today, about 60–70 percent of their orders are CoD, so one can imagine the growth potential that would have been forgone if this innovative feature was not introduced. In other words this means that CoD has been a big growth driver for Flipkart expanding the customer base exponentially and opening up an opportunity to delight them with their, by now famous, customer service.

CoD is an excellent example of designing a feature that enables a global trend like online shopping to be adapted for local socio-economic conditions. I was really keen to know how this thought came about for Flipkart. Did they have any apprehensions before they took the risk of sending a shipment to a customer not knowing if the customer will pay up. I was also curious about how they ran CoD-based operations on such a large scale. The answer that came was far simpler than I expected. The idea sprouted as they sat analyzing the inhibitions that customers have in online shopping. They figured that payment is a big concern and it was a genuine concern to an extent as payment systems were not as smooth and secure few years back. Success rate of online payments is very low i.e. a lot of online transactions do not get completed and lead to many multi-party issues involving customers, suppliers, and banks e.g. credit card charged but payment not received by the merchant. Every time a transaction fails, there is bound to be lot of frustration for the customer that would eventually impact the brand too. Credit card usage was and continues to be low and, of course, there is a huge percentage of the population with no access to credit cards. So, they tried to address the payment problem by giving customers an option to pay once the product was delivered to them. The CoD experiment began by offering the service in a small neighbourhood in Bangalore and it worked with no major hassles. In fact, more and more customers started coming back and bringing along new ones on board because of this facility, giving them confidence that they could make this work. So they expanded the offering to the whole city and then to another city before it became a default option. According to Flipkart, rejection rates are very low for CoD and negligible compared to the spike that it provided in sales. I would take that statement with a pinch of salt but I agree that the boost it has given to the sales may be worth the risk of rejected shipments.

Now what is interesting to know is the back-end systems they had to put in place to scale up this facility. They worked on providing training and technology support to the logistics partners to handle cash. A proprietary cash management technology was put in place to track and trace every transaction taking place on CoD with checks and balances in places to ensure minimum pilferage and losses. The analytics engine at the customer level checks the customer profile through their order history, their past behaviour to decide how many checks should be done before. CoD orders are accepted for these customers. For example, for the first orders placed on CoD, there is a small authentication process through a SMS code but this step is skipped if the customer profile is pushed out of the verification queue. Even though CoD is now an industry standard in India, no one so far is doing it at a scale at which Flipkart does. This obviously comes from the fact that they have their own logistics arm, technology support, and scale that bring down incremental cost with every new order. For most other players who tie up with logistics partners and collection agencies, CoD adds a fixed cost per transaction and a process that involves many parties. Flipkart also believes that they handle CoD in the most cost effective manner. Management of CoD at Flipkart is a proprietary process and gives them a distinct competitive advantage .

Businesswise I believe that beyond a certain threshold, CoD is going to give them financial returns as well as it saves the transaction fee that the credit card companies charge. Margins in retail are not very high and transaction fee charged by credit card companies is typically in the range of 2–4 percent of the transaction value. If the cost of CoD can be brought down to less than the credit card transaction fee, financial returns of CoD can be significant. Flipkart or any other e-commerce vendors are not talking about this probably because that threshold is yet to be reached. As and when it happens, it would be time for the credit card companies and payment gateways to innovate.

Elements of Customer Delight

30-day replacement guarantee

This is a feature aimed at making customers happy and confident about shopping with them. Introducing this requires building a complete reverse logistics system at the back-end. Typically an order ends with the delivery of product. The moment you introduce a replacement feature, you need to have a mechanism to pick up the product at a given time from the customer, take it back through your entire supply chain, and do adjustments in your various accounts while picking up the cost of the whole exercise.

Product and price comparisons

Product and price comparisons for similar products help customers in making an informed choice. Product comparison features come handy in product categories like electronics where a feature-to-feature comparison eases the decision for the customer. User reviews give the subjective or qualitative feedback on the products based on customers' personal experiences. The certified buyer tag tells the users that the person reviewing the product has actually bought the product from Flipkart and hence the review can be completely trusted. Comparison feature is in fact a big edge that online shopping has over offline where customers are limited by the stock that the retail store has and they have no structured way to do a feature-by-feature comparison of the products.

EMI facility

It requires technology that seamlessly processes EMI-based transactions between the company, customers, and the banks. Of course this is a one-time investment in building the technology to enable this feature. Once it is working well for one bank, it became a plug and play for the others.

Logistics

Consistent and dependable delivery mechanism enabled by effective management of logistics is Flipkart's biggest asset and an inherent character of their brand today. It is their ability to deliver on-time, every time, which keeps a lot of customers bound to them. Sometimes they are willing to pay a little more if the delivery is ensured as promised. Delivering consistently on-time has earned Flipkart the kind of customer loyalty that is very difficult to replicate. Flipkart management admits that they are obsessed with customer experience and the big part of it comes from their order fulfilment using efficient logistics. It also happens to be a key touch point they have with customers. Flipkart works with many exclusive logistics partners whom they support through training and technology. A parallel of Flipkart's logistics partners can be seen in auto ancillary industry that exists around an auto manufacturer—exclusively for them and totally driven by their requirements and their technology.

ROOTS IN TECHNOLOGY DRIVE THE MAGIC

On the face of it, Flipkart has a simple interface that is user-friendly and easily navigable. One can place an order with few clicks, add items to a wish-list for later purchase, or review products. Searching the products is simple, very similar to Google, but again it takes lot of complexity to exhibit simplicity. As a philosophy, they say instead of working on solutions that address a set of problems they work on building intelligent platforms that can provide multiple solutions to a wider range of problems or opportunities; thus building a higher problem-solving capability. Eventually they can also roll out some of these platforms as independent products. PayZippy, a payment gateway solution is one such platform that they have recently launched in the market that allows customers to store their credit card information on the website in a safe and secure way. Most of their software is based on open sources components.

Main functional components of technology at Flipkart are given in the table on the next page.

All these components work in a networked model, talking to each other all the time, managed by a 350+ team of technology experts that work in small 3–5 person teams across functions.

A/B Framework: Flipkart's technology team has an architecture based on A/B framework that allows their portal to have multiple live versions simultaneously. This is used to experiment new features and beta test them on small set of

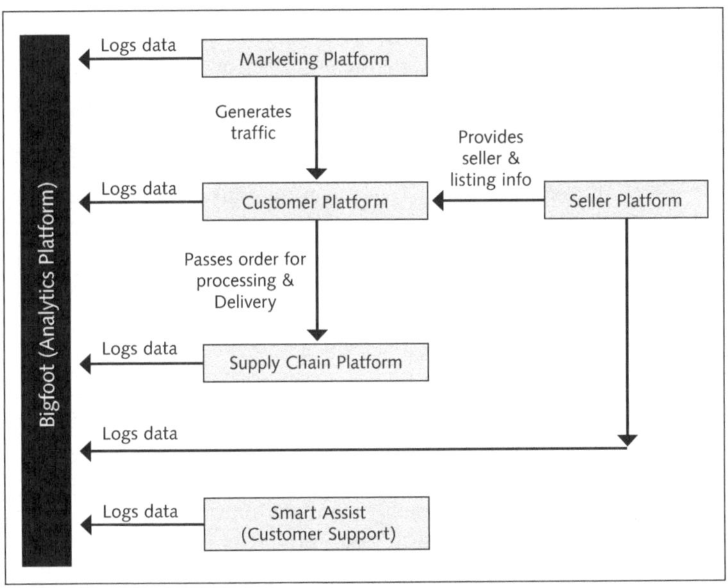

Fig 1: Flipkart Architecture

Table	
Marketing Platform	
	• Attracts customers through channels such as SEO, SEM, Social media, e-mails etc. • Contains strong intelligence about targeting the right customers.
Customer Platform	
	• Main touch point for all customers, and contains both website as well as mobile app. • A search engine to allow customers to find products. • A recommendations engine to recommend products and offers to customers. • A review and ratings service to help the customers make the right decision.
Supply Chain Platform	
	• Ecosystem of supply chain related technologies. • A fulfilment engine to orchestrate in-time delivery to the customer while increasing the efficiency of flow of goods. • A logistics engine to optimize the logistical operations of delivery partners.
Seller Platform	
	• Main touch point for all sellers on the Flipkart marketplace. • Cataloging systems to allow efficient and high quality product information. • Intelligence to dynamically determine seller quality and promote the best performing sellers to customers.
Smart Assist	
	• Intelligence engine for customer support systems. • Helps provide a very contextual and personalised experience to customers.
Bigfoot	
	• Central information management platform. • All systems pump data to this central data warehouse. • Helps bring out key data points to drive strong data backed decision-making in the organization.

users. Based on the customer response to the feature, they adopt, modify, or discard it. Instead of theoretically debating on a new feature, it is quickly put to a test with the live audience and a decision is taken based on the live user data. They improve upon the ideas that work and quickly chuck out the ones that do not. It allows the team to experiment quickly on multiple ideas simultaneously, and take decisions based on data rather than just a perception of what it can do. There is minimal disruption to business even if an experiment fails as it can be taken off easily and a very small percentage of customers are impacted by this. This is a formidable tool to do live market research using real customers although Flipkart still continues to invest in offline market research through traditional methods as well.

To realize the impact this feature has, let's look at how things would work in the absence of such a framework. Every time they would want to introduce a new feature, they would undertake a market research to understand how potential customers would receive it. They would then test it for say two weeks and any other feature would have to potentially wait for that time. Some features may need to be launched quickly, say in response to something that the competition is doing, but the environment may have changed during these two weeks. The number of experiments that can be done would be extremely limited and the time taken to take them live would be very high. Also, there is no possibility of doing a comparative analysis of parallel features.

At Flipkart, I was told, at any given time there are 20–25 experiments going on. Some features may be released to only

2 percent of the users on the system, but given their huge base even that is a substantial number compared to what you can target in a research group. These being live users, you get the best possible response to the experiment. Amod Malviya, the technology head at Flipkart, gave me an example of testing a feature where the menu is highlighted by darkening the rest of the screen when a user takes the mouse over menu. Now many of us may not have even noticed this change but apparently it works at a psyche level by improving your concentration on the menu, probably by removing other glaring distractions on the rest of the screen. They saw an increased conversion rate, and the feature was introduced for the overall website. Similarly another feature called Pop-up Cart was introduced to push up conversion rates. However, the shipping charges were not as apparent as in the original design and this led to a drop in the overall business metrics. Based on this insight, the design was tweaked till it gave a more positive outcome.

Technically speaking, this A/B framework is a part of their core technology layer with every other layer sitting on top of it. In simple language this means that virtually anything and everything can be tested using this framework. This was one of the first things that Flipkart had built as part of their web framework. Like other components this also is an evolving piece that initially required technical team support to run experiments and gradually that dependence is being done away with to enable business users to run it by themselves.

Impact of A/B Framework:

- More experiments.
- All decisions based on data.
- Minimal business disruption, if any.
- Experiments—a way of life, an element of culture.

Know Thy Customer

Every visitor to the website leaves his or her footprints in terms of data—where they came from, what they browsed, how much time they spent browsing, and what they finally bought. Slowly this data becomes statistics and by running a few queries on this big data, a lot of trends can be generated—both for individuals and for demographic groups. At the same time, performance of the internal functions can be assessed based on the same data like the total time taken to search the product and place the order. At Flipkart, a centralized analytics team works as business partner with functions to enable them with capability of analytics. Amod says there are investments being made into building an analytics engine for next generation analytics that would add many layers of depth to its potential. Analytics is another big advantage that online companies have over their brick and mortar counterparts, who have to rely on almost outdated data. Let's look at three primary ways Flipkart uses its analytics data:

1. *Live performance feeds* are displayed on the monitors in the office like a live display of business pulse. This works at

two levels. First it keeps throwing live statistics and any dip anywhere that needs immediate attention can be quickly responded to, making the business extremely responsive and hence effective and efficient. Second, it keeps everyone on the floor deeply connected to the business performance. It brings in absolute transparency to the employees giving them a sense of ownership. In their own words, they celebrate any good trend that comes up and attack any failures instantly.

2. *Function level analytics* are used by individual functions to take decisions. For example, if a product or a category sees a sudden spike in sales, the corresponding functions like inventory replenishments may need to be triggered off. Another example is product recommendation to customers either on the website or through e-mails based on their browsing history and buying patterns. Measuring the performance of the products, categories, and campaigns feeds into the future business planning.
3. *Organization-wide or horizontal analytics* are of course studied to take bigger business decisions. For example, from time to time Flipkart takes a call on minimum free shipping threshold. Regular users of Flipkart would remember that they had a minimum order value for free shipping at ₹100 that was over a period of time increased to ₹200, then ₹300, and at the time of writing this book, it stood at ₹500. The decision is taken after taking into account many factors like buckets of average order value, lifetime of customers in various segments, on ground logistics cost, and the general direction of the business strategy. Decisions like what kind of

delivery buckets can be promised to the customers on what product categories, or a general decision on what should be sold and what not—all these are based on the analytics.

Innovation process

One of my key interests in Flipkart was to find out how they nurture the culture of innovation. I did not find a clear structured answer except their annual Hack event where they spend two days and one night brainstorming on new ideas. What I did gather was an effort to expose employees to business by giving them visibility and transparency and a space to think about it at a level where they can come up with new ideas. There is a conscious effort in bringing synergy between the technology team and other functions so that they treat each other as partners. The technology team understands the business needs better when it understands the business and business partners understand that technology is at the core of an e-commerce business. Debates are encouraged. They anyway have a handy framework for quick experimentation. As a process for innovation, the only thing that I could put a finger on was that coming up with new ideas is part of their performance evaluation, but then we know of too many companies who have this but still have not much to showcase.

Rendezvous with Customers

In their first few years, word of mouth has been the biggest driver of growth for Flipkart. Every satisfied customer brought in more customers. There was no explicit marketing for the first few years. It was only when they had kind of inducted almost all the early adaptors into their fold that they ventured out to look at converting customers who are sitting on the fences and needed a bigger messaging to convert. Their current marketing plan is a mix of online and offline marketing.

Online marketing includes the obvious suspects like SEO, Search Engine Marketing, e-mail marketing, visual displays, advertising, and reaching out through affiliates. Search engine marketing leads to engagement and builds deeper brand building, and this is arguably the best online marketing tool, especially for the lifestyle category.

In offline marketing, TV commercials have been used to reach out to wider range of customers. The first set of TV ads were aimed at educating customers about Flipkart's value proposition like original products that came with manufacturer's warranty, cash on delivery, 30-day replacement guarantee with a tagline 'No kidding, no worries'. With this message, they were inspiring confidence in online shopping by saying it is safe and easy to shop online, and even kids can do it. The series also focussed on the new categories introduced at the store. The latest series of ads focus on creating a new branding around the slogan—'Flipkart it'. They have been creative in using kids acting out as adults with adult voices as a unique creative for the brand. Their series of advertisements now follow the same format with kids playing the roles of adults with new scripts for new messages or new launches. The format has already come to be associated strongly with the brand Flipkart. Another brand that has followed this for the longest time is Amul campaign with Amul girl, and incidentally that also uses a kid.

After a brief controversy about one of the ads, they experimented with releasing the new ads through social media and sought customer feedback. Ads were then tweaked based on the feedback and released on TV. This is a first by an Indian company where they have actively involved their customers in a marketing campaign. It also tells customers that they matter to the company more than just being follower or a fan on their social media channels.

In all my interactions with the company as part of writing this book, as an early customer or an affiliate, one thing that came across consistently is their DNA of experimentation. They started the company with limited technology and domain knowledge but with a great clarity in how they want the things to be done. Almost everything that they have achieved till date has come out of their experiments that succeeded. These successes must have come on top of a lot of failed attempts that may not have been spoken about, but it is their ability to experiment on a day-to-day basis and creating an environment where experimentation is the way of life that makes them stand out in the crowd.

Finally, I think it is their ability learn from their own mistakes and from what other people are doing right that makes them a high learning organization. Sachin is often seen mentioning how they learnt the fast delivery mechanism from Domino's who command a premium and high recall from customers because of their ability to meet 30-minute delivery promise every time. He refers to Airtel for effective marketing and Indigo Airlines for creating an end-to-end customer experience. Not many companies are designed to look at other companies across industries to pick what they are doing right and adopt that for their own business. Another observation based on the brands they speak about is that they are looking at active ideas that are working at the moment and not looking at what worked for someone in the past when business environment was substantially different.

As an early mover they have the huge advantage of scale and an ability to invest in the future, and that puts them in a unique position where they can work on expanding the horizons of e-commerce. They pretty much live in the public and media eye and we would keep hearing about them and hopefully continue to be delighted by their services.

References

Information provided by the company
Conversations with Amod Malviya, Ravi Vora, Payal Banerjee of Flipkart

http://articles.economictimes.indiatimes.com/2012-09-17/news/33902863_1_flipkart-social-media-new-campaign

http://www.business-standard.com/article/management/service-selection-and-price-are-the-three-pillars-sachin-bansal-113021700398_1.html

http://businesstoday.intoday.in/story/flipkart-online-shopping-e-commerce-order-books-online/1/20797.html

http://www.cio.in/case-study/flipkart-drives-innovation-through-intelligent-use-it

http://techcircle.vccircle.com/500/flipkart-to-head-towards-profitable-revenue-growth-not-just-revenue-growth-sachin-bansal-co-founder/

http://techcircle.vccircle.com/500/excl-flipkart-hits-rs-100cr-monthly-sales-mark-now-serving-seven-orders-per-minute/

http://www.thehindu.com/arts/magazine/article3290735.ece

http://www.medianama.com/2013/01/223-flipkarts-ashok-banerjee-timesofmoneys-kunnal-sharma-on-e-commerce-analytics/

http://www.nextbigwhat.com/flipkart-launches-ebooks-in-india-proprietary-format-297/

http://www.youtube.com/watch?v=YkU-E4bJYjg

Name of the company:	Flipkart.com
Website:	www.flipkart.com
Year of commencement:	2007
Founders:	Sachin Bansal, Binny Bansal
Headquarters:	Bangalore
No. of registered users:	10 million
No. of page views/per month:	More than 1 million daily visitors
No. of SKUs/products sold:	60,000 shipments daily
No. of product categories:	18

MAKEMYTRIP

Making Indians Travel at the Click of a Button

TRAVEL HAS BEEN AT the forefront of the e-economy, globally as well as in India. It is the first product consumers were comfortable buying online and the whole industry has responded by making everything in this domain available online. One big reason for this is because it involves a service sale and not a product sale. Customers do not need to look at and feel the product before buying it. From the online travel agents' perspective, there is no logistics requirement as the physical tickets have very smoothly graduated to e-tickets which can be delivered to the customers' inboxes. Additionally it brought down the cost of operations for travel agents significantly. Also, while travelling, a customer needs many types of information, including comparative data and all this can be done far more efficiently online than offline. Today, almost all travel products like tickets, hotel stays, and holiday packages can be bought online individually or as package deals. Financially, per transaction sale value is substantial, making travel a high revenue generating space though the margins vary from time to time and from product to product.

The Beginning of a Brand

MakeMyTrip can easily be called the pioneer in both the Indian digital business space and the online travel space, where they continue to be the leaders despite stiff competition from many new and old players. Deep Kalra the founder of MakeMyTrip was a very early starter. He started the company before the famous dotcom bust around the turn of millennium. The Indian market was not yet ready for the Internet-based businesses, payment gateways were yet to set their feet, and people were wary of using their credit cards. They did not know how to deal with an entity which only existed on their computer screens. Kalra spotted an opportunity in the US-India Travel market that had many NRIs travelling between India and USA on a regular basis. This customer segment was comfortable in making online transactions and was looking for better options to travel to India. MakeMyTrip provided them with a reliable options along with a 24X7 customer support to add further value. This gave MakeMyTrip an initial boost and helped them build a brand with a segment of regular travelers.

The success with the NRI market in the US, led to the launch of MakeMyTrip's India operations in 2005. As the cliché goes, opportunity meets the prepared. This was the time when the Indian travel market was going through many changes. IRCTC introduced users to the convenience of booking online by selling railway tickets online, and bringing in huge customer confidence. Many new airlines came into the scene with an interface to sell tickets online directly to the customer without the need of a middleman. With the advent of these mostly low-cost, no frills carrier (LCC) airlines came the need to compare fares and find the lowest one. MakeMyTrip responded to this need by building a flight comparison software that fetched real-time fares from both types of airlines—Low-Cost Carriers and Full Service Carriers. This may sound easy today but it was not so simple to executes it then as the data for both types of airlines was organized in different manners. Full service airlines had data on traditional GDS systems while LCCs on their own websites or servers. This innovation helped MakeMyTrip become the platform of choice for travellers who were delighted with both convenience and the money saved through flight comparison engine. Since then, MakeMyTrip has gone from strength to strength and has come to define the online travel space in digital India. Today, MakeMyTrip is one of the very few public listed digital companies in India.

What they Do

MakeMyTrip sells everything one needs in order to travel like air tickets, train tickets, bus tickets, taxis, hotel bookings, holiday packages, insurance and their combinations through multiple channels—online, mobile, and branded stores. As a business model this implies listing inventory of these products from various suppliers on their portal and selling them to users and earning a part of the sale as profit.

Air Travel	Hotel and Packages	Emerging Segments
• Domestic: Within India • International: From India • Inbound: Overseas to India	• Hotels: Domestic and Overses • Packages: - Domestic and Overseas - Conferences and Events	• Rail • Bus • Car • Ancillary Services/ Products

Fig 1: MakeMyTrip Product Portfolio

MakeMyTrip began with air ticket booking as its primary business. Over a period of time, booking air tickets has become a very low margin business. Airlines sell tickets on their own websites at similar or lesser prices making it difficult for the aggregators or agents to earn any substantial money over that. However, online ticketing has made customers more accepting to shop online for high-value transactions. This enabled operators like MakeMyTrip to add lines of businesses that

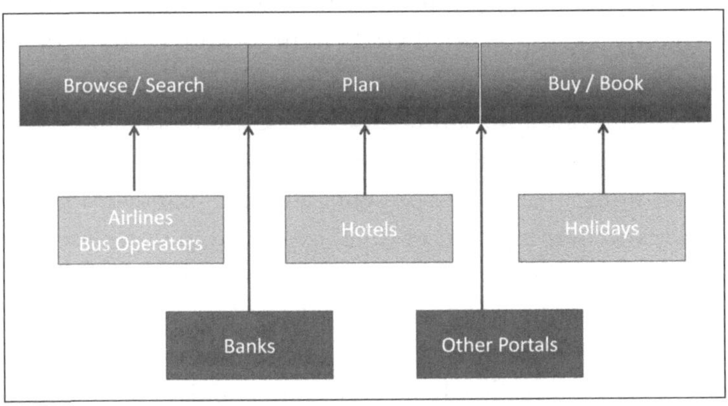

Fig 2: MakeMyTrip Business Model

include selling hotel accommodations, bus tickets, train tickets, and holiday packages. These verticals would provide the required growth and the long-term stability for the business. We need to remember that these segments are not really organized and come in all shapes and sizes making it a challenge to get the inventory in one place. The silver lining in this business is that tourism sector in India is just about opening up.

Offline Presence

MakeMyTrip kept growing by adding products to its online portfolio. It realized that there is a huge segment of potential customer base that is yet to join the Internet bandwagon and cannot be ignored. They also realized pretty early in their journey that they need to build an offline presence for their brand and should be available closer to the customer. Their first offline presence was established through an association with HPCL petrol pumps and their retail outlets In&Out. MakeMyTrip set up small kiosks in these outlets. An assistant at the kiosk would help customers with information about various products from the company. Customers could book their tickets or holiday packages right there. They started establishing their offline presence through branded stores in 2008, and over a period of time, expanded to stores in more than 50 cities across the country with a mix of 18 company-owned and 40 franchisee stores.

The major chunk of MakeMyTrip's business is B2C, i.e. the company directly sells to its customers and consumers, and only a small part comes from B2B segment.

Multiple Channels Approach to Reach Customers

Mobile Platform
Website
50+ Retail Stores
1000 people Call Centres
6000 B2B Agents

What Keeps them Ahead?

Over the years, MakeMyTrip has done many innovative things to keep themselves ahead of the competition and especially to make customers comfortable with purchasing online. I share some of the innovations here to give a glimpse of what it takes to maintain a strong position of leadership.

Route Planner

India has a limited number of airports and a relatively small segment of the population travels by air. Unless you are travelling between two big cities, you often need more than one mode of transport to complete your journey. There are many possible combinations that can be chosen. The choice usually rests on the time taken to travel and the cost involved. MakeMyTrip's route planner works out the best routes between any two points within India, combining the air, rail, bus, and taxi travel rates for customers and gives them a fair approximation of the time and cost involved for that combination. They also rate the routes on a scale of 10. This tool lets customers make an informed decision by comparing various transportation options. I tried fiddling around with the tool and was surprised to know about certain combinations that I would have never thought myself. The route planner, of course, links to the booking engine for each of the choices.

Making Hotels More Accessible

Empty rooms are dead inventory for hotels. On an average, hotels have an occupancy rate of anywhere between 60–70 percent. One of the insights that MakeMyTrip has from Indian customer behaviour is that 70 percent of the hotel bookings are done at the last minute. Marrying these two observations, the concept of *last minute hotel deals* was launched as a product. It lets hotel owners upload limited inventory at discounted prices at the last minute and customers get to see these deals while searching for a hotel for the same or next day. More than 30 percent discount is offered which makes for good value for both the hotels and the travellers. At the back-end, it requires MakeMyTrip to provide technical capability to the hotels to enable them to upload discounted inventory on the go, including from a mobile phone. As an added advantage, they are also given an option to display their last minute offer prominently to catch the customer eye.

When MakeMyTrip told me about their 100 percent money back guarantee on hotels, I expressed my doubts, as they were promising to refund money on behalf of hotels whose service is not under their direct control. They explained that the purpose of the money back guarantee is to ensure that customers get exactly what is promised on the hotel website and apparently it has led to increase in customer confidence. Similarly a *pay at hotel* facility has been introduced that comes at a non-refundable nominal fee of five rupees, but which ensures a confirmed booking and payment at the time of check-in. There is a map view of hotels to enable users to choose the hotels based on their current location. These small innovative features ensure focus on building hotel bookings line of business that has a huge room for growth for online travel agents.

Mobile Application

MakeMyTrip was one of the first companies in India to launch a mobile application before smartphones became the norm. As of now, their mobile application is the most downloaded mobile application in India with more than a million downloads. Apart from basic search, it allows proximity based search, restaurant search and instant checkout creating the same end to end experience for the customer as their website. The mobile app is already bringing in close to 20 percent of the traffic and about 10 percent of total transactions. Going forward these numbers are only expected to increase which means that the mobile app will have to keep getting better with zanier features

Payment

A sturdy, secure, and easy-to-use payment system is one the basic needs of an e-commerce portal. This is where the customer confidence can suffer the biggest setback if not handled properly. It is a given that vendors have to accept payments through all possible channels—credit and debit cards, net banking options from all leading banks, cash payment at offline branches etc. MakeMyTrip has an innovative feature called 'Easy pay', where customers can make part payments at the the time of booking for certain types of products like international air tickets. However, this facility is limited to customers with established credit history who the system thinks can be trusted for a deferred payment. Traditional modes like cash, cheques, drafts, and wire transfers are also accepted for the inventory that can be held and for which rates do not change very frequently. One of my questions to them, in fact, was why they do not have cash on delivery, and they explained that this is not possible because of the extremely dynamic rates that most of the products they deal with, have. By the time a ticket is delivered at the doorstep of a customer, the price has changed, creating a disparity between those who are holding the price and those who are paying instantly.

SMS-based Bus Ticketing

Bus travel is big in India with lots of big and small bus operators spread across the country. A good percentage of the bus ticket buying population does not have access to smartphones and uses phones with the basic calling and SMS facility. So, MakeMyTrip designed a simple application that works for all kinds of phones but specifically targets the customers who do not have smartphones. They developed a simple SMS-based application that can help book bus tickets by exchanging a few text messages. How well is this innovative tool received by the target customers, remains to be seen since this feature has been launched very recently. I tried my hand at using this service and was completely lost in the seemingly senseless SMSs that came my way.

Taming the Technology

MakeMyTrip may be the biggest travel brand in India, but at the core it is a technology company, which enables the travel products to be sold online. Let us look at the technology evolution at MakeMyTrip. This is one company that experimented with partly outsourcing the technology initially, but like everyone else had to bring it in-house eventually. Right now, they have a 300+ strong technology team that works on developing cutting edge products which keeps them ahead of the curve.

They have been using cloud-based technologies since the beginning. This helped them leverage the computational abilities of the cloud in orchestrating transactions for the products they sell. A lot of open source technologies are used to build applications. Sometimes, based on their requirements and design, they do outsource the development of certain pieces of technology to other vendors but the core technology is completely handled in-house. Besides agility and speed to market, in-house technology ensures ownership of the Intellectual Property (IP) associated with the technology. With an outsourced vendor even when the IP belongs to MakeMyTrip, the substantial knowledge of it lies with the technology company. For a technology-based e-commerce company this is a strategic differentiator which they cannot afford to lose to the market or to the competition.

Some of MakeMyTrip's technological challenges come from being an extremely high volume, high transaction website with a huge customer base. Given the nature of the business, traffic shoots up manifold during holiday season, discount sales hosted by MakeMyTrip or its partners or events that lead to spike in travel across certain sectors. These traffic spikes are managed by putting in place a redundant data centre which enables the website to scale up to five times of its steady state capacity, which in itself is a constantly moving target. Similarly, the website is prone to malicious attacks that can not only ruin the whole business but also pose a data security threat as a lot of confidential customer data is stored in their systems. Security strategy therefore, becomes very important given that the website has to be up and running 24X7.

Customized user experience is a technology-enabled feature which allows them to modify what a customer sees on the webpage based on data analytics like customer preferences. Order history gives data like spending history and periodicity of travel, browsing history indicates the potential interest of the user. Challenge comes from the fact that all data must be retrieved in real time for the customer from various systems that may be inside or outside the core system. For example when a customer is looking for flight+hotel, both data points come from different sources and put together may have a potential promotion as an offer that the customer came looking for. Both flight and hotel rates can change by the minute. Service-oriented architecture that is modular by design allows them to handle personalization on the go for each customer.

Partner Integration

Travel business is, by nature, a network-based business and depends to a large extent on all the partners who service different components of a customer travel experience. The integration between partners has to be seamless, secure, and easy-to-use for the customer. On the one end there are suppliers like airlines, hotels, bus operators who upload their inventory to the MakeMyTrip systems to be sold, and at the other there are financial partners like banks and credit card companies that enable payments on the systems and offer financing options. Furthermore, there are franchisees who sell inventory closer to customers. Supplier integration is tricky as it is transactional and interactive. While suppliers have control over what they decide to sell at the portal, they are enabled through business intelligence of the MakeMyTrip systems. It helps them take decisions based on data and the on-going trends, e.g. deciding the price of the product according to the demand. During very high volume transactions that take place

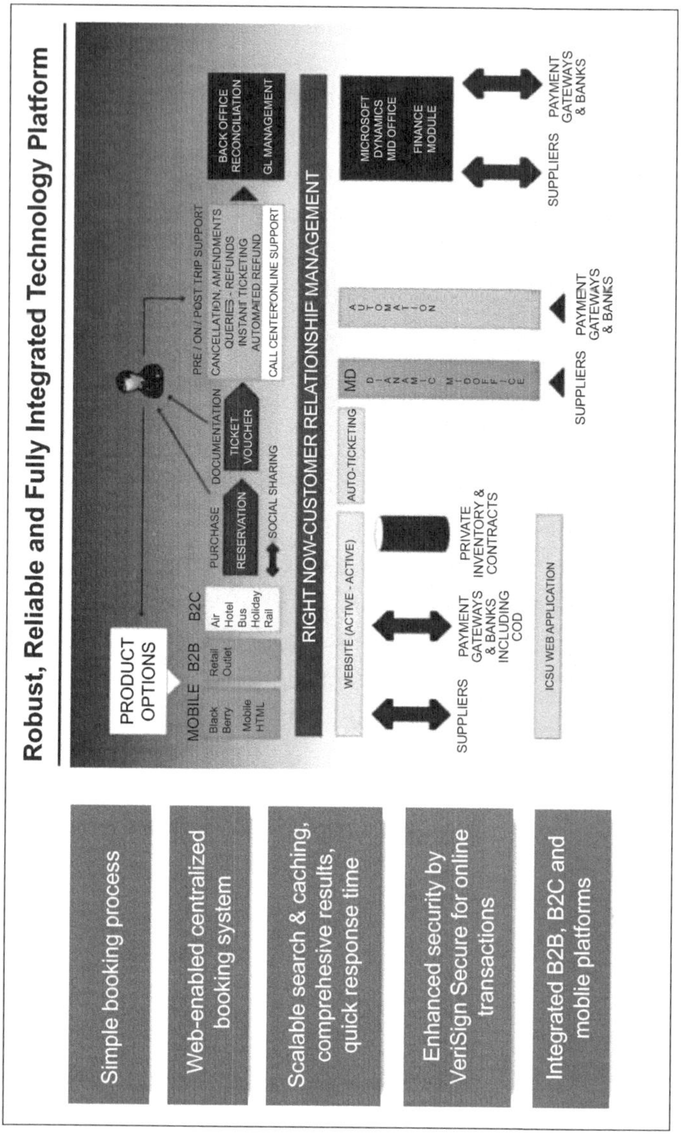

Fig 3: MakeMyTrip Technoloy Platform

during sales and holiday seasons, technology support has to be extended to partners to deal with the increased traffic. There is also integration with reviews sites like TripAdvisor for hotels, Zomato for restaurants, and services like Google Maps for location identification. What I found out in my conversations with various senior leaders in the company was an openness to partner with anyone who'd bring some value to the table for the customers and the company.

Reaching Out to Customers

Like most businesses, MakeMyTrip's customers fall into two broad categories. First is the set of existing customers who have either bought some product on MakeMyTrip or have registered themselves and hence there is some data available about them. These customers are sent regular updates about campaigns, discounts, and new products based on analytics of their buying behaviour and their browsing history. The other segment is the new and potential customers who are targeted more through brand building campaigns.

Manish Kalra, marketing head at MakeMyTrip, said that they want to be present everywhere where their potential customers are. So they appear on television, on radio, in print, in cinema halls, on cricket grounds, and, of course, on web pages through ads. All these efforts are targeted to get the customers to the website and enable them to buy the travel products. In the initial days, there were very few online customers, so online marketing was limited while traditional marketing like TV commercials was used extensively. Their advertisements focussed on the convenience of buying online vis-à-vis traditional mode of buying with a tagline 'Wish, Click, Go'. With increased Internet penetration, as the numbers grew online, they started online marketing that included conventional techniques like Search Engine Optimization, Search Engine Marketing, Targeted Advertisements through services like Google and visual advertisements.

By 2010, a lot of players had established themselves in the travel space, making it important for MakeMyTrip to form an emotional connect between its customers and the brand. They focussed on the power of making memories through travel, memories that people cherish long after the trip is over, memories that they like to recount to people who have not seen those places. Their campaign, hence, revolved around 'Memories Unlimited'. Lately, they have changed their focus to hotels and they claim to hold the largest inventory of hotels in India. Now their brand descriptor reads 'Hotels Unlimited' to give a push to the hotel line of business.

Analytics play a major role in online marketing. Based on the browsing and order history, personalized e-mail messages, promotions, and offers are sent to customers on a regular basis. For example, there can be customized offers on birthdays and anniversaries; there can be preference-based offers like some people may prefer beach holidays while others may like pilgrimages. Website experience is also customized, based on the data about the user. A dedicated CRM team, using various customer management tools, manages online users.

Travel Habits of Indian Customers

Fond of travelling—travel budgets not affected during recession
Need Indian food while travelling
Deep pockets but prudent spenders
Shopaholics
Plan at the last minute
Influenced by Bollywood locations

Promotional activities are also done with partners who cater to MakeMyTrip's potential customers on a day-to-day basis, typically with banks and other e-commerce companies. One can often find their promotional campaigns where small discounts are given to customers who use a partner bank's debit or credit card through a promotional code. Another common campaign is to partner with banks to offer interest-free EMIs for the holidays bought through that bank's payment channels. Matrimonial websites are other potential alliances to promote honeymoon tours and destination weddings. They have partnered with tourism boards to co-promote destinations with a combination of online and offline marketing.

As the market leader, MakeMyTrip tries to broaden the travel market by introducing new destinations and promoting them. For this they partner with tourism boards and airlines. For example they ran a holiday package campaign to short distance destinations like Bhutan, Ladakh, and Andaman Islands from key Indian cities using chartered planes. With a large customer base, it is now easy for them to custom design packages that can offer value to the travellers while ensuring it remains a viable business option for the company. For instance, a chartered flight makes sense only if you can run it at full capacity. If you can have a full flight, even hotels rates go down driven by economies of scale. Here they are also trying to sell to their existing customers who have already visited the popular destinations and are on the lookout for new adventures.

Social media is actively used as a channel to interact with the old and new customers. Sites like Facebook and Twitter are excellent platforms to hear what customers feel about existing products and what they are looking for in new products. Social media works both ways as a feedback channel and as an idea generation channel. All promotions, offers, and launches are routed through the company's Facebook and Twitter accounts. There is an effort to build customer engagement through online contests to maintain their loyalty for the brand and to ensure their active involvement. Whether all this leads to any direct sales cannot be ascertained at the moment but it definitely adds to the building of a strong online brand.

STILL WORKING ON...

Most of the challenges that MakeMyTrip faces are predominantly industry related; like limited reach of Internet, limited use of credit cards, and a small section of population holding passports. But they also feel there can be policy level reforms that can make payments easier without the need of entering, for example, input information on multiple screens, and avoiding jumping in and out of the core transaction system. This would in turn make customers more comfortable with online payments.

A lot of strategies and models used by MakeMyTrip have become de-facto standard for the online travel industry. You will find other players doing similar things like reaching out to customers through every possible channel and similar partnerships with product and service providers. However, being the market leader, MakeMyTrip has the scale and the first mover advantage over others and given their DNA to innovate, they are holding their leadership position very well.

redBus

If there is one business that I regret not making a part of this book, it is redBus—a company that I really admire. Started by three engineers, Phanindra Sama, Charan Padmaraju, and Sudhakar Pasupunuri in 2006, redBus is India's first, best-known, and the largest bus ticket booking service. redBus provides ticketing services to its customers through various channels like web, mobile phones, and retail outlets. While it makes bus tickets available at our fingertips, its biggest innovation lies in organizing a fragmented market with thousands of bus operators in big and small towns across India.

On the face of it, redBus manages more than 20,000 bus services daily from over 800+ bus operators in 22 states. It sells seats online as well as through a network of travel agents, post offices, mom-and-pop stores etc. They have about 30,000 point-of-sale outlets across the country through various models. redBus gets a commission for every ticket sold and that is one of its prime sources of income. At the back end, it has two complementary software businesses. First is its Software Solution called BOSS™—an ERP software application for bus operators. With 700+ operators using it across the country, it is a leading solution in its space. Second is a GDS business solution called SeatSeller™ that aggregates bus seat inventory for 40,000 agents like organized bus ticketing agencies, online travel agents, and organized retail stores across the country to sell. These software applications have put the small bus operators at par with the larger ones and made business more viable for them. For customers, besides the obvious ease of booking online, their solution has enabled the booking from any point to any point and has been especially useful for booking return journeys. If you remember, before online solutions, you had to be in the city of boarding to buy tickets and there was no guarantee that you would get the ticket. redBus has also introduced features that allow customers to choose seats while booking like airlines let you do. It also lets you choose a bus based on various factors like facilities available, pick up points, user feedback on the services, and punctuality of the service provider. As things become more and more transparent, bus operators will figure out that proving good services makes business sense and this would improve the overall quality of bus service in the country.

Based on their data analytics and research, redBus also advises bus operators on new routes to operate on.

BookMyShow.com

BookMyShow.com is an entertainment ticketing portal in India for all kinds of tickets like movies, sports events, plays, concerts, and festivals. This portal is becoming a one-stop shop for buying tickets of all kinds of public entertainment events. It is also one of the earliest startups and a true pioneer in its category, having its beginning well before the dot com bust of 1999. With an easy to replicate model, they still hold 90 percent share in the ticketing market.

Movie tickets form their biggest and most regular inventory to sell. This is not a surprise as they have an inventory of over 1000 screens across 250 cinemas in 75 cities and are associated with all major cinema chains like Inox, Fame, Big Cinemas, Fun Cinemas, DT Cinemas, and Satyam Cineplex. This is followed by their exclusive association with India's largest theatre venues like NCPA and Prithvi in Mumbai, Indian Habitat Centre in Delhi, EpiCentre in Gurgaon, and Rangashankara in Bangalore. BookMyShow sells tickets for over 500 events every year, which includes events like Sunburn, Sula Wine Fest, Auto Expo, The Comedy Store, KOD-Zangoora, and NCPA-SOI. They claim to sell 75 percent of all sporting events tickets and their most famous partnership is with Indian Premier League. During sporting events they also have on ground tie-ups with various retail chains like Café Coffee Day etc for sale of tickets. About 85 percent of their revenue comes from sale of movie tickets and of the other 15 percent, about 45 percent comes from large format events like IPL, Formula One Indian Grand Prix, and music-related events.

They have traffic of 33 million page views per month on an average, and an active customer base of 3 million, a lot of whom are repeat customers. Their Facebook page has 2.4 million followers, making it a strong channel to promote the events that they sell tickets for. With 26 percent of their transactions happening via mobile, they top the mobile transaction charts in India.

REFERENCES

Information provided by MakeMyTrip and its website

Conversations with Manish Kalra, Amit Somani and Sanket Atal of MakeMyTrip

Information provided by BookMyShow

http://www.medianama.com/2011/08/223-makemytrip-launches-loyalty-program-deals-new-site-soon/

http://www.medianama.com/2011/08/223-chart-of-the-day-makemytrips-billing-per-transaction-for-air-tickets-vs-hotels-packages/

www.redbus.in

http://www.bookmyshow.com/
http://forbesindia.com/printcontent/35183
http://www.business-standard.com/article/companies/hotel-occupancy-room-rates-set-to-hit-a-new-low-112081300062_1.html

Name of the company:	MakeMyTrip.com
Website:	www.MakeMyTrip.com
Year of incorporation:	2000
Founder:	Deep Kalra
Co-founders:	Keyur Joshi, Rajesh Magow, Saching Bhatia
Headquarters:	Gurgaon
No. of offices:	62 stores across India, 2 in US
No. of employees:	900+
No. of page views per month:	7.2 million unique visitors per month in fiscal year 2013 according to comScore

BIGBASKET

Groceries at Your Doorstep via Your Computer Screen

GROCERIES ARE PART OF our day-to-day needs. Since the beginning of civilization, the friendly neighbourhood trader procured different items from the widespread producers and sold them to us for a profit. We never had to look beyond the immediate neighbourhood to fulfil these needs. In fact, when this industry began to get organized about a decade back, the retail stores still came to our neighbourhood. Some of these grocers gave us the facility of home delivery but preferred if we walked to their store and picked up our groceries ourselves. Groceries are probably the easiest, and yet most difficult, things to sell online, as we shall discover in this story of an online grocery store that is doing reasonably well.

BigBasket.com is India's leading online grocery store that, as of now, delivers groceries across three cities in India. Though it started only in 2011, and is less than three years old at the time of writing this book, its management team comes with a long expertise in the field of online grocery businesses. Four of its founders—Hari Menon, Vipul Parekh, V.S. Ramesh, and V.S. Sudhakar—had started one of the first online businesses in India way back in 1999 under the name Fabmart.com, and started retailing groceries online in 2001. Their experience was helpful but back then India wasn't ready for e-commerce. The dotcom bust did not help either. They took the business offline and started a chain of physical retail stores across south India called FabMall in 2002. This retail chain was merged with the Hyderabad-based retail chain Trinethra. At their peak, they had around 300 stores. This business was eventually sold to the Aditya Birla group in 2006 and is still running under the new brand name of 'More'. The team was still gung-ho about the idea of an online grocery store, and in 2011 they again came together to create BigBasket.com along with a new partner Abhinay Choudhari. Between them they have more than 45 man-years of experience in online and offline grocery retailing in India which came in handy in their second innings as they quickly established supplier and investor relationships.

Selling groceries online has both its pros and cons. As low volume requirements with low economic value of the products accompanied by low shelf life are involved, customers are willing to try out the online model. If the grocer can give them good service, they will tend to stick to that grocer. Beyond getting the orders online, it is a complex business of managing disparate inventories with different storage requirements, sourced from multitude of vendors that need to be picked, packed, and delivered according to the customer order at the right place, right time, and in the right shape with expected quality.

Everyone buys groceries, so ideally anyone can be a

customer, but given the comfort levels with buying online, the first set of customers for this business are the same as those in most other categories of e-commerce—upwardly mobile, working couples with many demands on their time. The primary proposition that grocery retailers can have for the urban population is the saving of time in purchasing the mundane items online, as long as there is service and quality guarantee. Grocery shopping at urban stores demand precious weekend time, most of which is spent standing in queues for hours. Compare it to the scenario of someone delivering the same stuff, with a much wider range of choices, at your doorstep at your preferred time.

GROCERIES BUSINESS LANDSCAPE

BigBasket is the biggest player in groceries both in terms of their operations in multiple cities and the range of products they offer to their customers. Most other players that exist today operate locally in one city or, more often than not, in a small area within a big city. Physical retail chains also offer home delivery within an area and a part of this may shift to their websites in the future. As of now, the space is clearly divided between offline and online retailers and there are no players that operate in both segments. The reason is simple but not very obvious—the two business models are entirely different. In the offline model, the business is about sourcing, maintaining inventory, and managing the store operations. In the online model, it is about sourcing, inventory management, and servicing the orders. In the offline model, store operations is a big cost element especially as the real estate in prime locations comes at a premium while in the online model it is the cost of logistics that demands efficient management. Skill sets required to operate the two models of business are completely different. If an offline player has to introduce an online channel to complement its offline presence, it would need huge investments in technology and logistics. It would also need to bring synergies between the two different ways of running the same business. Similarly, it would be true for online players if they wished to have an offline presence. One indicator of the maturity of online grocery space would be when offline stores start moving to online models. This would also indicate that customers are as comfortable buying online as they are with the real-time stores today.

Offlive Vs Online Grocery Stores

Offline Grocery Options	Online Grocery Stores
Organized retail chains	Multi-city grocery stores
Kirana stores	Single city/small locality stores
Farmer's markets	Niche products stores e.g. organic products only stores or tea only stores
Vegetable hawkers	Single brand stores

The local online stores will continue to exist as of now and would come with an advantage of quick servicing of orders as the area served is small and so is the number of Stock Keeping Units (SKUs) served. The challenge of these players would be to scale up to match the range of products offered by the big players like BigBasket. Future may see consolidation where these players may either merge with the bigger players or learn the ropes and scale up themselves. However my gut feeling is that there would be place for both these formats. As customers, we'd need big ones for the choice they give and small ones for speed and personalization. So I might order my weekly groceries from BigBasket but may want to source my fresh produce from smaller players. We already see some maturity setting in the physical stores with many chains like *More* cutting down on the number of stores they have in order to be more profitable.

An online grocery business still has to be city-wise as the products cannot be sent by courier and have to be delivered fresh. Having a multi-city presence comes with its own challenges and advantages. Entering every new city is akin to opening up a new operation, as the supply chain needs to be entirely local both for the nature of the business that has a fair segment of fresh produce and to comply with the local laws that restrict the flow of agricultural produce across state borders. Warehouse, inventory, and logistics have to completely operate locally. The advantages come in the form of large volume of non-agricultural products that sell across locations that provide economies of scale when dealing with large suppliers like FMCG companies. Branding is another advantage as the brand moves with customers as they move between cities. In the connected world, a multi-city brand gets more visibility and referral business over a local business that cannot go beyond a limited geography.

BigBasket management strongly feels that their business may look simple but it is very difficult to replicate. To begin with, capital can be a strong entry barrier for starting an online groceries business, as it is extremely capital intensive. Equally important are strong skill sets in supply chain, merchandising, and operations. Managing complex supply chains across locations and the last mile logistics make it a difficult business to emulate. If you can crack it, though, the market is huge. Vipul Parekh, VP of Finance and Marketing at BigBasket, says that their home base Bangalore alone has a market of more than ₹5000 crore to tap. What works in the favour of an online grocer is the fact that order values are small and the items routine, so customers are willing to try it out. Groceries are the smallest shelf life items in a household, so even if the experience is bad, customers can go back to their neighbourhood store without much grief. Secondly, since these are routine predictable purchases, technology can always help as it is good at replicating repeatable processes.

Groceries in Numbers

Organized food and grocery retail market is about $12 billion at the moment, growing at about 30 percent. Online retail is a very small part of it at the moment but is expected to grow faster and reach $17 billion in next 5 years.

TAKING THE BASKET TO THE CUSTOMER

An online grocery store is more of an offline business enabled by an online platform to receive orders and the software to smoothly run the back-end operations. The offline component of it is far bigger and complex than the online one. Let's look at the key components of an online grocery store.

Procurement

A grocery store has vendors across the spectrum; right from highly organized and well-established FMCG companies to unorganized vendors like farmers at the grassroot level. Both these vendors are equally important and products from them usually feature together on a customer order. With large players, the prices can be negotiated on the basis of volume for delivery across the warehouses. However, large players cannot deliver just in time, so a certain level of inventory of their items must be maintained based on the periodicity at which they deliver. So if a company supplies once in a week, the retailer must maintain 7-day inventory and if they supply once in a month, they have to maintain an inventory of one month so that orders can be best fulfilled. At the other end of the spectrum are the local suppliers like that of fresh fruits, vegetables, and dairy products. These products should be bought as fresh as possible and that means they should stay in the warehouse for as little time as possible. The supply chain team needs skills to deal with the systems and processes of big companies and at the same time an understanding of the local markets to know where and from whom to procure the daily fresh stock of perishable items.

Every city has its unique requirements according to local tastes and traditions. For instance, pickle consumed in various parts of the country is very different, or when it comes to rice—Sona Masuri is primarily consumed in south India while it is

Basmati in north India. The mix of various grains and other items is highly dependent on the local consumption habits. For the established brands too, the regional preferences differ a lot. According to BigBasket, about 30 percent of the products are unique to a city. It is also important for the sourcing team to gauge the quality of crop they are buying against factors like chemicals used or varieties of produce available. Region-wise they need to have an understanding of customer preferences, and have a working relationship with regional suppliers. I found out from the BigBasket management that they are very particular about selecting their buyers, as they are crucial in ensuring the quality of products sourced and at the right price. Good quality of products positively impacts customer satisfaction and lowers wastage due to rejects or returned orders. Most of their buyers come with 8–10 years of buying experience either from an agricultural background or from big FMGC companies and retail chains.

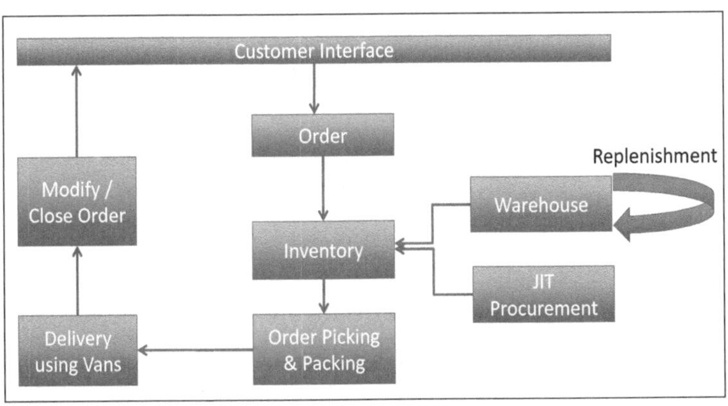

Fig 1: BigBasket Business Flow

Inventory Management

Inventory Management is again local for each city of operation. Even the blanket agreements at company level are eventually sourced at the local level according to the local requirements. The number of SKUs being sold is very high, a significant percentage of them have very low shelf and some of them need special handling like freezing. As of now, BigBasket has anywhere between 6000–8000 SKUs and this number is expected to go up to 15,000 as they expand their offerings in existing markets and as they enter new markets. Beyond a point, managing this kind of complex inventory manually is not possible as the business demands greater efficiency and productivity. BigBasket has effectively used technology to manage inventory automatically that includes placing automatic orders as the inventory reaches re-order levels. As of now, about 70 percent of their SKUs are part of their inventory and 30 percent are procured just in time, though the latter also spend 2–3 hours in the warehouse as they are washed, cleaned, checked for quality, graded, picked, and packed for customer orders.

Logistics and Order Fulfilment

Unlike most other e-commerce businesses, order cycles are very small in groceries businesses. Most of the items sold pertain to daily needs, and households order them on a regular basis. If the order cannot be fulfilled within a few hours, the provider would lose it to the competition—offline or another online vendor. Hence, there is a need to manage the logistics effectively and with a tightly controlled delivery mechanism in place.

BigBasket follows a hub and spoke model to manage its logistics. Warehouses act as the hubs where the orders are picked and packed, and the delivery routes of the vans are the spokes that connect to the customer homes. Each city they service has multiple warehouses as hubs and each one covers a certain area of the city. Size of the warehouse depends on the area and the number of households being served. All the elements of logistics are completely owned by the company. Delivery vans are specially designed, low cost, and temperature-controlled vehicles with a freezing and chilling chamber so that freshness of the frozen products is not lost till they reach the customer's doorstep. BigBasket feels that logistics and technology are core components of their business and hence cannot be outsourced. Moreover, most logistics providers would not be able to cater to the specific needs of the groceries business like short order delivery time, different packaging sizes, difficult to pack products, products that cannot be packed together, and cold chain requirement.

How fast can the order be delivered to the customer is a key to order fulfilment. Most online grocery stores started by giving a generic commitment of delivering within a given time say within 4 hours of placing the order. This leads to logistics chaos, as they never knew when and where the next order would come from. At some times during the day or week, they would need more vehicles than they have while at others the vehicles would lie unused. This would lead to delays in servicing orders during peak time and thus result in overall inefficiency. BigBasket delivers orders in 4 slots during the day, two in the morning and two in the evening. Customers can choose the slot while placing the order. With the slot system, BigBasket is able to service up to 99.5 percent orders on-time. They attribute the 0.5 percent delay to circumstances beyond their control like traffic jams, heavy rains, or vehicle breakdown. This is an innovation that gives customer a choice and the company a firm handle on planning and productivity. The idea of slots allows them to close the slots as they reach the delivery capacity; it allows them to place local orders according to the orders received and plan the routes of the vehicles in a way that minimizes mileage hence saving fuel and time for the delivery team. Depending on the addresses of the orders for a slot, route planning is automatically done by the software and handed over to the delivery team going with the van. In case of any delay, the back-end team can track their GPS enabled vehicles and inform the customers. Going forward, they may be able to convey more accurate delievery times to the customers, probably within a 15-minute window.

Vital Success Factors

Same day delivery
Choices wider than neighbourhood stores
Freshness of produce

Quality Assurance

In case of lifestyle products, customers do not have the need to touch and feel the products as they are familiar with the products, specially the branded packaged items. However, when it comes to groceries, with no defined standards of quality possibe, they are more concerned about the quality of the products and whether they are fresh and perishable. They need the product to be fresh, ripe or unripe as required. If the company can assure them of quality here, they are willing to let go of the need to touch and feel. BigBasket has started grading the products based on factors like ripeness, for example, a banana can be ripe—ready to be consumed, semi-ripe—consumed over next 2–3 days, or unripe—to be consumed as such. Customers can choose products based on their requirement and also know what to expect when they are delivered, minimizing the expectation and delivery gap to an extent. An attempt is being made to build confidence through a 'no questions asked' return policy with refund of the entire value of the product. At the same time, they have invested in a farm to door cold chain that ensures freshness of the fruits and vegetables till they are delivered. Experienced buyers coupled with a strong quality control process ensure that returns are few and far between.

No Explicit Cost Marketing

BigBasket is not indulging in any big-ticket marketing expenses. It is depending on three main factors for reaching out to new customers:

- Word of mouth: A belief that if investments are made in servicing the existing customers well, they would do the publicity for them.
- Delivery vans: Branded delivery vans roaming around the city are moving hoardings with no extra costs.
- Search Engine Marketing: Since the order placement is all online, they have invested in online marketing, but not in advertising as most other e-commerce players have.

This shows that they are putting their money in ensuring that the existing customer is happy and talking about them. Even their social media presence, both on Facebook and Twitter, is more in the form of a response to queries of customers who prefer to use social media for communicating. They are not running any marketing campaigns, barring some local radio ones, as of now. This sounds conservative compared to what other e-commerce players are doing, in terms of creating noise about their brands at all possible places, but then they are in the basic needs segment and not in luxury or customer choice segment.

Eco-consciousness

From the very beginning, BigBasket was firm about not using the ubiquitous plastic bags for deliveries. They made a one-time investment in plastic crates and baskets that are re-usable. Fresh produce is packed in perforated zip lock bags. Customers are encouraged to return the packaging after use. For delivery, total order is carried in different crates—not mixing the items that should be carried separately like kitchen items and toiletries. These crates are obviously re-used on a daily basis. This is small innovation today that may provide big returns eventually for the company, directly in terms of costs saved or carbon credits. Even with their route planning they do effective savings on fuels and this is not accounting for the fuel that their customers end up saving by not taking out their individual cars for each order they get supplied at home.

DRIVING EFFICIENCY WITH TECHNOLOGY

Any online business is eventually a technology-based and technology-dependent business. Customers interact with the company through a layer of technologies and they are serviced through yet another layer that the company uses to run its back-end operations. Orders are placed using either the portal or the mobile application, the latter allowing them to place orders on the go. Customers can also place their orders on phone but it is not something that the company encourages or the customers prefer. The website is a simple portal that lets you add items you want to buy to a basket as you browse through the various categories of products. Once you are done, you can choose a delivery slot and a payment method to complete the process. Cash on Delivery is a hygiene factor now for online portals, so keeping in line, BigBasket also gets paid for about 60 percent of its orders in cash after delivery. By the time this book comes out, the credit card on delivery would be operational too. The portal allows customers to save standard shopping lists to save time. BigBasket's basket feature can also be used as shopping list like the one every kitchen has to record out of stock items.

Technology is the core component of the business and hence is managed in-house. Some software components like inventory management and CRM have been bought from off the shelf vendors but are being managed completely in-house. Similarly the mobile application was designed in-house but the development of the same was outsourced to an external vendor. The ownership of all the software pieces remains completely in-house. I asked pointed questions about why keep it in-house and why not outsource it to the many vendors in Bangalore, where their head office is situated. The answer was that this ensures speed, agility, control, and flexibility which can be an issue with outsourced vendors. Releasing new features of the product takes longer time when it is managed by an outsourced partner and sometimes as a live business you need to do technology tweaking on the go.

For online stores like BigBasket, technology plays a big role in managing inventory and logistics by making these processes error-free, bringing down the cost of managing them, and saving costs through improved productivity of the workforce and the assets. It is practically impossible to manage the huge inventory of 10,000+ SKUs and order them on a daily basis. The sheer number of SKUs, and many of them similar looking with minor variations like different flavours of the same product, makes the order management prone to frequent errors. Manual ordering can lead to wrong orders that do not appear wrong on the surface like picking a wrong flavour of an ice cream with similar packaging. Cascading effect is that the product can keep lying in your inventory forever. This, in turn, means an unwanted cost while the absence of the right product means that the customer orders cannot be fulfilled.

Order picking is completely automated from breaking down the order into various categories of products and then routing to fulfilling centre. Picking is done automatically through hand-held devices and pickers are even told the shelf location of particular products in the warehouse to minimize their walking around. All the items are then scanned using bar code readers and put in different crates so that different types of items are not mixed—say you would not want to place a floor disinfectant with fresh fruits. There is complete tracking of who is picking what from where. After the picking, orders are assembled and if there are any changes in invoice the order value is recalculated instantly. Typical invoice changes occur due to big difference in the weight or quantity of fresh items that are difficult to procure in exact quantities, change in quantity due to lack of availability of enough quantity, or a minor change in the prices. Order modifications happen automatically with corresponding adjustment in the customer account. Assembled and adjusted orders are then ready to be delivered.

Route planning for the GPS-enabled delivery vans is done using routing algorithms to ensure maximum efficiency. It is important to understand here that the delivery vehicle needs to take a different route every time depending on the addresses on the order list. Orders are mapped to the vehicles and at any point in time, the company can track the expected time of delivery if the customer wishes to know. Each delivery person carries a smartphone with a delivery application installed on it. This application has details of the route they need to take, the orders to be delivered, money to be collected, and a form to take feedback from the customers post-delivery. The customer has to enter a pin on the device to confirm delivery and this acts as proof of delivery and order completion. If there are any items not accepted by the customer for quality or other reasons, the delivery staff can modify orders using the application and alter the customer invoice. On a scale of five, if the feedback rating is three or less, an alert is generated and a customer service agent from the call centre calls the customer to understand and address the reason of dissatisfaction. I once rejected a bunch of bananas that were too ripe for consumption and immediately a credit note was issued to my account. Moreover, the local service manager sent me another bunch of bananas at no cost. When I called to enquire, he said, 'Ma'am you wanted bananas today and though I may have returned your money, your need is not fulfilled. So, I have sent you bananas'. I was impressed to say the least. For the record, this incident took place before I started working on this book.

Pramod Jajoo, the Chief Technology Officer at BigBasket, passionately spoke about the sophisticated technology that he and his team manage. I wondered about the costs involved. Without getting into the numbers, Pramod said that the cost is justified by the accuracy and efficiency that it delivers. About the initial investment in technology, he said, the website existed in its earlier avatar as shopasyoulike.com for more than a year and serviced a small area within Bangalore. So the base platform was built and tested over a period of about 18 months before it took the new name of BigBasket and was launched in December, 2011.

ANALYTICS

As the customer data grows larger, analytics will help grow the business with more precision. Here are some of the basic analytics that BigBasket or similar companies can do with ease.

- Customer profiling—based on who is buying what and where.
- Recommendations based on past history.
- Specially designed promotions and discounts.
- Test marketing for new products from suppliers.
- Order data.
- Unfulfilled requests that can be catered to.
- Inventory management.
- Merchandizing planning can be fine tuned.

When I look at my order history on BigBasket, I know how much of what I have consumed. Sometimes I raise an eyebrow and say to myself that I have been consuming too much of fried snacks, or too many potatoes have been coming home. I add some more fruit the next time I order or some green leafy vegetables. If I can alter my decisions based on a small list of items that I see myself consuming, I think there may be potential in sharing their consumption patterns with customers who may want to see their analytics. I know that companies like BigBasket are still thinking about analytics as a tool to enhance business or make it more efficient. I am not sure if it works in their favour if they let the customers analyse their own consumption pattern, but as customers we would appreciate this analysis and, if I am not thinking out aloud, I am sure many research agencies and policy makers would welcome such data. Of course, we have to wait till the data grows to that level.

On a closing note, BigBasket is also an example of an online e-commerce business that is a combination of deep domain knowledge of grocery retailing business combined with a smart use of technology. It is a complex business that uses technology as much as an interface with its customers as it uses it to manage its operations. Online grocery stores are an evolving entity; how much market they will take away from the physical stores and at what rate, how the two of them will co-exist—only time will reveal. We as customers can probably expect the best of both worlds when there is a store at our hands and another at an arm's length.

References

Information provided by the company
Company website
Media reports on the company website
Conversation with Pramod Jajoo and Vipul Parekh of BigBasket.com

Name of the company:	Innovative Retail Concepts Pvt Ltd
Website:	www.BigBasket.com
Year of incorporation:	2011
Founders:	V.S. Sudhakar, Hari Menon, Vipul Parekh, V.S. Ramesh and Abhinay Choudhary
Headquarters:	Bangalore
No. of offices:	3
No. of employees:	600+ as on November 2013
Cities present in:	Bangalore, Mumbai, Hyderabad
No. of registered users:	1,50,000 as on November 2013
No. of page views per month:	4 million approx.
No. of SKUs/product sold:	12000+
No. of orders per day:	Average 1800 per day

CARATLANE

Diamonds Galore

SELLING HIGH-VALUE, DESIGN-INTENSIVE, lifestyle products like diamonds and jewellery online, where people cannot touch, feel, or try them, sounded almost impossible to me till I studied a few portals doing exactly that. As I studied these businesses, I noted the key changes happening in and around this industry and its customers. Over generations, we have trusted only our family jewellers. The range available to us was limited by the knowledge and inventory of this small-time jeweller. Our tastes were defined by what he could offer to us and new designs were a rarity. Then came Tanishq from the house of Tatas and they, kind of, organized this fragmented industry where every small vendor had a set of households as captive customers. They brought in the concept of brand in the precious jewellery segment. Women are the major consumers for jewellery. With the evolving socio-economic profile of women in the society, their jewellery preferences are also getting diversified and women are looking for new designs. This is creating an unmet need in the jewellery business which opens up an opportunity for innovation in such businesses. Some traditional jewellers and some new age entrepreneurs are exploring this space to cater to the new needs of Indian women and to give them more options than they have ever had. We look at one such business in detail in this chapter.

CaratLane is India's leading online jewellery retailer that sells diamonds, gold jewellery, and gold coins. They have been around since 2008, when it was still 'early days' for the niche online retail stores. Their product portfolio includes a range of solitaire diamonds, solitaire-based jewellery, ready-made diamond jewellery, gold and engraved jewellery, designer collections, and gold coins with an option of limited customization. Their supply chain includes 4000 vendors of solitaires from across the world, an in-house design team, in-house manufacturing facility, and customers across the Indian cities served through the technology platform with support from the logistics team.

The founders of CaratLane—Mithun Sacheti and Srinivasa Gopalan—form a unique combination of domain and technology expertise. Mithun comes from the family that owns Jaipur Gems and brings with him the inherent understanding of the jewellery business coupled with his education as a Gemologist. Srinivasa is an experienced technology professional and understands the technology requirements of an e-commerce venture.

MAKING INROADS IN A TRADITIONAL BUSINESS

To understand the jewellery business, we need to first understand the nature of its product. Jewellery is a luxury item. People buy jewels to pamper themselves or their loved ones. It is not a necessity. People are usually in no hurry to buy jewellery, except during weddings in the family and those too are mostly planned events. India has a very strong tradition of buying gold and diamond jewellery on festivals and on special occasions like marriages or births in the family. It is also used as a gifting option amongst close family members. Buying jewellery serves two purposes—as an adornment for the owner and as an investment in precious commodities, a kind of systemic investment plan. Jewellery businesses have been the domain of traditional jewellers who have been associated with families across generations and a lot of them operated from their traditional marketplaces called Jauhari Bazaars. If you walk through the old markets in the cities, you can still spot a Jauhari Bazaar where you see small shops with workshops in the back. You can buy, exchange, repair, redesign, or sell your precious jewellery here. Trust factor plays the biggest role between the buyer and the seller. Buyers believe they can go back to the trusted merchant for exchange and get a fair value. Observed from outside, this makes the market look very unorganized and the choices for customers limited to what the merchant has to offer. The first major change in this industry came when the Tata Group launched their branded jewellery store, Tanishq almost two decades back. It played a key role in moving the customer preferences to branded jewellery through innovations like Karatmeter that allows testing of the purity of the metal, a key concern of buyers. It also leveraged the overall trust that the Tata brand carries in the country. Tanishq also sells online now, but it is more of an extension of their offline businesses.

CaratLane is the next generation jewellery store that is completely an online business. Even when they open experience lounges to be closer to the customer, to let them see and feel the product, the order processing still happens through the portal and the order is delivered at the customer's doorstep and not at the experience lounge.

Products offered at CaratLane include:

- Solitaire diamonds of all shapes, colours, cut, and clarity grades, with sizes starting from 30 cents going all the way up to 10+ carats
  - Customized setting based on choice of solitaire and design
- Specially designed jewellery collections in gold, gold and diamond, gold and other precious stones
  - Designs based on research of trends and tastes
- Gold coins
- Independent collection of:
  - Earrings
  - Finger rings
  - Pendants

Their diamond range makes them the largest repository of diamonds in the world. They procure diamonds just in

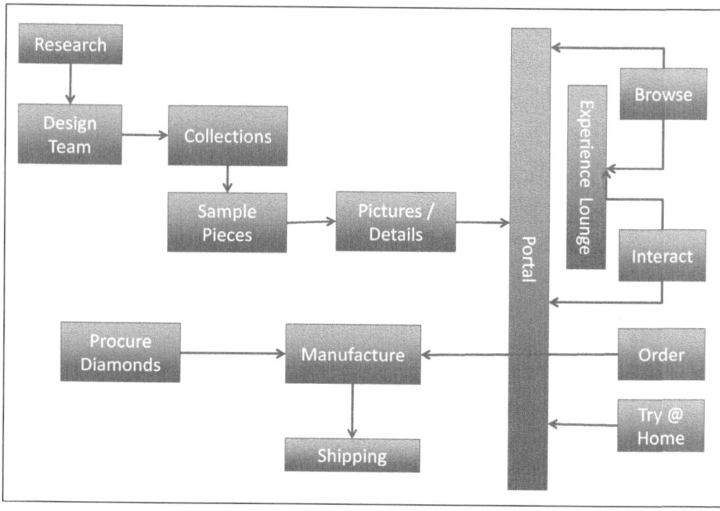

Fig 1: CaratLane Business Process

time based on customer orders implying no need to hold any inventory and that brings down their costs drastically. There is no capital held in the inventory and there is no inventory carrying cost.

FIGURING OUT THE CUSTOMER

In this gold-obsessed country, almost anyone with just enough money to afford gold would qualify as a potential customer. Serving the needs of every customer is a daunting task. A business needs to focus on a category of customers that they can serve best. CaratLane is focussing on young, upwardly mobile section of the population that is looking for original, contemporary designs in gold, diamond, and precious stones.

Siddharth Kapoor, VP of Marketing at CaratLane, told me that there are two levels at which they are trying to analyse the customer insights they get from the data generated by the website visits, online chats, and phone conversations besides the hardcore sales data.

At first level, they are trying to get customers to buy jewellery online, and here they have no precedence and limited market research data exists. There are two known fears of customers—buying jewellery from someone not known and buying jewellery online. CaratLane is trying to figure out other inhibitions that come in the way of a customer buying jewellery online so that they can address them effectively. They study various data points available to them like click stream patterns of the visitors, chat transcripts, and phone calls coupled with the feedback, complaints, and compliments they receive from their customers. All these data points are analysed to derive insights. For example, they figured out that it is difficult for customers to judge the size of a piece by looking at the picture or by reading its dimensions. So they added pictures of models wearing the pieces so that customers get a more realistic feel of the size along with a better sense of how it would look when worn. Similarly to enable customers with a real-time view of the solitaires, they are now launching a multi-angle view of the stones through which customers can virtually rotate the stone as if they were holding it in their hand and see it from all possible angles. To begin with, they had the same price point for different sizes of the same product, say finger rings. Variable pricing for different sizes was introduced based on customer feedback that pointed out that the amount of gold used is different in different sizes. Another example that Siddharth quoted is that of choosing the right diamond given a desire and a budget. Most people need to decide on a tradeoff between the quality and size. They need help from someone who is an expert and can be consulted. CaratLane addressed this in two ways. One, they created documentation on tips and tricks for choosing diamonds on their portal. This educates the customers about various aspects one needs to be aware of while choosing a diamond and the informed questions they need to ask when buying. This documentation in itself can help take decisions. Secondly, they hired trained gemologists in their sales team who can help customers in choosing the right diamonds.

At the second level they are trying to get an insight into customer preferences to figure out what they are looking for in the products. They would then use this data to design their collections and product catalogue in such a way that it is in tune with customers' tastes and preferences. For example, if young couples are looking to seal their relationship with solitaires then they put together a huge collection of it. If working women need jewellery to complement their wardrobes for different occasions like work and leisure, they have collections to meet those particular needs. This is going to be an on-going industry research at any point in time.

Bringing Men into the Picture

CaratLane started conscious brand building in early 2013, more than five years after they started the portal. What I found interesting about their branding philosophy is their focus on both men and women. They are targeting the young and upwardly mobile by offering them diamonds and jewellery to celebrate their personal milestones. They emphasize on traditional events like marriage proposals, birthdays, and anniversaries but have also added new age milestones like winning a deal, getting a promotion, and other milestones customers might have defined for themselves. This strategy is based on an insight that young Indians are are celebrating their relationship moments more elaborately. There is a constant urge of going beyond the ordinary way of doing things, when it comes to celebrating milestone moments.

Most jewellery brands tend to focus heavily on women, who are the prime consumers of the product. CaratLane on the other hand, is trying to target men too by helping them choose the right jewellery for the women in their lives. Men form about 40 percent of CaratLane's customer base, though I assume this figure includes group buying by families led by men. Their marketing campaigns too aim to establish CaratLane as a brand that helps inexperienced men make good jewellery buying decision. For example in their 'Making a Proposal' campaign with the solitaire offering, their first TV commercial showed a man proposing to a woman with a solitaire from CaratLane.

Offline Reach

A 360-degree marketing approach of the company includes a TV campaign, outdoor hoardings at prime sites and key spaces in relevant media. They also use mediums like digital and mobile marketing, direct marketing, and smart Out Of Home displays. The idea is to reach out to the target group and compel them to checkout the website or walk in to the experience lounge. To augment their offline connect, CaratLane regularly organizes outreach programmes at societies/communities, exhibitions, shopping malls, corporate campuses, and high-end residential societies. In alliance with private banks, they reach out to their elite customers and engage through specially designed events like Diamond Appreciation Workshops. Sometimes they conduct wine and cheese crash courses on diamonds for priority banking customers of some partner banks. They participate in various community programmes in their target segment in neighbourhoods of key cities like Chennai, Hyderabad, and Bangalore by putting up a stall. As people throng to these programmes in all their finery to celebrate the festival, they can walk up to these stalls and obtain information about CaratLane and its collections. In a small way they make their presence in shopping malls and corporate campuses through contests and events.

Online Alliances

CaratLane partners with other prominent online brands to offer value that works at multiple levels:

1. Reach out to the customer base of their partner brands through specially designed offers for them. It allows partner brands also to reward and engage their existing customers in a new way

2. Enables CaratLane.com to acquire new customers in the above process
3. Strengthens the brand through better visibility

In simple words, these co-branded campaigns work for both partners as they reach out to both companies' customer base and increase visibility for both brands. Some of the brands that CaratLane has worked for are MakeMyTrip.com, ICICI Bank, American Express, Platinum Guild International, Zivame.com, and Basicslife.com.

KEEP IT SIMPLE, TECHNICALLY

Without repeating the importance of technology for an online portal, let me give you the technical lowdown on CaratLane. CaratLane's online portal is built on an open source technology platform called Magenta that is now owned by eBay. They use a framework called LAMP (Linux, Apache, MySql, php). Magenta has been specially designed for e-commerce websites and users who have to just plug and play. A product just needs to be configured for its look and feel and it is ready to be launched. Of course, customizations will always follow. An in-house team of about 15 engineers develops and maintains the portal. Work on the portal started way back in 2007, almost a year before the first version was launched in 2008. It was outsourced to a technology partner who provided the technology services till 2012 when the management decided to bring it inside its own fold. This was a point I wanted to explore as it is evident that all successful digital enterprises run in-house technology divisions.

Guru, the technology head of CaratLane, relates control and flexibility as two key factors in favour of having technology teams in-house. The biggest disadvantage with outsourcing technology is the loss of agility. An upcoming portal needs dexterity in switching or changing set operations, whether to launch new features or to respond to competition. There is a constant need to re-prioritize the features that are in the pipeline. Till the product reaches a fair level of maturity, it is very difficult for the product team to concretely visualize the product requirements—especially short-term requirements. Lots of new ideas are generated on an everyday basis and they need to be experimented with. When technology is outsourced, the provider requires written specifications from the company on which they base their project and resource planning. Any change to these specifications needs to go through the management process and usually takes up a lot of time. So the choice really boils down between Big Bang approach with an outsourcing partner or short and agile steps with an in-house team.

The in-house team at CaralLane now works on a small release cycle. Cycle time for releasing new features has come down from 1.5 months to about a week. Sometimes they have even launched new features in less than three days. This allows the management to prioritize the release of features based on the strategy direction or market conditions. Quick launch of a new feature can give a first mover advantage to the business. Most of the releases are done at night so that there is minimum disruption due to glitches, if any, as a majority of the customers are based in India, and website traffic is relatively low at night. Given the product category they deal with, traffic is generally not as high as other e-commerce portals, at least till now.

A CUT ABOVE THE REST

A leader always does some things differently and that is why it leads the pack. Let us look at some of the innovations that keep CaratLane ahead of its competition and better prepared for the future.

Large Collection

Variety is an online store's big advantage and not many offline stores can compete with them on this front. A network of 4000 suppliers of diamonds makes CaratLane the largest diamond store in the world with about 1,25,000 solitaires to choose from. This is a very difficult advantage to beat for its competition. Unlike traditional jewellers, they need not push the stock they have to the customers as they source the diamonds from suppliers based on demand. This, in the true sense, provides the customers with the widest range of possible options. This advantage comes from the strength of their supplier relations and their ability to source the diamonds on demand.

Lower Costs

The just-in-time and direct procurement of diamonds from vendors helps CaratLane bring down the costs substantially.

Customers get a direct benefit of this cost saving; in fact, their advertisements clearly mention a claim of being 25 percent cheaper than competition. This claim of 25 percent intrigued me and I wanted to understand the dynamic behind it. Calvin John, VP of offline marketing at CaratLane explained that for CaratLane, unlike physical jewellery stores, there isn't any inventory holding cost for extremely high-value items like diamonds, real estate cost of running and maintaining a luxurious store in a prime locality, or personnel and operational costs associated with brick and mortar stores. They conducted some surveys in key jewellery markets across the country and the figure for the savings varied between 20–40 percent.

25 percent Lower Costs: The Game Behind the Claim

- Direct sourcing from solitaire vendors, eliminating intermediaries
- In-house manufacturing facility
- No high inventory holding costs—biggest cost for traditional jewellery retailing business
- No real estate cost
- No high overheads like human resources, operating costs of running stores

Customer Education

CaratLane understood that most customers depend on a jeweller's advice while buying diamonds and this stems from the lack of basic knowledge about diamonds. With the intent to bridge this gap and enable customers to make an informed and educated choices, they launched a knowledge series on understanding diamonds. As I browsed through their website, I learnt that a diamond can be judged based on shape, cut, colour, clarity, carat, polish, symmetry, fluorescence, table, and depth. A tips and tricks section gives simple tips on what to look for before buying a diamond. While some of these aspects are self-evident, some need a little more understanding. For example there are conflict diamonds or blood diamonds that have a violent history associated with them. Many people have reservations in buying them and would like an assurance that the diamonds they are buying do not come with bad vibes. Though this knowledge is extremely helpful to customers, CaratLane would have to keep innovating here, as static content can be replicated by competition in no time and this content can be referred to while shopping at competing websites.

Delivering Choice and Convenience at Home

Cash on Delivery (CoD) now comes as a customer expectation for e-commerce portals in India, and CaratLane delivers on this expectation too. Cash on Delivery is limited to under ₹50,000 at CaratLane as there are obvious limitations with handling big amounts of cash. CaratLane has a 'Try at Home' feature that allows customers to choose upto five items to be sent to them to try at home and make a choice. This allows them to take the opinion of family and friends who are big influencers in high-value jewellery purchases. These two features are paramount to customers who get to choose and try products, and also pay for them in cash after delivery. In fact, the only inventory that CaratLane maintains is that of Try at Home pieces and display pieces at their city experience lounges. According to the company, Try at Home feature can work wonders for converting customers who, today, are sitting on the fences. Try at Home is available for all items priced above a certain price point and this helps establish a comfort level for customers before they make high-value purchases.

Most orders are made to order in their manufacturing facility at Chennai. Average time to manufacture and deliver an order is between 15–20 days. This is a substantially long time, and which I think acts as a limitation for CaratLane, compared to physical stores, where customers can walk in and walk out with the piece or inventory based online retailers that deliver in about three-days time. In my opinion, CaratLane should work on bringing down this time to at least a week. This would allow them to cater to customers looking for instant purchases.

Designer Collections

2500 BC, Summer, Fleur, Everyday Diva, Mayur, Italian, and Traditions are some of the designer collections available on CaratLane. Calvin John passionately speaks about the research they do to come out with new collections, and the stories that their designers craft with metals and stones. There are different collections like the ones that are inspired by Indian architecture are called Eterna or Fleur; and is inspired by floral shapes. They have a team of designers who are working on these collections based on research. One example of their research process was that of looking at Bollywood characters and the kind of jewellery they would like to wear. Take Preity Zinta's character in Kabhi Alvida Na Kehna where she is a married, career-oriented woman who manages an ad agency on her own in New York. The jewellery of an independent woman living in a cosmopolitan city needs to reflect and accentuate her personality. CaratLane is trying to go a few levels deeper by evaluating category needs of different women in today's world. They recognize that the jewellery needs of a banker differ from a woman working in a creative role or a high flying professional's requirement would be different from that of a school teacher. In essence, they are trying to fill in the gap between the cosmopolitan design sensibilities of a modern woman's wardrobe and the traditional jewellery designs available in the market. They are making contemporary designs that are lightweight, and hence low priced, and can regularly be bought like other accessories.

Jewellery collections are turned around every 15 to 20 days, to keep the brand fresh and dynamic Customer feedback indicates that this is a big differentiator for them and customers keep coming back to check new designs that they do not get so easily at traditional stores.

Experience Lounges

Offline experience lounges are being set up to showcase the products to customers that they can try and order. This is combining the best of both worlds online and offline with limited inventory cost. Customers can touch and feel the product before placing an order online. Lounges are designed as an extension of the online browsing experience that subconsciously makes them more comfortable with the website. The only downside I see is that customers may want to buy the product they have in hand and not wait for 15–20 days before they can have it.

Hygiene Factors

- Multiple payment options including Cash on Delivery
- 30-day return guarantee
- Lifetime exchange guarantee
  - Packaging
  - Under camera
  - Temper proof travel safe metal boxes for shipping
- Insured Shipping
- Certification of purity for diamonds and gold coins
- Assurance of conflict-free diamonds

Still to be Conquered

Given the limited number of online jewellery retailers, the real competition for companies like CaratLane is still the neighbourhood traditional jewellery stores. These stores are not only always available closer to the customer but because of the physical presence are also more trusted. CaratLane and other online jewellery retailers will have to build the brands through customer service and quality that customers would trust as much as they trust the neighbourhood store.

The challenge is to gradually build customer confidence for buying high-value precious jewellery online. CaratLane is trying to lure customers by offering designs that are not available with traditional jewellers and by offering the largest range of solitaire diamonds possible. However, full customization as per the customer needs is something that is still missing in their offerings. They offer only limited customization. Would customers switch to mass designs that they can potentially see on others as well or would they prefer their own designs is something only time will tell.

I found CaratLane's story fascinating because they have cracked a category that in my mind was one of the most difficult ones to crack. It would be interesting to see hereon how they scale up from this base, how the emergence of online retailers impacts the offline ones, and if offline retailers will jump on to the online bandwagon and reach newer markets through them. Since this is a design-heavy space, will it lead to the emergence of a new breed of designers who can sell their designs through these portals? Most importantly, I am sure the modern Indian woman is happy to see designs that suit her wardrobe better, fit into her budget, and can be bought at her own convenience.

REFERENCES

Information provided by the company

Conversations with the Calvin John, Siddharth Kapoor, Gurukeerthi Gurunathan of CaratLane

CARATLANE.COM

India's Trusted Online Jeweller

Name of the company:	CaratLane Trading Private Limited
Website:	www.caratlane.com
Year of incorporation:	2007
Founders:	Mithun Padamchand Sacheti and A. Srinivasa Gopalan
Headquarters:	Chennai
No. of offices:	4
Experience Lounges:	Hyderabad and Delhi
No. of employees:	150
Manufacturing units:	Chennai
No. of registered users:	Over 3 lakhs
No. of SKUs:	1,00,000 solitair diamonds and over 2,000 jewellery designs
No. of collections:	18

PART 2

CONTENT

CONTENT

Creators Go Online

CONTENT ENTERPRISES ARE CENTRED around creative professionals, people who create content for various mediums to consume. Adding the business angle means creating content or curating content for a certain audience to consume. In the traditional world, the onus of content creation rested with people who had the knack for it—filmmakers, writers, painters, and designers. Their job was to create content and hand it over to someone who would distribute it, and based on how the content was received by its consumers, receive financial returns on it. Let's take newspapers for instance. They create content based on news and current affairs and the second part of their business is distribution of newspapers across the country by a network of big and small distributors. The whole business is funded by advertisements placed in the newspaper and small amounts that people pay for subscription. For films too, content is created by production houses and then distributed through a team of distributors who sell the film at cinema halls and

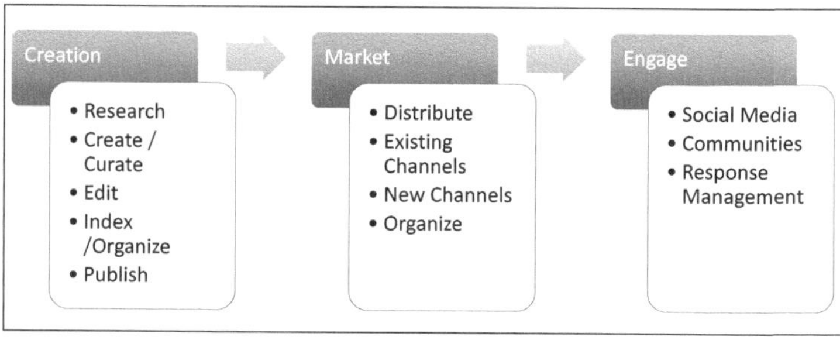

Fig 1: Content Lifecycle

get financial returns. Switch to the digital world, you find that content creation has been democratized and does not remain a bastion of a few. Here, the distribution of content is through technology and technology-enabled channels.

Majority of traditional content businesses have been running all these years supported by advertisements as the key revenue model, and the norm seems to carry over to new media as well. Advertising on websites makes business sense as it provides a perfect platform for businesses to reach out to exactly the audience they want to reach. Technology-enabled online platforms allow granular visibility to the user's profile like where the user is, what is his demographic profile, and what time is he found online. This is exactly what an advertiser needs for a targeted marketing. High traffic on websites justifies the marketing budget for the complimentary brands and businesses like brands catering to kids can place their advertisements effectively on parenting websites or mommy blogs. This is unlike traditional media where the reach is far wider even today but the real target audience is usually a small percentage of that. This essentially implies a waste of effort and resources on people who were outside the target segment.

Creating content in the pre-Internet days was limited by many entry barriers, which came primarily from the limited space that was available to hold the content. A newspaper or a magazine had limited pages that they could circulate; Radio and TV channels had only 24 hours that they could fill every day. The Internet removed these barriers completely. Now, there is endless space available for all kinds of content. There are easy-to-use tools available to help create, publish, and market content and all this can be achieved in a very economical way. This has opened a whole new world for individuals or groups of individuals who create content. They can now publish their creative works, share it with potential audience, and in the process get connected with countless people who consume their content. Some of the common formats for publishing online include blogs, e-magazines, photo galleries, and online music and video channels. Blogging has created a new breed of cyber celebrities, many of whom would have been lost in the crowd but for the Internet as a medium that has made it possible for them to voice their opinions or share their expertise. Some experts go to the extent of saying that anyone with an online channel to voice their opinion or share their knowledge can be counted as a media channel.

Content entrepreneurs are in the business of creating and monetizing content. They may either sell the content they create or attract advertisers with their engagement with an audience that regularly consumes their content. Content can be in the form of written word, images, music, audio, videos, games or a combination of two or more of these.

The interactive nature of web content adds another layer of content called conversational content or user-generated layer of content. This layer comes from the users of the content who share their opinion through comments or feedback. Most commonly this layer is used to spread the word around by encouraging users to share content on their personal social media channels. It totally depends on the businesses how they use this layer. User-generated content layer differentiates an online content business from an offline one which, more often than not, ends with broadcasting.

Most content businesses I studied, started with the entrepreneur himself being the content creator. They soon realized that as an individual, or even as a small group of individuals, it is not possible to scale your business. For a business to take shape, the amount of content required is huge along with quality that can compete with the best. So most of them have gone beyond themselves and have added content created by others to achieve scale. Common ways to curate content for a content-based business are:

- Co-creation: Create content with the help of a larger team around the business focus.
- Aggregation: Aggregate content spread across the web on a theme or a niche.
- Curate: Host content contributed by independent content owners on your platform.
- User-generated content: Conversational content generated by the users or followers of the portal.

Value chain for online content entrepreneurs involves managing the complete chain of the process from ideating about the content to creating , editing, publishing, distributing, marketing it on multiple channels, engaging with the consumers of the content, and answering to all their responses responsibly. In a traditional offline setup, these are all individual functions handled by different people, so the content specialists focus only on their area of expertise, i.e. creating the content. For their online counterparts though, the roles overlap. Everyone needs to have a basic understanding of technology and the ability to handle it. Those who are not very conversant with technology will have to learn it to an extent. A content creator's role does not end with creating the content; as authors they needs to engage with the audience and interact with them on all channels that distribute their content. They need to study their response and take that feedback into their next content creation.

Technology requirements for content entrepreneurs are not very high compared to the other two categories in this book. They primarily need a sturdy placeholder for the content supported by an engaging design. Placeholder technologies like blogging platforms, video channels, and photo sharing softwares are easily available—a lot of them are free as well. It seems that the base technology has more or less reached a mature stage although continuous improvements will continue to happen at their own pace. The challenge is to keep track of all the small innovations that keep cropping up like small snippets of technology called plug-ins that can be game changers for the way content looks, feels, and engages.

The open source culture of content sharing keeps throwing up new plug-ins that can be plugged into the base technology platforms of content businesses. In fact, software engineers writing codes are themselves creating content in the form of these small pieces that can be used by anyone.

What is of utmost importance for a content business besides the quantity and quality of content is how the content is organized on the portal and how easy it is for the users to locate what they come looking for. Design, thus, plays an important role in content-based enterprises. It impacts how the users engage with the content, how easily they can search for relevant content, how well they can connect with other users who have similar profiles as them, and how often they come back. In cases where content also has a user-generated layer, design impacts how easily users can contribute to that layer. Content businesses are also adding intelligence to their portal design by dynamically choosing what the user sees when she first lands on the page or if the page can be customized based on who the user is and where she is coming from.

Key revenue streams for content businesses include:

- Direct sale of content; like ImagesBazaar sells images.
- Subscription model wherein against a fee, content can be licensed for use for a limited period or for limited purposes; like music portals.
- Advertising
  - Paid targeted advertising-based on the nature of content, like advertisers at Zomato pay to be seen by people who are located in the vicinity of their restaurants and hotels when they are searching for options to eat out.

This increases the possibility of diners choosing them over other eating out options in the area and an instant conversion from their advertisement.

- Niche audience for a category of advertisers; like CommonFloor has a niche community around property needs and, hence, is an ideal platform for real estate companies to advertise.
- Ad networks are are generic models available to all kinds of publishers—from personal blogs to best performing gaming websites. Ad networks use technology intelligently to dynamically place the right ad for the right audience in a given geography, for a certain demographic at the right time. By using ad networks that work on revenue sharing models, publishers do not have to reach out to the advertisers individually.

In this category, most prominent offline players have already established their online presence. Most major newspapers and magazines are already online and most entertainment businesses have a YouTube channel. It is relatively easy to co-exist on both offline and online platforms for businesses and even cross promote them. Pure play online players are gaining their own strength that comes from having complete focus on only one channel. It would be interesting to see how the two will converge or co-exist.

Mobile devices are fast becoming the preferred platform for content consumption. People are increasingly using mobiles as primary gadgets to search and browse through content. Almost all players in the content space have either a mobile application or have enhanced their websites for optimized viewing on the mobile or tablets.

Comparative content is another type of content that sits above the base content and generates comparison among similar offerings, allowing users to make informed choices. Independent comparative content portals are emerging in some segments like financial and consumer products. In others, they are embedded within the product or service offerings; like most portals selling electronic gadgets let you compare features. Where the product is standard, like say books or even specific models of consumer goods, price comparison websites come into play. They are very popular in the western world but no significant players exist in India as of now. This is a secondary or a tertiary segment that would emerge once the base portals attain maturity. Core revenue generation model for comparison sites is usually lead generation for the e-commerce portals and getting a commission on the sales generated through them. Of the established comparison portals, PolicyBazaar is a significant player in insurance products segment while in horizontal portals, CompareIndia has some visibility.

Content starts being profitable after it has attained a certain level of user base and can generate enough daily traffic for the advertisers to show interest. Content portals and social networking platforms share a very interesting relationship—they feed as well as compete with each other. Content portals compete directly with social media portals to grab eyeballs of the users. At the same time they also distribute their content by sharing it across these networks and encourage their consumers to do the same. Niche content-based portals use content distribution networks to build audience. While doing so they need to ensure that traffic comes to their websites and their content is not hosted by any other portal. Advertising networks like Google Adsense also work on the same principle and their payouts become substantial only after enough traffic is generated by the content. Direct advertising is not applicable to all kinds of publishers but businesses are trying to come up with hybrid models where revenue can come from a mix of ad networks, direct advertising, and paid subscriptions.

Among the various content entrepreneurs I spoke to, there were some common insights like content should have either global appeal or hyper-local appeal. Entertainment still remains a key vertical with various formats like videos, games, music, and, of course, readable text. Text-based content is the most prolific on the web, as it is easy to create and only needs an opinion or a point of view in the writer's head. At the base of this segment are a plethora of blogs that are written by mostly individuals. At the other end are the news-based portals and niche content-based portals on various topics like cricket, or portals which specifically address women. Images compliment the text-based content and also exist on independent portals either as a commodity to be sold or to tell a story. With mobile phones making cameras ubiquitous, the picture content being shared on the Internet has grown exponentially. This is also true for video content to an extent, but professional quality video content needs cost-intensive production facilities and a creative concept to work with. The biggest advantage of video content is that it is not dependent on language tools and can be made in any language; the limitation though comes in the shape of low bandwidth. Online games are pure technology-based content that did not exist in this form and shape in any offline avatar.

Creating a large quantity of content is one strategy that almost all content entrepreneurs use as it is usually impossible to tell what content is going to hit the bull's eye. So as you create more content, you increase the probability of some content going viral and generating traffic on the portal. Almost all successful companies in this space look for a network of creators to contribute to their content portfolio on a revenue sharing model. Repetitive use of popular content is a must for the content channels to become profitable, as creating content is a cost- and effort-intensive process.

If it is easy to publish at the click of a button, it is as easy for anyone to copy your content at another click of a button. Piracy or copyright infringement can be a drain on a content entrepreneur's resources and bandwidth. As we shall see in the cases discussed in this section, some formats are struggling with piracy; some have found ways to leverage the pirates as networks; while others have chosen to ignore it as a necessary evil of the game.

When I began speaking to various content-based businesses, I wanted to cover different types of content. By the time I sat down to write this section, I had discovered many new types of content and concepts they employ that this section looks far richer. There were many small businesses that have excellent concepts but are yet to achieve a scale where they can make a substantial difference.

ImagesBazaar to me is a poster boy of pure content business. They have not just made a profitable business out of studio images, but have also organized a scattered industry into a single platform. Almost every business I spoke to was ImagesBazaar's customer and had used their images. To me they are also an excellent example of leveraging the network of photographers and other stock images players. They have plugged themselves into the global scene by partnering with global leader Getty Images. They are also leveraging the power of other smaller Indian stock photography companies by hosting their images on their site. Like an agile and responsive business, they have kept up with the times by venturing into microstock photography. I admire the sheer focus that they have on India and Indian images.

Zomato was not a part of my initial list, but as I spoke to them, they came out as the strongest contender in this category as they are the only company that has gone 'global' in the true sense of the word. They are an example of building content around one niche—restaurant food in their case—and becoming the default choice of people looking to eat out. As a corollary, they become the default choice of restaurants and hotels to advertise. They are also an example of building layers of content, with a core layer of content that they tightly control and the rest of the layers coming from their users who create active review data and give them tips on adding core content.

Games2win is a company that thrives on being creative in coming out with the fun, casual games. They are an example of creating content that has global appeal for an age group, albeit sometimes with a little contextual tweaking here and there. The content on Games2win has its own niche within the gaming space and they are focussed only on creating games for their audience. Their innovation which was built to combat piracy, and eventually end leveraging the pirate's network to their advantage, is worth a look. Their story, over the years, has many examples of experiments that they tried and failed at, the trick lies in accepting the failure and moving on. Though I'm not an avid gamer, I did play a few on their portal while doing research and found them pathetically addictive. Now I know why they are amongst the most visited websites in the world.

Chai with Lakshmi is an online chat show, similar to TV chat shows, run by Lakshmi Rebecca. She is almost a single woman army working on bringing small but meaningful conversations to our computer screens. At the time of writing, this is probably the youngest and the smallest business in terms of revenues or even impact. I had the choice of replacing this case with another bigger one, but I was too impressed by the mission Lakshmi was on, that had conversations at the core to make India more inclusive. Debates, arguments, and discussions are at the core of a democracy even when they are not political topics. To me her conversations also cross-pollinate ideas by spreading them. She is putting the spotlight on people who are deserving but don't get a platform to voice their views. Her Inclusive India initiatives take this to another level and my own conversations with her brought out her vision that I feel is going to go places in the future.

Some of the content categories that could not be a part of this book are text-based content companies like news portals, live music portals, and entertainment portals.

ZOMATO

Spoiling you with Food Choices

FOOD IS A BASIC human need. We need it at least three times a day, if not more. Look at it from the business lens and literally every human being is a potential customer. To be practical, everyone in the vicinity of the food offering is a potential customer. It is no wonder then that Zomato—a portal that brings menus and other useful information about restaurants, both big and small, to its users at the click of a button—is one of most visited websites, especially just before lunch and dinner time every day.

It all began with a small observation that young Deepinder Goyal had while standing in a cafeteria queue at his office where everyone wanted to have a look at the same menu. He thought of a simple solution—why not scan all those menus and put them on Intranet for everyone to see and reduce this congestion at lunchtime? Soon he joined hands with his colleague, Pankaj Chaddah, at Bain & Company to experiment with this idea outside the company. Together they started spending their weekends collecting menus from restaurants across Delhi and NCR. In July 2008, they launched Foodiebay with menus from 1200 restaurants along with details like location, contact information, average cost of meal for two etc. By the end of 2009, they had included restaurants from Mumbai and Kolkata too and were ready to take the plunge into making it into a commercial business. Soon, Gunjan Patidar joined in to take care of technology platform. 2010 was a milestone year when the cities of Pune and Bangalore got added to their portfolio and investors like Info Edge (India) Ltd became interested in investing in the business. Foodiebay was re-christened as Zomato to make the platform open for verticals other than food, though right now they seem completely focussed on food and see enough potential in the space to stay there for the foreseeable future.

With capital in hand in 2011, Zomato added Chennai, Hyderabad, Ahmedabad, and Chandigarh to its menu and launched the mobile version of the website. Info Edge gave them another round of funding and they expanded their team and started focussing on marketing, brand building, and development of Zomato portal as a product. That year they experimented with selling online tickets for events like New Year parties that are a big craze in restaurants around the year-end holiday season. In 2012, they went international with Singapore and Dubai restaurants added to their portal, while the former had to be dropped out, the latter became the harbinger of international growth for them. At the time of writing, Zomato has expanded its services to 7 countries overseas—UK (London, Manchester, Birmingham), South

Africa (Johannesburg, Cape Town), New Zealand (Auckland, Wellington), the Philippines (Metro Manila), Qatar (Doha), and Sri Lanka (Colombo) besides 15 cities in India, and they are working on their plans to enter Continental Europe, South-East Asia, Latin America, and Australia.

Their vision is to be the go-to source for users whenever they are looking for any information related to any restaurant by being the most comprehensive online restaurant and nightlife guide and a food discovery platform. As per Alexa, they are already amongst the top 2000 websites in the world[1]. When they began, India was the boundary of their dreams but today with presence in 7 countries, they want to take what they have done in India to the world. The focus remains on content and not e-commerce. Having said that, one never knows how things turn out and when some complimentary opportunity for e-commerce comes knocking on the door.

Is there Money in Uploading Menus?

Zomato is a content business. This means they create and curate content and this content is their core asset. How they present the content to the users is where their key skills lies and this is what keeps bringing the users back to them. The number of visitors hitting their portal—looking for food options just before they want to eat, makes Zomato a perfect place for food businesses to advertise. Selling ad space on their electronic real estate is their key source of revenue. There are two primary

[1] www.alexa.com rankings

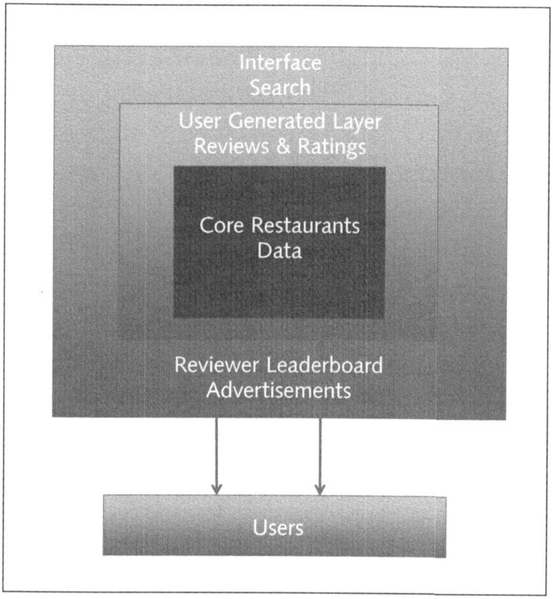

Fig 1: Zomato Business Model

sources of content that Zomato has as of now—curated content from restaurants and user-generated content.

First and most important is the curated information about restaurants that includes their menus, the type of restaurant it is, its address, contact details and location on map, the cuisine it serves, open and close timings etc. This information is completely handled in-house through a dedicated content team that personally visits all restaurants to collect information, and not just once, but every 90 days. Upgrading the information is important, as changes are a way of life. Restaurants can upgrade or change menus, revise rates, add options, move location, or even shut down. This content is at the core of Zomato as a business. The listing of restaurants is free and this will continue to be free so that users can get an unbiased listing of all possible food options. Any eating joint with a menu can be listed here. There are no premium or paid listings to keep the core data absolutrely neutral. For the same reason, no reviews are written by Zomato itself.

The second type of content comes from Zomato's users who can write reviews for restaurants they have eaten at. A typical review has an objective rating on a 9-point scale and a subjective review detailing the experience of eating with an option to add photographs of the restaurant or the food served. This part is purely generated by the users based on their personal experience of eating at a restaurant and Zomato plays no role in creating or playing around with this content. Only moderation they do is to ensure that there is no spamming and that no expletives are used. They, however, do classify users on the basis of the number of reviews they have written and the number of followers they have. Users at the top end of this hierarchy are called Super Foodies and Connoisseurs, and they get to rate restaurants on additional parameters like ambience, food quantity, quality, price value, and service too. These users can report spurious reviews too.

All the content collectively comes and resides in the Zomato servers and here begins the task of organizing and presenting this data. The engineering and design teams at Zomato work on presenting the information to users in such a way that it is most useful for them. In the beginning, they had a simple listing of menus, but they soon realized that people want different types of restaurants and need some classification to find what they are looking for. For example, some may be looking for a bar to spend time with friends, some may be looking for dining out options, some for basic food on the move, while others sitting at home may be looking for home delivery options. So they started classifying the restaurant based on what they offered. Location based restaurant search soon followed as did the other features like user reviews, location, cost, and tags like veg/non-veg, air-conditioned/non-air-conditioned, WiFi available or not, cash or card payment options etc. Like a true software product, features kept getting added on the go and it can be safely assumed that they will continue to be added.

Recently, Zomato has brought in the social angle into their user community that gives users another reason to come back to the portal besides hurried search for food options. Users can follow fellow users with similar tastes, recommend places to each other, or simply discuss food. These communities of foodies in every city that Zomato is present in builds a strong followership for them. By using social media identities of users, they intend to connect friends from other platforms on Zomato as well. According to the company, after the introduction of the social feature, the review rates have increased. Users started following each other and started building their followership. Personalized ratings allow users to view restaurant ratings only from their friends and people they follow on Zomato. This validates the accepted notion that we tend to trust reviews from people we know more than anonymous reviews. Zomato claims that they are a one of its kind food-based vertical social network in the world.

The product overall offers people looking for food options an easy search where they can have a look at the menu and other things and decide on where they want to go to eat. The ease with which they can find what they are looking for and the authenticity of the information are two cornerstones that can make or break a platform like Zomato. The ease of using the platform brings back users and gives them a reason to stick around. The more authentic you are with the content, more users trust you and the more they trust you, more they recommend you and bring more users to the platform.

Once the users arrive, advertisers can't be far away. For all food-related businesses, including restaurants, there cannot be a better platform to advertise than a site where 14 million people visit just before they have to eat and make a decision on where and what to eat. This high amount of targeted traffic that Zomato gets at meal times makes them an ideal choice for restaurants to advertise on. Zomato has made this even more attractive for the advertisers by providing hyper local advertising options. So, if a user comes from a particular locality in a city and is looking for certain type of food options, the advertisements and promotions shown are of local restaurants in the vicinity of that user. The advertiser gets a perfect place to advertise for its niche target segment and at the perfect time. Users also get to see the options that they can potentially use and not some random advertisements. A dedicated sales team takes care of selling ad space. 99 percent of the ads on Zomato are by restaurants and only 1 percent are from other segments like credit card companies.

ICING ON THE CAKE

Rating and Ranking: As the database on restaurants grows, the importance of ratings and reviews goes up as users use them as a criteria to make choices. Zomato is working towards putting objective and, as far as possible, transparent criteria for their ratings and rankings. For example, their weekly listing of top 25 restaurants in every city involves parameters from user behaviour that they choose to disclose while still keeping confidential the weights and patterns. This tells the users how the restaurant gets featured in the list but keeps some salient features hidden so that foul play and potential spam can be avoided.

Criteria for top 25

Top 25 trending restaurants in this city are selected on basis of user behaviour on zomato for this week. These user actions include a weighted average of:

- Pageviews of a restaurant on zomato website and mobile apps
- Organic searches for the restaurant
- Number of reviews (with 4 & 5 stars) and votes for a restaurant
- Average time spent by a user on a restaurant's page

Lot of other interesting user behaviour patterns which determine where our users are going, but too proprietary to disclose here. Also, we can't really disclose the weights of all these parameters—that would lead to a lot of spam!

Source: Zomato Website

For subjects where malaise like spamming or fake hits is a low probability, they have chosen to be as transparent as possible like their classification of reviewers in various categories and their dynamic city-based Leaderboard. A city-based Foodie Leaderboard shows the Top 25 reviewers of a city and this keeps changing dynamically based on the new reviews written. It gives the top reviewers visibility and connects more visitors to their reviews. Here we need to understand that fresh reviews are the most relevant as environments at restaurants change constantly.

1. FOODIE

You'll always be a foodie
Your average caveman. Doesn't care what he eats as long he gets something. Fights for his survival, doesn't help the community much (by writing reviews).

2. BIG FOODIE

20 Reviews + **20** Followers
A bit more evolved than the caveman. Staple diet includes a slew of burgers and pizzas. Can sometimes tell good food from bad. Gets better with time.

3. SUPER FOODIE

40 Reviews + **50** Followers
Known to be spotted at a good restaurant or two; friends respect his/her opinion and eat bad food when he/she says so. Acts pricey at restaurants and writes good reviews.

4. CONNOISSEUR

80 Reviews + **150** Followers
The ultimate snob. Knows his/her food. Can give restaurants a tough time. Widely respected in the Zomato community.
Super Foodies and Connoisseurs also get a chance to get their reviews featured in the Connoisseurs Guide to Eating

* Zomato Website

Leaderboard

Leaderboards showcase foodies who write a number of great reviews. Here's how we decide the leaderboards.

Review (> 50 words)
10 Points

Featured Review
25 Points

Write For a Bite winner
50 Points

Thanks on a review
4 points (thanks by Connoisseur)
3 points (thanks by Super Foodie)
2 points (thanks by Big Foodie)
1 points (thanks by Foodie)

Only 4 reviews per day per foodie (and reviews above 50 words) are considered towards leaderboard!

Reviews are subject to moderation. Users who don't write a review for a month drop off from the leaderboard.

Source: Zomato Website

A bit of offline activity is being explored through printed food guides for some cities. How these guides are received in a market that is already crowded with many food guides is yet to seen. I find it a bit contradictory to their base business model of giving instant, up-to-date information based on the user's specific needs. However, it may prove to be a good brand-building exercise as part of overall marketing strategy and it may come at no extra cost. They can always sell ad space in the guide through their existing relationships with restaurants.

Competition: There is no direct competition online for Zomato as no other food website has a sharp vertical-focussed approach. However, there is generic competition in all-purpose listings on the web that cover restaurants to a great extent. Globally, Yelp has majority of the listings in eating out space but it is not a food-only directory. Google itself is competition, as people tend to search restaurants directly on Google. So, the differenting factor for Zomato is that they are able to design the whole product around food and restaurants that provides users an easy search for restaurants. Qualified ratings and reviews help them choose their options. The fact that they collate and maintain all the information gives them an edge over other searches making them a platform for food discovery, a place to find out what is new and what is trending.

THE FAMILY RECIPE

Authenticity of Content

Users come to Zomato because they trust the information it provides. They expect the information to be correct and up-to-date, otherwise it would be useless. This means that the company has to ensure authenticity of data at all times and this is not easy in a highly dynamic environment where restaurants open and close, update their menus, and change prices every few days. It is also important to ensure that all possible restaurants are covered and not just technology savvy ones. This is a key reason why they collect all the primary data about restaurants themselves.

At the time of writing, Zomato had more than 1,00,000 restaurants listed across cities and countries and, to me, it sounded like a mammoth task to manually manage the content for so many entities. I asked them if they would like to eventually automate the content collection process and maybe open up a window in their system where hotels and restaurants can manage their own data. Their answer for the foreseeable future was no, and they had their reasons for it. They emphasized that the whole content about restaurants is core to their business and they must have complete control over that data to ensure that the data is correct. Their team hits the streets and goes door-to-door to collect menus, pictures, map coordinates, and other information straight from the restaurants. However, established, tech savvy restaurants do send them updates whenever there is any change. Before entering a new city, Zomato's content team visits the place a few months in advance to source, moderate, and update information about restaurants. At the time of the launch, about 80–90 percent restaurants in the city are listed along with their customary details.

Managing User-generated Content

Leaving your content platform open to users is a double-edged sword. On the plus side they add a whole new dimension to the content by sharing their experiences of restaurants, highlighting the best and the worst of the place, and giving recommendations. On the flipside, Zomato can becomes a platform for restaurants to compete through better reviews and ratings. Restaurants would also like to promote themselves through Zomato. This can lead to spurious content being generated. This, if left unchecked, can eventually overshadow the authentic user reviews and take away the very essence of reviews. This content is also prone to spamming by people who may have had exceptionally good or bad experiences at some restaurants. Manual moderation is not possible as the number of reviews is huge and at one level they must be left as they are for them to be relevant. Zomato uses a mix of technology and strategy to handle this. Through technology they track where the comments are coming from, if similar comments are coming for the same restaurant and if there are potentially fake Ids beings used to post comments. As part of strategy, they keep their ratings criteria confidential.

I am sure managing user-generated content would require constant innovation at Zomato's end. As they keep refining the system by putting checks and balances in place to check spurious activity, people will keep cracking the code, figuring out some loophole, or a way around to break the system. This cycle would go on, unless they come up with some breakthrough innovation. At this point in time Zomato has tried to work around the system by classifying reviewers amongst their users into various categories based on the number of reviews they have written, the number of people who follow them, and the regularity of reviews written by them. They are given names like Foodie, Big Foodie, Super Foodie, and Connoisseurs. When people see the reviews, they can see the tag of the reviewer which reveals if they can trust the review. In a new feature, Zomato is also integrating user reviews with restaurant owners where they get notified for each review and can respond to the reviews publicly.

Global Cuisine

Zomato is one of the few digital companies from India that have launched themselves globally. At the time of writing, they are operating across 11 countries and 35 cities. I spoke to them about the challenges of going global. From our conversations, it emerged that every market presents two clear challenges which the organization has to be flexible enough to work around. The first challenge is, of course, the regulatory requirement, where you have to first figure out and then adhere to the regulations. They can come in the form of a need to setup a local office in certain areas in the country or a need to hire local staff or something similar. These requirements are more often than not non-negotiable, so it is important for a company to identify them before entering a market and plan accordingly.

Second challenge comes in the form of understanding the

market i.e. the content base, that is restaurants in this case, and the users who would be consuming the content hosted. The product needs to be customized for local user needs. Overall the product may look the same, but the nuances should take care of local requirements. For example, in most Indian metros, the home screen shows options of Home Delivery, Go out for a Meal, Go out for Drinks, Catch up with Friends. In London, instead of Home Delivery, there is a Takeaway option. In Sharjah and Ahmedabad, the options are limited to Get Home Delivery and Go out for a Meal. In Auckland, the options change to Order Takeaway and Visiting a Cafe. Similarly the filter for food changes with the place. In India a veg/non-veg filter is important; in UAE, they have a filter for Halaal food, while in western markets this becomes Vegan food or organic food. Zomato uses the same version of the product, but puts location-based filters for the choices.

Before zeroing in on a new location to launch, Zomato conducts a business evaluation. Key parameters of this evaluation involve the culture of eating out in restaurants that indicates if people are really looking out for options to eat. If people go out to eat, do they have their favourites places that they stick to all the time or do they like to explore new options. This in turn, is directly related to whether restaurants would like to advertise their business on the website or not. Zomato's team gave me an example of Singapore, which was one of the first cities outside India that they wanted to get into, but had to give up as people preferred to eat out in their neighbourhoods and in their trusted eateries only.

Improving the Search

Making search more and more relevant for the users is a constant challenge for content entrepreneurs. At Zomato, they learnt that the name of the restaurant and the locality are two basic searches for users. This is followed by the type of restaurant, that dine-in, takeaway, or bars. After this, they look for features like WiFi, air-conditioning, and live music. Searching for location itself is city dependent; for example in London, people search by zip codes as everything is mapped to zip codes there and people are used to searching like that. In Dubai, addresses are mapped to closest transit or metro stations. In India, we still have landmark-based addresses that are more recognizable than the real ones. So the search for restaurants has to be localized based on local habits.

Tempting the Customers

Zomato as a product is centred on the most basic human need—food. Word of mouth has literally worked wonders for them and will always remain a key marketing channel for them. With the introduction of social network like features, the word of mouth gains precedent as foodies discuss food and restaurants. Zomato does most marketing and PR activities in-house including creatives for their campaigns.

The usual suspects in digital business like Search Engine Optimization & Marketing and Social Media Channels are obviously used since the beginning on a continuous basis. To build the brand outside the computer screens, they engage in time-tested marketing channels like TV advertising to remain on top of the users' minds. On TV, they follow a very niche approach of targeting only food-based programmes. For example, they sponsored *Masterchef Australia*. As a young company, they are experimenting with various mediums to reach out to their audience and to build a recognizable brand in their minds. They are also trying to reach out to their potential customers by partnering with other high traffic networks like MakeMyTrip where their restaurant data is integrated within the packages offered by MakeMyTrip. Let me give an example which demonstrates their frugal but innovative approach in using the marketing or user engagement channels. Television commercials(TVC) can cost a bomb. Zomato attempted to crowdsource the TVC creative via a contest. These commercials were aired on programmes which were all about food, so it made an instant connect. This gave them a two-fold result—one the cost of getting TVC creative was very low and second it engaged their users in the process, building a stronger bond with them, as they became a part of the brand through their creativity. Building a brand name and brand ambassadors at the same time is a very smart move.

Zomato actively engages its user community on Facebook and Twitter. Let me quote an example of using social media intuitively and intelligently. On the day Bal Thackeray passed away, all of Mumbai city came to a standstill, and almost all establishments were closed. Zomato engaged their users in Mumbai to tweet about restaurants that were open and were serving food. A separate page was created and shared on various channels so that people had information about where they could get food that day. This instant reaction to a situation where many people were looking for options to eat helped them build a bond with the users and gave a message that they care about people's needs and are not just making money out of their presence on their website. Zomato.xxx is a site dedicated to Food Porn. Here users can post mouthwatering pictures of food using #Zomato hashtag on Instagram along with their names and messages.

The mobile app of Zomato is a big hit with its users as they can look for restaurants on the go, or locate a restaurant close to them by sharing their location. All of Zomato's web features are available and fully supported on the mobile app and it brings in upto 40 percent of the total traffic on the website. Social media remains a channel to communicate with existing and potential users. Like all others, they also use it as a channel to listen to the users, the suggestions that they make, ideas that they share, and the feedback that they give. One good thing that I picked up from their social media thought process was not to spam the followers with product updates and not use the medium for advertising their clients. Being a young company, they keep the fun element on the forefront and somewhere that ensures customer loyalty for them. They have found Twitter to be more conversational while Facebook more of a platform to share updates about the company like new features, new ad campaigns, posts from their blog etc. I found their blog quite engaging. If you read it chronologically, it is a great place to get insights into the company's thought process as it evolved. I also got to know about their upcoming features through a post that talked about a dish-based search across restaurants. I got to read about their focus on improving spam management as they realize Zomato ratings can impact the restaurants' business.

TECHNOLOGY SPREAD

The technology is completely managed in-house for Zomato. A 15-member team manages its portal, design, infrastructure, and mobile application. They experimented with outsourcing design earlier but it did not work as they felt they needed a far tighter control on it and is now in-house. Zomato uses open source software for its platform. One big challenge for them technically is managing spam in user reviews which is growing and will continue to grow as they gain more and more traction. They use the tested techniques like filtering out user sessions from same IP addresses, putting policies in place that gives more weight to users who review regularly rather than those who come sporadically with spikes in activities. There are automated spam alerts based on algorithms that help them contain the spam as much as possible. A potential threat is plagiarism that they need to keep track of, as it is not very difficult to copy data. Their blog talks about an interesting plagiarism case where a competitor blatantly copied their data. They discovered this by bugging their data and publicly wrote about it.[2]

The second technical challenge is to manage spikes in traffic just before lunch and dinner times. Now with their

[2] http://www.zomato.com/blog/

being present across different zones on the globe, this would mean many spikes during the day. Gunjan Patidar, CTO of Zomato, said that close to 80–85 percent of their traffic is during these two time bands. Server latency has been built by locating servers close to the locations to keep the speed of queries fast enough for the users.

Servicing a user query by sensing what the user is looking for and managing the data that is being constantly generated are constant opportunities for their technology team to work on.

The Succulent Future

The Zomato team is focussed on expansion both on its product features and geographies that it can target.

As of now, they are not doing much with the analytics on the data they have, besides using it in a small way in generating ratings. But I would assume that they would have good data on eating out habits, on food preferences by various demographics, on restaurant landscape of the locations they operate in—all of which could be industry data that many people may be willing to pay to access.

For you and me as consumers, they are spoiling us with varieties of food options by bringing them to our closest screens.

References

Information provided by the company and its website

Conversations with Gunjan Patidar, Pankaj Chaddah of Zomato

http://www.SocialSamosa.com/2012/07/zomatos-social-media-strategy-explained-interview/
http://www.medianama.com/2013/06/223-chart-zomato-revenue-split-fy13/
http://www.medianama.com/2012/04/223-zomato-launches-printed-food-guide-monetization-international-expansion-wp7-app/

zomato

Name of the company:	Zomato Media Private Limited
Website:	www.zomato.com
Year of incorporation:	2008
Founders:	Deepinder Goyal, Pankaj Chaddah
Headquarters:	New Delhi
No. of offices:	22
No. of employees:	650
Cities present in:	35
Countries present in:	11
No. of restaurants listed:	1,81,000
No. of registered users:	1.6 million
No. of page views per month:	60 million

GAMES2WIN

Bringing Out the Kid in you

ONLINE GAMING IS AN Internet era phenomenon. It is one of those spaces that were invented as soon as Internet started gaining mass adoption. India took time to jump the wagon on many Internet-based trends but in gaming, it kind of had a headstart. There is no wonder then that gaming companies from India are playing in the global arena. Gaming is a content business very tightly coupled with technology and latest gadgets. Gaming started with hardcore console games, and was followed by computer games that have both hardcore games as well as casual games. Hardcore games need a lot of time to play, are complicated, and need you to develop certain skills to play at higher levels. Casual games are small, fun games that emulate real-life situations on the computer screen, and let you have some fun for some time. They do not require much skill to play and just about anyone with basic computer knowledge can play. Casual gaming is easy to handle, non-stressful gaming, where the player is entertained through the gaming experience.

From a business perspective, console games are not as popular in India as they are expensive. Online games which require nothing beyond a simple Internet connection have as huge a potential as the broadband reach. Studies suggest that playing casual games is a universal addiction with as many as 1 in 2 people playing these games online. Now mobile games have given a mini console in every hand that can be used on the go, while waiting and just about everywhere. Demographics in India is massively skewed towards the young that form the prime segment that likes to play games. However, not many have the spending power to spend on high-end games. So, for the Indian youth, casual online and mobile games are the choices and hence hold a business potential. Alok Kejriwal thought along the same lines when he launched Games2win in 2005. Today this company consistently holds a rank among the Top 20 gaming companies of the world, has a truly global user base, and traffic that most businesses can only dream of.

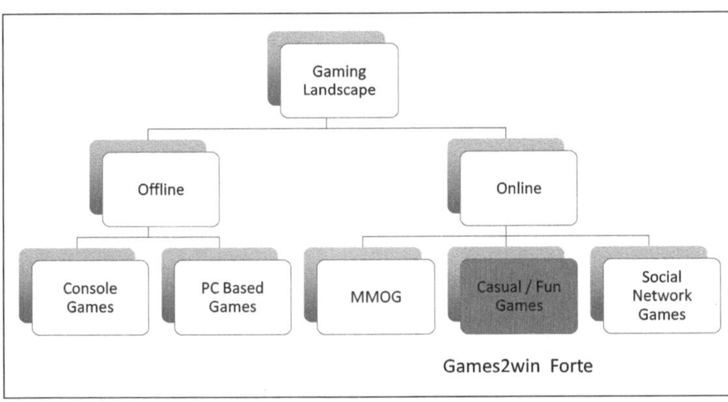

Fig 1: Gaming Landscape

ARENA

Like most content businesses, gaming is also primarily a advertisement-driven business. In one line, gaming business would read—create games, let people play them for free, drive traffic to the website, advertisers will follow, and so will the revenues. Now let us study this model further and see how they do it.

Creating games is a nothing but writing software programmes that work according to a player's commands, calculates scores, and has different difficulty levels. What a programmer needs input on is what the game should do and what it should look and feel like. What a game should do comes from the game researchers and designers. What it should look like comes from the art designers. At Games2win, most of the games are created in-house but since the beginning, their model has been open to independent developers to host the games on their portals. They have also tied up with other portals to distribute their games to get wider reach. There is no way to predict what is going to click and what not in a content business. If you look at offline entertainment-based content businesses as well, the predictability of what will work is very low. To tackle this probability in their favour, Games2win focussed on quantity and released as many games as possible in different genres. Their forte emerged from the consumption trends. Casual games, that are now the company's focus, require a small investment and have lower risk associated with them. They take an average of about 100 hours of development time and require funds somewhere between ₹3–5 lakhs per game. It costs almost double of that cost to develop mobile games.

Their foray into topical games started with a game called 'Revenge of Tandoori Chicken' that featured the bird-flu hit chicken as the hero. Games2win followed it up with some games on trending controversies, especially those involving celebrities and Bollywood antics. The games were a hit and this has been a popular genre since then mainly because it entertains players and involves them in topics of current interest. Bollywood and Cricket—the two obsessions of this country—followed by politics, remain the biggest content providers for topical games. During cricket World Cups or other sport tournaments, Games2win comes out with its own parallel games for its users to play. They also figured that not everyone in India enjoys playing action-packed games. There is a huge market for light, fun games inspired by everyday life. So there is Gully cricket along with regular cricket. There are games that celebrate historical moments like Apollo 11 celebrated Neil Armstrong's mission to the moon.

Another set of popular games are theme-based games with an Indian theme but global appeal. Bombay Taxi, one of the all-time popular games, is a parking game, something that every city dweller around the world connects with. The game lets people enjoy dealing with obstacles in parking. The problems that people face in Mumbai are different than those faced elsewhere so this game was morphed into Parking Frenzy—a game with universal appeal and it went on to become one of their best games ever, consistently ranked No. 1 on various rating parameters and at app stores. Similarly, Super Mom is an unusually popular game. What I found pleasantly surprising about the consumption patterns of their content was that people around the world, especially young girls, love Indian content. The games built around romance and marriages remain a favourite among varied age groups. The company has leveraged this fact and made it a vehicle for growth in the gaming space. Games2win feels that people come to play games that challenge them while also being entertaining. Alok feels that the entertainment needs of the youth are the same across the world. He says his biggest source of insight about children and young adults have been his own daughters and their friends. He closely observes their behaviour and, along with the insights from the data, that is all he needs to come up with ideas for new games. Of course, he keeps an eye on the upcoming trends as well through various media and online channels including Google and YouTube trends.

NUTS AND BOLTS

Games2win's business model can be defined as a SNAP model where SNAP stands for Studio, Network, Applications, and Portal. Studio is the creative part of their business, where games are researched and designed. This includes creation of artwork for the games like graphics and character design. Then, games are coded and tested here before they are ready to be launched. All the games are conceived and designed in-house including the artwork for them. About 50 percent of the development is handled in-house and the rest is outsourced. Although the cost of development is far less in-house, it

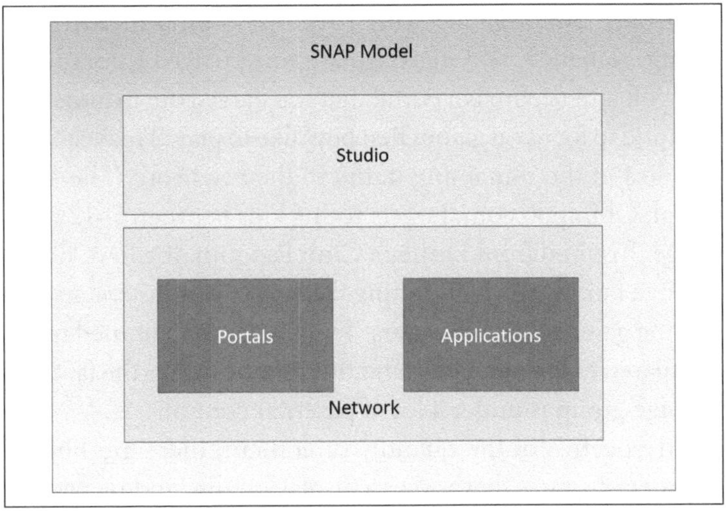

Fig 2: Games2Win SNAP Model

makes sense to outsource some work, so that the size of the team is small and manageable. According to Alok, their core competency is designing games and they are not looking forward to becoming a production house, so some outsourcing of the code development fits well into their vision.

Network consists of applications and portals through which they reach their audience. Applications can be on mobile platforms or on popular social networking sites where people can play these games. Portal refers to the three portals, owned by the company to target different segments of users. The most popular portal of course remains their main portal, that is Games2win.com that accounts for three-fourths of their traffic. This portal is very popular with teen girls across the world. Softer games which revolve around dressing up, dating, romance, and marriage are most played games here. Gangofgamers.com is a portal that was carved out to target the boys and to focus on games that boys like to play. This accounts for most of the remaining traffic to their network. The third portal, Chimpoo.com, targets young kids between 5–12 years of age. Inspired from Disney's Club Penguin, it allows kids to live in a fantasy world by letting them take various avatars and playing games as those avatars. This portal has a limited reach compared to the other two, and this may be due to the fact that this age group is under a lot of parental control.

Irrespective of the quantity of content, there are limited number of games that you can display on the landing page or homepage of the portal. This calls for careful curation from the large inventory and takes whole lot of business intelligence to decide what should appear where, when, and for how long. Games2win follows a content calendar that controls what gets displayed on a daily basis when the users open the portal. I was intrigued if this is automated or managed manually and the answer was a curious mix of both, once again re-iterating that you can achieve a lot with automation but you still cannot undermine human intuition and intelligence. So, they display a mix of what their algorithm says they should from the library and few intuitive experiments like introducing new games, inserting old games with new thumbnails, or anything else that goes with the current trend like a cricketing season or election time or launch of a movie. Sometimes there are wild card entries to test some games.

Peak traffic: Monday 2–4 pm—from the office cubicles
Average gamer in US: In the age group 28–35
Average gamer in India: Teenagers

Games2win follows the freemium model to a large extent, where games are free for the users to play but businesses pay to reach out to these players by placing advertisements. Games are free for users on all the three portals of Games2win. A small part of revenue comes from the sale of in-game virtual merchandize that players can buy to play the game. As for advertisements, they can be placed as pre-rolls and post rolls with games, inside the games without being interruptive, or on the portal. They have even made the skin of the portal available as potential ad space. For mobile games, the revenue comes from paid downloads from online stores like iTunes or Android app stores. There is evidence to suggest that users are more willing to pay for games on the mobile than on the web. This is the only company that I know of that has put its ad space inventory as well as rate card out there for public consumption, along with the contact details of all its senior management. One of their diminishing revenue stream is building advergames i.e. games made for brands for the purpose of advertising and promotion. To begin with, this was one of the models they had explored given their genesis of Contests2win.com but as of now this is a miniscule part of their portfolio.

Casual Gamer: Plays less than 4 hours a day, no loyalty to any game, is under 35, and spends 12–25 minutes a day on single users game.

The competition for Games2win is any other alternate channel of entertainment that can divert consumers away from them, including films. Direct competitors for them are other gaming companies like Zapak, Indiagames, and Electronic Arts. In the virtual world, the competition will always be global no matter where you sit and code from.

Games Evolution

- Genre: Hardcore to Casual
- Device: PC to web to mobile and tablet
- Platform: PSP to Orkut to Facebook
- What has not changed: Games are free but items of game come at a cost

Experimenting with Different Strokes

Games2win has an interesting array of experiments that they have carried out in the last 6–7 years. While most companies tend to talk about what worked for them, and keep quiet about failures, in this case I found well-documented failed experiments on their website. This proves as a perfect case study that shows that a small number of big successes come out of a long series of experiments. Let us discuss a few of them.

Games2win had launched a vertical search engine for finding free flash games called GameCurry which could find games based on the type and genre of games with a crowdsourced layer of user-generated game reviews. It should have allowed the not-so-popular games and old forgotten games to be monetized by the developers, but soon realized that no one came looking for a particular game. People either know exactly which game they want to play or want to explore and stumble upon new games. So players would rather visit their favourite games portals and discover a new game than go searching for it. If and when they did go searching, the big brother Google sufficed. After a while, Games2win closed down this portal. Appucino is another of their experiments. It was a location-based network built with the intent to make players located near each other play games together. This included games within games. The network is still alive and active without an explicit focus from the company.

Professional gaming was experimented by launching a platform called T7 or Temple of 7. They launched a team of exclusively signed professional gamers to compete internationally. The idea was to groom professional gamers, open doors of opportunities for them, and get them corporate sponsorships. While gamers got recognition, salary, and support to pursue their passion, the company got a share in their sponsorship deals. It was expected that the games and gamers would command a visibility in the market that would help push games in the long run. I feel this idea was good, but

Alok told me that there were cultural barriers, as gaming is still not seen as a serious career by most parents for their children. There were no precedence available for the families to look at and deals could not go through. This concept was tightly tied with Massively Multiplayer Online Games (MMOG) which are video games that can simultaneously be played by a large number of players, usually on the Internet. Players cooperate and/or compete and interact with each other, creating a kind of small social network of the players of the game. This networking can create stickiness for the brand and that is directly proportional to the stickiness for the advertisers. But the concept of MMOG never picked up in India and Games2win dropped the idea of both MMOG and T7.

Categories of Games

Action	Adventure
Arcade	Car
Cricket	Dress-up
Escape	Funny
Kids	Make-up
Matrimony	Romance
Puzzles	Sports
Shooting	Topical

Making the World Play

Going by the kind of print and electronic media coverage they have had over the years, I would say PR has been Games2win's biggest marketing weapon. Going through their well-documented media website, I could chronologically figure out the launch of games and other initiatives like InviziAds, GamesCurry, GangofGamers, and Chimpoo. Games as a concept and space were a new animal and had to be introduced to the potential users. I discovered their interesting history of trying various things at marketing games to the users.

Way back in 2005, Games2win collaborated with TV channel AXN to promote a games-based show called GameMax that gave a lowdown on the latest games and previews on the global gaming industry. AXN hosted GameMax Gaming Championship in India. The contestants were chosen through an online gaming competition featured on Games2win. Four customized cricket-based games were specially created for this campaign. It attempted at interactivity with the audience using a loop of 'watch the show—play the game—get on the show'. By 2007, they had built a base of games and players, but Internet penetration was still a limitation. A lot of people used Internet cafes, so Games2win tied up with them to improve infrastructure so that people could go there for playing games and not just checking their e-mails. In 2008, they hosted the ICL application on Orkut in association with Essel group that helped them leverage the popularity of cricket league.

Games2win's marketing is completely focussed on making the games or the content go viral through online communities and forums. They strongly believe that the content has to remain free for users to come and play without hesistation. Today, Alok says, the best marketing strategy for them is to make compelling content that engages their users, so that the rest follow. His vision to make Games2win the greatest company in the world translates to as many players as possible, playing his games. I believe he is right as everything else like traffic, rankings, and revenue flows from this simple metric—how many players are playing your games at a given time.

MAKING THEIR OWN RULES

InviziAds

InviziAds may be their single biggest innovation that protects them against the biggest challenge for a gaming company—piracy. No matter what you do, it's impossible to protect your games from being pirated or scraped by smaller companies or individuals. This would typically mean a loss of revenue and traffic for a company which has invested heavily into creating a game. InviziAds is a small tool that puts coded advertisements in the games that can be controlled by the source company for display. This ensures that even if games are pirated, the traffic and ad revenue still come back to the source company, and the advertisers actually end up getting a larger reach through the games. In fact, now they want more and more companies to pick up their games and distribute them across. However, there is a flipside—it somewhere ends up promoting piracy and that may keep away some advertisers on principle.

Data indicates that 'in-game' advertising provides superior returns to advertisers because of high CTRs (Click Thru Rates). Advertisers can select their geography of choice and then target consumers playing games in those markets through controls that allow them to decide when and where the advertisements are displayed. They can even optimize between advertising networks through Wise In-game Network (WIN) that chooses the right network to display advertisement intelligently. This is based on the fact that ad-networks optimize different types of visitors. For example, Ad network CPMStar provides best revenue for US traffic, for campaigns in the US between 8am and 8pm. Similarly other networks have their best performing times and geographies. WIN will automatically switch on the right network, at the right time, depending on where the visitor comes from.

Games2win originally seeded the InviziAds business using its own games but soon it opened up to the rest of world. InviziAds is now an independent offering for game developers and publishers who can sign up for free and use the technology on a revenue sharing model. InviziAds allows developers to insert an ad code in their games before releasing it to the outside world. Then depending on their deals with other gaming partner portals, if it is license or revenue share or both, they can turn these ads to be either visible or invisible on these portals. InviziAds allows developers to generate revenue from their games even when they are no longer on their own site. They have the option to either drive traffic back to their site or to allow InviziAds to optimize 3rd party ad-tags and generate revenue. Advertisers can also run campaigns with target audience through not just one website but many websites that the games travel to. At the time of writing, InviziAds-powered games reached over 15 million gamers worldwide, across 6,500 websites.

This is a brilliant example of tapping into the viral nature of content. This solution was designed in-house, although it is not unique anymore given the democratic and replicable nature of technology. It is how they applied the technology and the solutions available and made it work in their favour that makes all the difference.

Re-use of content

In the content business, one of the key success factors is the number of times you can sell the same content, either to a different audience with minor tweaking or to the same audience again and again. Games, if interesting, keep the players hooked. For the first 6 years, Games2win was focussed on creating as much content as possible. They were releasing close to 100 games a year, or about 8 games a month. In the last two years they have slowed down a bit and have reduced that rate to about half. Their data indicates a very long tail of consumption of games and they say that 80 percent of their revenue comes from 80 percent of their content, debunking the famous 80-20 rule. This indicates that a lot of their content remains relevant for a long time and players are not really losing interest in them. Another insight shows that players tend to forget games and with some minor changes here and there, the same games can be presented again to the players. Games2win uses multiple strategies to increase the reusability of their content.

Context-based customization can also take the same game to a larger set of audience. Let's take the example of a game called 'Stock Market Suicide' that came during the economic downturn in 2008. The game had investors jumping from the BSE building as they lost all their wealth. On the ground, it had Finance Minister P. Chidambaram and Prime Minister Manmohan Singh trying to save them. For its US audiences, the game featured Federal Reserve Chairman Ben Bernanke and President George W. Bush. Not all the games are localized though. As with any content, a small percentage of content becomes a hit and subsidizes the investments made in the rest of the content. So Games2win picks up the games that are going viral and gives them the cultural twist for different audiences—in a way tapping into the wisdom of the crowds.

Another method of reusability is releasing the same game in different languages, so the core content is taken to new audience with each language. All the games are translated in 25 popular languages around the world and the content is localized on the go, based on where the user is coming from.

As the playing platform moves from computer to mobile, they are refurbishing a lot of their old and popular games for the mobile platform. As Alok put it succinctly, 'We are super-curating our own super library.'

Women as Audience

Traditionally gaming companies have targeted men or boys for gaming, and that is why we saw lot of action-based games like shooting, racing, or sports-based games. Games2win changed the focus to include women by introducing intuition-based games and softer games involving marriage and romance which caught the attent of women and girls. This had a two-fold impact—one, it got a dedicated audience since not many people were catering to women gamers and it was a white space waiting to be tapped. Second, women are a bigger target audience for advertisers, as for most consumer brands, women are the biggest decision-makers or decision-influencers. So by focussing on women, they created a more promising proposition for their paying customers. They extended this to young mothers when they launched Chimpoo—a platform for young children where in all probability mothers would accompany the children in playing games.

Insight Technology

This small survey-like feature allows them to ask questions to the players. Answers when aggregated over a certain demographic can give insights to businesses and policy makers. Some examples of amusing insights from their previous surveys are:

- Filipinos fear God the most
- A church in Vietnam is visited more than a church in America
- Western European regions have most school haters
- Lemonade beats Coke in America during summers

In the future, this can be a potential channel for conducting sample surveys on the chosen demographics. It is only a matter of time that it is recognized and pursued as a revenue channel.

The Challenges before the Next Level

The negative perception about games being addictive and promoting sedentary lifestyle remains a challenge for the gaming companies. Not that these perceptions have really impacted the playing patterns or checked the rise of gaming. It is also interesting to note that they were the least impacted during times of recession. Games2win likes to believe that games can be an exceptional way to reach young audiences and convey messages in a non-preachy way. For example, after a hilarious game called 'Singh is King', on Prime Minister Manmohan Singh's political career, many users came back, curious about inflation, so in a very subtle way, it created awareness about the concept while users played and had a good time.

I thought making games on celebrities and public figures was potentially risky. I actually expected some stories on how they were sued or asked to remove some games, but the company says they have never faced any such problem. Once or twice, a celebrity has threatened to sue them but it has never actually happened. In fact, according to Alok, they all love it when a game is made on them, as it means free publicity for them. When I asked them about games made on public figures like the Prime Minister, they said they actually wrote to the PM's office to try and play the game. So, it seems games are actually taken lightly and in the spirit of fun and entertainment as intended.

As someone who has never played online games, studying Games2win was a fun learning experience for me. I learnt that making games that go viral is no child's play but a lot of kids playing your games can build you a fortune.

REFERENCES

Information provided by the company and its website
Conversation with Alok Kejriwal, CEO Games2win

GAMES2WIN.COM

Name of the company:	Games2win India Private Limited
Website:	www.games2win.com
Year of incorporation:	2006
Founders:	Alok Kejriwal and Mahesh Khambadkone
Headquarters:	Mumbai
No. of offices:	2 (Mumbai and Delhi)
No. of employees:	95
No. of mobile games:	99
No. of games on the website:	873
No. of page views for October 2013 for web:	16 million
Top geographies for the company:	India, USA, Brazil, Russia, Turkey, United Kingdom, China, Pakistan, Thailand, France

IMAGESBAZAAR

Clicking India and Indians

VISUAL CONTENT TAKES CENTRE stage in the online world. It is one of the three key contents online—text, pictures, and videos. Once upon a time, before digital photography made photographs ubiquitous by giving technology in the hands of people, writers used to write words and words to describe what they saw, so that readers could visualize the same in their minds and understand. Today, even when we have the words, we want the perfect picture to go with them. The world has moved to looking for a perfect picture to compliment its works. Add to this the fact that we all have cameras in our hands and anyone can take a good picture anywhere. Study of social media's most engaging content clearly shows that pictures are far more engaging than any other type of content. Text and video content need a user's time and attention while a picture in a fleeting second can convey the message or a feeling.

Prior to the Internet era, print media was the biggest consumer of pictures. With the advent of digital era, many platforms need picture-based content. So on one hand the number of people creating pictures has increased exponentially, and on the other, the number of platforms that need pictures for consumption have also increased at more or less the same rate. This creates a need for a platform that stocks pictures from several photographers that can be bought and used by the consumers. As a business, a photography platform would have its own nuances and that is what we explore by understanding the business of ImagesBazaar—India's biggest stock photography portal.

Sandeep Maheshwari's ImagesBazaar is one of the pioneers in digital stock photography in India. It boasts of a database of the highest number of ready-to-use Indian images in the world. More than 8000 clients in more than 45 countries are using images from ImagesBazaar. For the creative professionals around the globe, it is a go-to platform for sourcing Indian images and videos. On the other end, it brings together photographers and helps them showcase and sell their work to prospective clients. ImagesBazaar works with a vision to take India to the world by being behind every possible visual communication about India or Indians. In other words, they want the world to see India through the pictures they host.

I found the story of Sandeep Maheshwari, the quintessential college dropout turned young entrepreneur, very fascinating. Like many aspiring photographers, Sandeep also started out as a freelancer. His home was his studio and as a fashion photographer, he shot a lot of portfolios for aspiring models. There was decent money in shooting portfolios but there was something missing as he discovered that more than 90 percent of the models who got their portfolios shot, never got any assignments. When he tried searching for a reason, he found that clients were sceptical of working with fresh faces for their ad campaigns as a photo-shoot costs a lot. If they are unable to use the pictures from the shoot, all the money goes down the drain. One fine day, an ad agency chose to use portfolio pictures of a model shot by him for their campaign rather than going for a fresh shoot. This made Sandeep think of a business idea—if he could make thousands of portfolio pictures shot by him available on a website, clients could easily choose and buy photos, saving a lot of time and resources. He could pay the models for the shoot and then own the images to be sold later through the website. This is how he stumbled upon the stock photography industry and soon realized that it was already a more than 10,000 crore industry, globally. An Indian equivalent with Indian images was conspicuous by its absence. If you think back and remember images used in marketing communications like print advertisements in the eighties, there were quite a few non-Indian faces used, and it was primarily

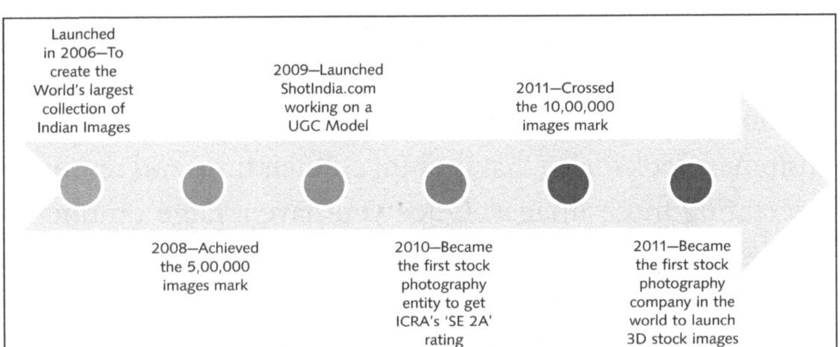

Fig 1: Journey of ImagesBazaar

because Indian images were not readily available. Thus began the idea of building exclusive Indian content online which could service the needs of Indian advertising and marketing industry by making stock images available to them. This was sometime in 2005 and by February 2006, ImagesBazaar.com was launched. Today, in India, ImagesBazaar is the largest stock photography company in terms of revenues, website traffic, quality, and quantity of images. They roughly add 800–1000 new pictures to the portal every day.

Sandeep's journey tells us how he kept looking at the gaps in the field that he chose to be in. As he kept addressing these gaps taking along others from photography fraternity, he kept building a scalable business, kept reaching out to more and more customers while focussing on the quality of images that he stocks.

BEHIND THAT PERFECT PICTURE

In a line, the business model of ImagesBazaar can be summed up as creating and selling pictures. Scratch the surface, and you realize that one person can create only limited content and hence must rope in other creators to generate a number of photographs. Research is required on the kind of images customers look for, so that they invest their time and resources in creating those images. Once you have a large number of images on your website, you need to organize and present them in a way that it is easy for a customer to find the right images that he needs. All this requires investment in technology and design.

Stock photography comprises of primarily two types of images—creative images and editorial images. Creative images are used in advertising and marketing campaigns. They typically use a model—usually a person but can also include private properties. A release, that is essentially consent of the model or property owner to use the image for commercial purpose, is required to use these images. These images are usually captured as a part of an organized shoot around a particular theme and style. Editorial images are candid images that are used with news-based articles mostly for reference. No styling is done or even required in editorial images. ImagesBazaar identified that there was a void of creative images required by the advertising and marketing agencies in India. From the content perspective

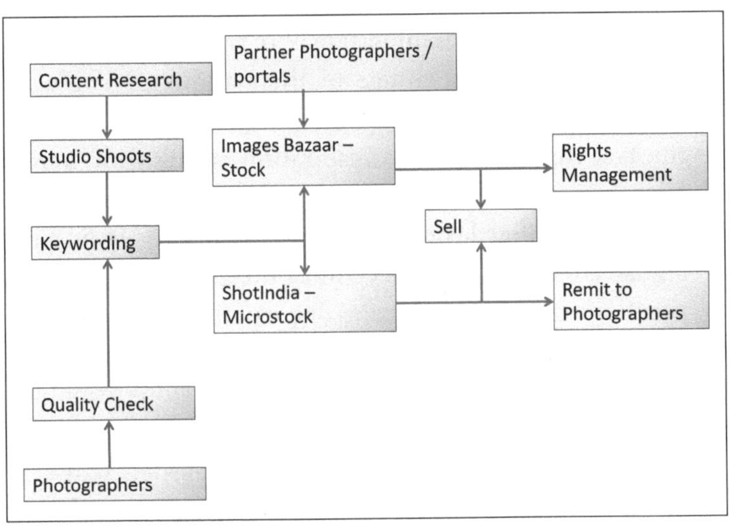

Fig 2: ImagesBazaar Business Process

they identified that quintessentially Indian images that highlighted the local cultural ethos were missing.

I could have never imagined the various factors that affect a photo shoot till I learnt about the content research at ImagesBazaar. Let's look at some of them:

- Most important factor is the reigning fashion trend. Garments used must be in-line with what's in trend currently, and new images need to be created as soon as the trend changes. Sometimes images may even lead certain trends.
- Forthcoming festivals and occasions need to be catered to. This also includes trending activities around the country like say protests or vigils by the youth of India.
- Advertising trends by studying some of the most successful campaigns worldwide, ensuring accordance with global trends. This becomes important as in this hyper connected world, a small percentage of their audience is always global and must connect with the image. Not to forget the fact that many times inspiration comes from across borders.
- Shifts in the lifestyle of rural and urban India e.g. holidaying abroad is on rise, so they need more images showing Indians vacationing in foreign locales or preparing for one.
- Content needs to be constantly updated when changes take place in technology e.g. shift from landline phone to mobiles to smartphones and tablets must reflect in the images.
- Looking at their own search logs on the website. Analysing the millions of searches taking place every month on the site and consolidating the data to come up with ideas regarding

the missing images on their site—basically figuring out what customers came looking for and did not find.

- Most importantly, inspiration backed by intuition.

In the absence of stock images, customers looking for Indian images had no option but to go for a fresh photo shoot every time that involves hiring models, photographers, makeup artists, stylists, location and art directors, props, etc. It is a time consuming and capital-intensive effort and needs to be repeated every time you need new images. So, solutions like ImagesBazaar drastically brings down the cost, time, and effort for the clients. Cost of using the images or videos can come down from millions of rupees to a few thousands and the time taken from weeks to a few minutes.

Microstock photography is a new concept, born in the Internet era where portals stock photographs from all kinds of photographers—professional, amateur, or hobbyist. The business model for microstock photography remains the same, except that these pictures are not professionally shot. Hence, they are priced very low compared to regular stock photographs. This is because of the low-cost of producing those pictures as well as the large number of these images available. The world is moving towards microstock photography which implies that pictures are available at very low price points. Compared to price points of large players like Getty Images, Corbis, and ImagesBazaar, Microstock images can come at as low as 10% of the cost of professional images and sometimes even lesser. This trend could either be seen as a threat by large players or embraced as a line of business to cater to the market at the lower end as well. ImagesBazaar chose the latter and launched their microstock website ShotIndia. Through ShotIndia, they allow photographers—amateur as well as professional—from across the country to upload their images and share 50 percent of the revenue from the image sale with them. Each picture has to go through a quality check before it is accepted by the portal to ensure overall quality of images on the website. They have over 15,000 registered users on ShotIndia and a bank of nearly 1,20,000 pictures at the time of writing this book.

Pricing of images is based on exclusive and non-exclusive rights for an image. For non-exclusive images, there are multiple options for the users to choose from depending on where they want to use the image and the dimensions of the image. Exclusive rights come for a period of time ranging from 3 months to 8 years and the image is taken off the portal for that period. Every single image is a product and has an identity on the portal. They are working on offering a subscription model that allows customers to use certain number of images for a time period for a fixed fee. It brings down the cost of copyrighted images for the clients, and gives them greater flexibility to choose images on the go. I believe this would also help leverage the long tail of images that they have built over the years. Subscription model is already in place for ShotIndia where customers can choose from various options depending on the number of pictures and image resolution for a one year.

Both these ventures are very clearly focussed on India, and may include SAARC countries. My obvious question to them was whether they see themselves going global and creating global images as well. A very clear answer that came from them was that there is still so much potential in India and around that is untapped, so geographically they want to remain focussed on India. However, they do have expansion plans. The next big space they want to capture is video content that includes videos and interactive media. This is where they think the future of content belongs.

ImagesBazaar has tied up with Getty Images and some of their images are hosted on their portal. So when you buy Indian images from Getty Images, in all probability you are picking up images off ImagesBazaar. They, in turn, also host images from other stock photography websites to increase the breadth of their own portfolio. Basically they understand that there are big established brands in the global market and it may be difficult to break into that space, but you can always collaborate with them for the niche content that you have to make the best out of both the worlds. Their content gets an established platform with a global partner and they get both revenue and exposure.

ImagesBazaar has a team of around 100 people and about 50 percent of them are in the creative department. This includes creative researchers who research for the type of the content required, art directors who create storyboards, stylists who take care of costumes, production managers who manage the shoots, model co-coordinators, makeup artists, support staff, and, of course, photographers. There is a post-production team of about 25 people that works on the images before they are ready to be put up on the portal. A keywording team of 6–7 people, supported by 5–6 people that comprise of the IT team, works on making images search-friendly. ShotIndia is managed by a small team of 5 as it only requires quality check and rest of the activities are automated. Sandeep proudly mentions that their attrition rate is close to zero.

Typical Customers

- Advertising agencies
- Creative professionals in design
- Corporate marketing firms
- Printers and publishers
- Web-based professionals
- Small and medium businesses

Range of Creatives

- Creative images
- Candid images
- Videos
- Animations
- Illustrations
- 3D imagery

10,00,000 images and videos shot by over 15,000 photographers and filmmakers from all over India.

Perfecting the Frame

Online content must be organized and indexed in such a way that it can be searched easily and appropriately. If the content takes too much time to be found, it will alienate the users over a period of time. Moreover, if the content is too cumbersome to search, it may eclipse the audience it deserves.

Sandeep Maheshwari says, 'It is easy to say that we have created more than 10,00,000 images and videos in the last few years but just imagine the kind of effort that goes into creating just one perfect shot. Every single image on our site was just an idea or a concept till the time it was conceived and materialized by bringing together a highly professional team of photographers, models, make-up artists, stylists, art directors, creative researchers, production managers, assistants, spot boys, location coordinators, shoot coordinators, model coordinators, graphic designers, key wording team, etc. In other words, we have created more than a million innovative and truly unique concepts in a few years.' In a typical shoot, they shoot anywhere between 1500–2000 pictures, of which about 70-80 images are selected for uploading on the portal, and out of these, only 2–3 are highlighted on the main page of a category. When Sandeep was describing this process to me, it gave me an idea of the kind of effort and resources that go into creating a picture.

Capturing India's diversity is another big challenge. Think for a moment, is there any one image that can represent India except may be the map or flag of India? With India becoming a tempting market with its growing middle class, many big global brands have entered the Indian market. They wanted to go as local as possible with their ad campaigns and for this they required images that were local, using local models, and authentic locations. The ImagesBazaar team says they have travelled the length and breadth of the country to capture its diversity and have worked with models from all regions. This adds to the cost of the production of the images, but also adds value to their portfolio of images. So, India's diversity is as much a challenge as an opportunity.

Plagiarism is an industry-wide problem. People do not think twice before downloading images from online portals and using them without taking either permission or buying rights. A part of this problem comes from the low awareness of intellectual property rights (IPR) in the country and the fact that people assume that everything on the Internet is free to download and use. ImagesBazaar has faced its own set of issues with plagiarism. They are using watermarks on their images and putting copyright notices on with each picture. A message below each image informs the visitor that it is a criminal offence to use the image without buying rights for the same and can potentially take them behind the bars. The fact that justice in India isn't handed out easily and court cases can take forever to settle gives people another reason to carry on with plagiarism. I can only hope that technology can eventually come up with a solution for this menace.

TECHNOLOGY FILTERS

ImagesBazaar claims to be one of the fastest stock photo websites in the world. If you look at their design, it is no-fuss and simple website, with no advertisements. Once you are looking at the images, everything else recedes into the background. Images do appear quickly. Come to think of it, creating and hosting content is one thing, what matters most from a business perspective is that a client should be able to find the relevant image and he should be able to do it fast enough.

To help prospective clients find the right image, search has to be optimized. The search is based on keywords that are associated with the image, so assigning the right keywords to an image becomes an important task. There is a bit of research involved to see what kind of words customers come looking for and what are the results they finally choose based on those words. There are synonyms for each word, and different cultures use different words for the same description. For example, some people may enter the keyword women and others, females. By taxonomy, female is a superset of woman, so when a search is done on female—all woman-related images should also turn up. Add the right context to this and you may get the right image. ImagesBazaar has invested in the theory of right keywords and has a dedicated team that assigns keywords to each image that you see on the portal. Every image has roughly 50 or more keywords associated with it. Some typical keywords tell characteristics of the image like number of people in the picture, the background, type of image, type of model, locale, style, and what the image conveys. At the back-end, control vocabulary software tools take care of indexing and retrieval of the right images. Latest images appear on top as they capture the latest environment and are more sought after by regular clients, but it is not difficult to find old images, if so required. The key here is to make sure that the customer gets a match from the stock to the requirement he came looking for. Categorizing the images at the top level and archiving old images is also a part of organizing the content intelligently. Some other built-in features to aid search are auto complete in search box and an option to see most viewed images and images similar to the one open.

Speed is the key to success of portal is something that Sandeep realized very early in the life of ImagesBazaar. The fact that India did not have great Internet bandwidth may have actually helped design the solution. Sandeep almost gave up photography, and learnt programming to be able to manage the technology and improve the speed of the site. If you recognize a potential customer pain point, you can convert it into an advantage for yourself if you can address it.

Most technology requirements are managed in-house, though they do engage external vendors for some application development on a case-to-case basis.

SHOOTING FOR THE CUSTOMERS

In the initial days, it was not easy to sell the pictures and there were two primary reasons for it. One, there were not as many people looking for pictures online and two, ImagesBazaar had no brand presence. Since the portal was, and to some extent still remains, synonymous with Sandeep Maheshwari, he tried to gain some limelight by attempting something unusual like creating a world record. He applied some creative thinking to see what he can do to bring focus on ImagesBazaar, and all the people involved. He used to charge models about ₹5,000 for shooting portfolios and there were many who couldn't even afford that. He went back to his database and called up all those models and offered to shoot their portfolio for just ₹500 if they helped him create a world record. On the day of record creation, he ended up clicking more than 10,000 shots with 122 models in less than 10.45 hours. With the ₹500 that each model paid him, he managed to recover all the money he had invested in creating that record. The record brought in much needed media coverage, and this lead to more business.

Since then there has been a conscious effort to make ImagesBazaar a leading brand and they have used all possible channels to spread the word about themselves. I remember seeing a full-page ad in *Times of India* with a collage of their own images saying 'freedom to download', a moment for them to celebrate 10,00,000 images online. On TV, they have sponsored shows like *Storyboard* and *All about Ads*. In print, you can find them being mentioned off and on in places like Brand Equity and other business pullouts. In digital media, they frequently get mentions in industry publications like Afaqs. They, of course, send their digital catalogues as direct mailers to their existing and potential customer base. They do their bit of Search Engine Optimization and Search Engine Marketing. About 10–15 percent of their revenues go into marketing and they find print campaigns to be most effective. However, they have no sales team and they reach out to their perspective clients only through marketing, supported by a diligent customer support team. On social media, they have literally no presence and they do not see a ROI on the effort spent there at this point in time.

To me, what was most amazing about the ImagesBazaar story was the way they brought order to an unorganized space. In the process, they created a whole new market while putting Indian content and Indian ethos at par with the best content available across the globe. For scale, they leveraged the power of networks, and plugged themselves into global networks at one end, and allowed independent photographers to plug into their network at the other end. The focus on customer pain points led them to find the best technology solutions to enable them to find relevant images as quickly as possible.

Almost every other company I spoke to had used images from ImagesBazaar and had positive things to say about them, which just goes on to show what an impact they have on the market.

References

Information provided by the company and its website
Conversations with Sandeep Maheshwari of ImagesBazaar
www.shotindia.com

imagesbazaar

Name of the company:	Mash Audio Visuals Pvt. Ltd.
Website:	www.imagesbazaar.com
Year of incorporation:	2003
Founder:	Sandeep Maheshwari
Headquarters:	New Delhi
No. of offices:	1
No. of employees:	92
Cities present in:	New Delhi
No. of registered users:	1,08,000
No. of page views per month:	21,90,000
No. of clients:	12,000
No. of images (ImagesBazaar+ShotIndia):	15,00,000+

CHAI WITH LAKSHMI

Conversations with the Heroes Among Us

VIDEOS ARE ONE OF the three prime forms of online content. Till some time back, creating a video needed both skill and special equipment, but today we have the basic video cameras embedded in our mobile phones. This gives everyone a chance to experiment with creating videos and sharing them. Digital technology provides many video-hosting platforms that allow anyone to showcase their videos, be it for personal or professional purposes. YouTube, followed by Dailymotion and Vimeo, has many video entrepreneurs who are running a full-fledged businesses through their niche video channels. Most popular videos still come from the entertainment space indicating that consumers still think of them as entertainment bites. Education is emerging as another key focus area and lots of educational videos are being created, right from nursery rhymes to science lessons. Video and audio are a form of content that go beyond language and literacy barriers, as no additional technology is required to create content in any language. I chose an online chat show to study this segment of content for various reasons other than the fact that this show is a pioneer in its vertical. In India, we strongly associate chat shows with television and are still to move online to consume this content. There are not many online chat shows outside of the pure entertainment segment. This was one chat show that was focussing on inspirational conversations with real people who are doing some remarkable work.

TEA-TIME CONVERSATIONS FOR THE NEW AGE

Chai with Lakshmi is an online talk show conceived, produced, and anchored by the gorgeous Lakshmi Rebecca. Like TV talk shows, it comes in seasons and episodes called Webisodes. Each episode is shot in an elegant teashop or lounge of a high-end hotel with the host talking to another Indian, who has an inspirational story to tell. The objective of the chat show is to put a spotlight on real life heroes who are all round us but usually go unnoticed. Lakshmi is working on bringing out their work and its influence through conversations over chai, the quintessential Indian beverage to chat over. In the introduction on her website, she says, in the era of everything going online, she is bringing the tea-time or tea-break conversations to you, online. Tea refreshes and recharges us and conversations de-stress us, making tea-time a much awaited and celebrated part of our hectic, modern lives.

The talk show connects us to people with whom we would probably like to have conversations and for whom we have some potential questions to ask. For example Shubhendu

Sharma of Afforestt who has planted 36,000 trees in urban centres and is working on bringing back 30 percent of total forest cover that India needs to balance its ecology. He has used Japanese Miyawaki method of tree planting to grow urban forests. Do we not have questions like how do you do that in a city like Bangalore? Can I also do something like that in my neighbourhood? In few minutes, Lakshmi's guests like Shubhendu tell their stories, share the lessons they have learnt on the way, and sometimes engage with their audience by inviting them to participate in their missions. You can actually sit with a cup of chai and watch these conversations that the host and guest have over their cup of tea. You can participate by leaving comments or engaging with the guests on their websites or communities as the case may be.

Lakshmi started her career with social work and transitioned into social research when she was a part of making documentary films for BBC, Discovery, and Channel 4. This was followed by her foray into modeling and anchoring shows before she took a career break to do her masters in International Marketing at Sheffield Business School. After a few years in marketing, research, and consulting, she felt an undeniable urge to bring together her experiences and create something bigger that would offer growth and satisfaction at multiple levels. She thought of an online talk show and started experimenting with her first few videos, and was soon sucked right into creating her own branded show—Chai with Lakshmi. She now runs a production house called Red Bangle that produces videos for clients on demand as a service. Chai with Lakshmi is Red Bangle's first in-house product, or its first brand. When an entrepreneur calls a venture their first baby, you know you can expect many more from them. In this chapter we will focus only on Chai with Lakshmi online chat show and its journey so far. We would also see how producing a quality show needs vision, direction, and strategy, and involves more elements of business than simply pushing the content and expecting it to go viral.

Running a TV-like Show Online

As India's first online general-interest chat show, Chai with Lakshmi targets educated Indians around the world in the age group of 25 to 45. It brings insightful conversations for its target audience on topics that are interesting and real. Although the show follows a television-like format, it has been adapted for the web audiences based on their viewing preferences and consumption behaviours. A television episode usually lasts 26 to 46 minutes depending on whether it is consuming a half-hour or one-hour slot. On the web, attention spans are far shorter and distractions are far too many in the form of multiple open windows. So what the audience needs is small crunchy bits put together in 2 to 13 minutes capsules. The challenge, however, is to capture the essence of the conversation in that small window of time and keep the conversation meaningful.

According to Lakshmi, there is a huge demand for this type of content among educated urban Indians. This is substantiated by the fact that many such forums are coming up online and witnessing ample traction with the audience. So quality becomes a key differentiator for the channel especially when you want to run it as a viable business. So, for Chai with Lakshmi, Lakshmi chose to create broadcast-quality content that is no-fuss, contemporary, and contains relevant infotainment. She narrated how she started with a small hand-held camera with basic video quality, and a plan to do three webisodes a week. Soon she learnt that the effort involved in producing a good episode is far more than she had estimated. Besides production, there is a substantial effort required to market the content to reach out to the target audience once the content has been uploaded. She brought down the frequency to twice a week and finally settled for one webisode every two weeks, so as to focus on quality of production and on distribution of the content. There is a blog-like approach to the portal, where videos are released like new posts.

The chat show now follows the concept of seasons. The team works for Webisode schedule of a season and takes breaks in between seasons. Lakshmi explained to me how they need dedicated time for pre-release activities like research, coordination, and video production, followed by post-production activities like audio podcasts, transcripts, teaser clips—the smaller video clips that get distributed via syndication platforms, and the website's blog space. There is a lot of back-end work that goes into each of these activities and hence they need the team's time and focus. There are non-production related activities that demand effort on a continuous basis like maintaining an activity level on social media, engaging in business development, and managing public relations. Shooting a video in itself is extremely time-

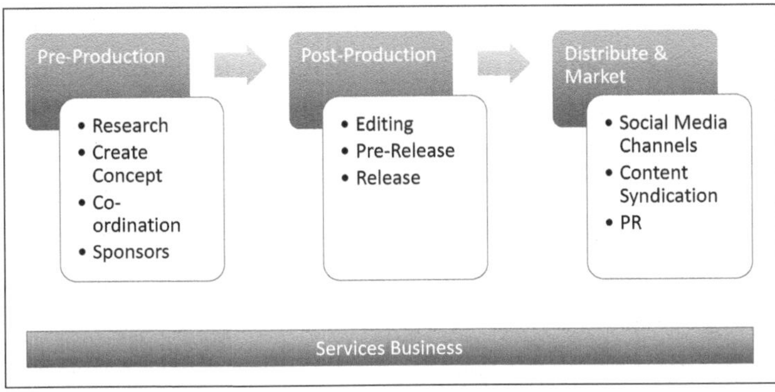

Fig 1: Chai with Laskshmi Business Process

intensive for the filmmaker who, in this case, also happens to be the anchor of the show and behind the scene entrepreneur. The quality of videos is absolutely professional which makes it expensive both in terms of time and money. It is at par with a full-fledged TV talk show, except one that happens to use web as a medium for broadcasting itself. Lakshmi explained to me that as an anchor she even has to look good on the show—now that is something that people like us do not even realize is an effort, but when you link it to the business, it matters.

The show started by featuring primarily urban Indians and targeted urban audience, as that is where Lakshmi herself belonged to and that is where she felt there was a void to be filled. However, she soon realized that there is a need to be more inclusive and she spread her wings to include rest of India as well. She launched a campaign called 1,000 stories on Inclusive India that aimed at publishing 1,000 positive stories of Indians who are working towards making India's society more inclusive. They want to produce content that is positive, sensible, and inspiring and not just entertaining. This was the original thought behind the show, so this campaign is nothing but a natural progression to scale up both the sources of the story and the field of impact. The idea also stems from too much negative news that we see in the mainstream media and total absence of positive news and minimal focus on change-makers.

At the time of writing this book, Chai with Lakshmi has about 120 episodes online spread over 4 seasons.

MAKING IT WORK COMMERCIALLY

From a bird's eye view, the business model can be summarized in one line—create content and monetize it. Let us look at the various cost elements and the revenue channels for this kind of a business.

Costs

- Pre-production cost that includes the cost of research and concept development.
- Production cost includes equipment cost that can be either a one-time capital cost or a recurring rental cost. The actual shoot takes time and effort that translates into cost for the production house in the form of staff, logistics, and administrative cost for activities like coordinating with the guests, location, and wardrobe sponsors.
- Post-production cost involves studio and software cost.

- Marketing cost comes in terms of time and effort of the team.
- Keeping a live website up and running it all the time needs investment in technology, and on regular intervals the upgrades will involve costs for design and development.

Revenue Channels

- Primarily, the source of revenue is ad networks which in this case is Google Adsense, since Chai with Lakshmi is a YouTube-hosted product that in turn is owned by Google.
- Some revenue comes from the distribution and syndication services used.
- Sponsors associated with the brand contribute to the revenue directly.
- Ticketed offline events: The show has recently taken an offline avatar to engage with users in real time. They now host ticketed events that have some of the people featured engaging in real time conversation with the audience. This works both as an additional revenue channel for the show and as an offline outreach channel.

Newer revenue channels will emerge as distribution across platforms grow and new avenues open up.

My sense is that if Lakshmi is able to build a strong brand around positive, inclusive India through her dedicated campaigns like 'Inclusive India', she may invite interest from large media houses to run their positive news section someday. Of course, how much commerce can be built around this concept would drive the final course.

Chai Store was supposed to be the e-commerce arm of this venture. The idea was to sell merchandise around tea on the portal like handcrafted teacups and various varieties of tea etc. I thought this was a brilliant idea but Lakshmi has kept it on the back burner for now. She says for handcrafted products, the cycle from design to manufacturing to storage, packaging, and shipping was just way too long and she would probably try it at a later stage. For the time being they are going with a range of show-related merchandise like launch T-shirts to promote their Inclusive India campaign.

The Technology Mountain

A content entrepreneur's key technology requirement is a placeholder for her content, and thanks to many existing technologies, there are quite a few available to choose from. Chai with Lakshmi show is hosted on YouTube at the moment. There is a team of three people taking care of the portal.

Looking at her website and her YouTube channel, I think there is a lot that she needs to do to organize her content. She needs to understand the long tail of Internet that works very differently from the television content that depends primarily on the telecast schedule. On the Internet, all the content is available all the time and, as an entrepreneur, one needs to leverage this. I could see the latest webisodes on the homepage and I could jump to other seasons but there is no way to find a video by my interest. For example if I am looking for conversations around education or survivor stories or stories from a particular geographical location, I cannot find them.

I have to hope to stumble upon them. She probably needs to do key wording and tagging of videos pretty much the way ImagesBazaar tags its images so that customers can search them easily. I strongly feel she needs to use technology smartly to organize and recommend videos based on some analytics. I also found the interactivity very low and unintuitive. Follow-up conversations have the potential to make the content go viral.

Overall, technology is under-leveraged in the venture, but then it takes only a minor shift in focus to work on these shortcomings. A strong technology partner can bring in the required thrust and the content can have a much better reach which in turn will make better sense for the businesses to be associated with the brand.

Getting Viewers On-board

Lakshmi thought monetizing content would be easier than it turned out to be. She expected big brands to see value in sponsoring episodes or seasons just like they do on television. What she learnt in the process is that marketing spends of brands are purely driven by numbers. To get them interested in your venture, you need to first drive numbers in terms of eyeballs or visitors on your portal. To be fair to brands, it makes sense for them be associated with a show only if they are assured of a certain number of viewers being reached through the content.

Lakshmi actively reaches out to the audience through various social media channels. They use all the popular social media platforms like Facebook, Twitter, Pinterest, and Google+ to reach out to the customers. They put a collective 100+ messages every week across platforms, not including the syndication work. Lately, they have introduced a monthly Twitter chat on their Inclusive India campaign that tends to engage conversations around the topic, and also bring out stories from the fraternity that can become a part of the show. For the Twitter chat they have partnered with initiatives like Ashoka Foundation, Mahindra Rise, and many other social entrepreneurs. She also tied up with content syndication agencies that distributed her content through their content marketing strategies. In about two years, Chai with Lakshmi is clocking about 2–3 lakh views per month. Small and local brands have started associating with her. Her latest videos have Taj group properties as the venue. She believes that it is a matter of time that big brands will start associating with Chai with Lakshmi.

Lakshmi thinks that what works in terms of traffic is simple but really a long-haul strategy: find something you love doing, do it well and just keep at it. At some point, you'll go big. According to her, depending on your platform, that 'point in time' can vary between 2 and 10 years. Online content is really not a game of quick money and anyone who thinks it is, is really just fooling themselves. Do I agree with her? I am not sure, because I see many examples of businesses doing this faster by using the right strategy. She probably needs to understand the pace in digital world is way faster than electronic media.

Working Around Challenges

Most common challenge for Chai with Lakshmi is the same as most early stage startups—funding. The venture is completely self-funded at the moment with some help from family and friends. Lakshmi is doing a parallel service offering of film making for corporate clients through the parent company Red Bangle. Most of her funds come from video films she makes for others and that funds her own baby, Chai with Lakshmi. This is potentially an option for entrepreneurs in the early stage, as institutional funding usually comes only after you start generating enough revenues. In fact for Lakshmi, Chai with Lakshmi as a brand brings in more customers for her services business while services business funds the products during its initiation run.

Getting sponsorships for episodes or seasons is another on-going challenge. This is a common challenge for small and medium content entrepreneurs—to have enough number of visitors viewing their content. This leads to a question if the established offline players establishing their online presence will dominate the online world too? On one hand Internet gives power to individual content creators to have their own place in the sun, but on the other hand it also requires them to market themselves aggressively to be relevant and economically independent.

Piracy that is a challenge for most content entrepreneurs—does not really bother Lakshmi. The reason being the format of the content that ensures that even when pirated, she being the anchor holds the brand intact. There may be a small loss of ad revenue due to distribution of downloaded versions, but that kind of gets offset by the fact that content is potentially reaching wider pockets and still contributes to the brand value.

Success for Lakshmi has come by way of recognition through awards like The Manthan Award—an international award for digital initiatives amongst others. Some of her focus areas for the show include entrepreneurship, sustainability, and inclusiveness. Most popular videos on the channel so far are those of Inspiring Indians. I believe that this channel or others like this can become a cross pollinator of ideas among the audience and between the storytellers themselves. This would be the real ROI of portals like this one, a positive social movement that feeds itself.

Edewcate

My search for an education and animation content company led me to meet the entrepreneurs behind Edewcate—a YouTube channel that thrives on providing educational videos and animation-based content. Their content ranges from traditional classroom subjects like Mathematics, Physics, Chemistry, Biology, Elementary Sciences, Social Sciences to languages—both Indian and foreign—to general areas of interest like sports, human anatomy, general knowledge, and other parallel learning topics like yoga, cooking, and music. Their wide range of subjects makes them attractive for audiences ranging from young ones to the older populace—anyone who wants to learn is a potential user. Content on languages and other modes of cultural learning appealed to the huge expatriate Indian population in the US, UK, Australia, and Gulf countries. Their first video was test launched on YouTube in January 2008 and since then their channel has clocked over 140 million views. This amounts to nearly half a billion minutes of content consumed, with about 90,000 dedicated subscribers, and viewers across 125 countries. Edewcate is also the world's most viewed nursery rhyme channel. You can watch more than 400 nursery rhymes from around the world in more than 15 languages including English, Hindi, Telugu, French, Spanish, Japanese, Turkish, German, Korean, and Mandarin. We must understand here that to convert video content into multiple languages requires more than just literal translations. The accents of the audio must be taken into account for each region otherwise it can alienate the audience. This is a brilliant example of content that keeps the users coming back to the channel almost every day and of reaching a global audience through the same content.

Technically, Edewcate prepared themselves well for the future by opting for full HD videos even when they were not really the norm, so they could be viewed with the same quality on big screens. The high bandwidth requirement for video content remains a challenge but these should get resolved as we move to 3G and 4G services. Their primary source of revenue is Google Adsense as partners of YouTube. This strategy does not require any explicit marketing efforts and lets them focus completely on creation of content with high quality and low-cost. Of course, they do collaborate with schools for licensing their digital classroom products.

I heard some major expansion plans from Vandana Bandaru, the CEO of this company, and it would be interesting to see how they manage multiple video channels in different spaces, and how they cross promote them to generate greater viewership.

REFERENCES

Chai with Lakshmi Website

Edewcate YouTube channel

Conversations with Lakshmi Rebecca and information provided by her.

Conversations with Vandana Bandaru and Satyadev Chada of Edewcate and Information provided by them.

chai with lakshmi

refreshing conversations

Name of the company:	Red Bangle
Website:	www.chaiwithlakshmi.in
Year of incorporation:	2011
Founder:	Lakshmi D. Rebecca
Headquarters:	Bangalore
No. of offices:	1
No. of employees:	4
Cities present in:	1
No. of seasons:	4
No. of episodes:	120
No. of registered users:	Around 10,000
No. of views per month:	50,000

PART 3

CONNECTORS

CONNECTORS

Bridges and Catalysts

IN THE GOOD OLD days, our social networks were primarily limited to families, friends, neighbours and colleagues. The number of people we interacted with at any point in time was limited to those who were in the immediate vicinity or may be a phone call away. However, with the advent of social media, our interactions with other people has multiplied manifold. People whom we have met even once get added to our digital social networks and are not lost after the meeting. Digital communication has made everyone equidistant as we use the same mediums to interact with people in our own cities as well as those located across the globe. The digital space has given birth to many communities by enabling connections between people who may not have met otherwise. In its early days, Internet resembled other media channels where one could broadcast to readers online through a website, an e-mail campaign, or a e-brochure. This was followed by an era of limited interactivity where the readers could speak to the author and publishers by leaving a comment or an online feedback for anyone to see and respond to. This evolved into discussion forums and social media platforms where users could speak among themselves. This created a space that connected people who were potentially looking for 'each other' but had no way to discover each other except through organized channels like clubs or organizations.

In this section, we look at the Internet portals that play the role of connectors. They connect people or parties that are looking for each other but have limited ways of reaching out to the other in the offline world. They can also take the form of small niche communities that come together for a common purpose and end up being a part of a specialized community. This common bond leads to a highly engaged social network providing unique networking opportunities to their members irrespective of whether these communities are geographically dispersed or hyper-local.

Connectors started as online classified advertisement listings, with job portals like Naukri.com and matrimonial portals like Shaadi.com. Real estate portals soon joined them and now we have many niche communities around cars, education, food, health, and entertainment. There are many horizontal portals like JustDial.com, Asklaila.com, or Quickr.com that let you put advertisements across verticals. Sulekha.com is one of the oldest players in horizontal classified portals. Horizontal portals lack an advantage of building communities around a niche. Players in this segment have existed since early Internet days in India and have reached a mature business state. Niche portals on the other hand focus on one vertical, or a very narrow sub vertical at times, and become the go-to place for members in that space. Besides being the connector for players in their segment, they also become a knowledge centre for their domain. Using technology, these connecting portals host an array of tools that help users make informed decisions from the choices available e.g. a real estate portal gives you a map based search or a matrimonial portal has tools that highlights profiles where partner preferences of both profiles match the best. The simplest form of these tools involves comparative features and complex ones can go to the extent of scenario analysis with some built-in predictive algorithms. As Internet penetration increases, the horizon keeps widening for these portals. The same would apply to technology evolution like at the moment there is a significant shift from computers to mobile phones and tablets and almost all players are working on tapping on that traffic source.

This section of businesses can also be looked at as consumer-oriented. A big percentage of them are C2C (consumer to consumer) businesses and connect consumers to consumers without involving any businesses really. Take, for example, real estate portals that connect owners of property and their potential buyers and tenants. Matrimonial portals are pure C2C enabled by a technology platform. A key characteristic of these platforms is the search on a large database of potential choices that is further enabled by matching technology that assists in shortlisting of the choices. Some portals have a C2B (consumer to business) component as well where they leverage the strength of their communities to attract businesses and benefit from them.

In a way, all the players in this segment are competing with popular search engines that are the default choice for search. The advantage of niche portals lies in providing specialized, advanced search. This is coupled with a technology layer that does the first level matching based on preferences, thus giving users a narrowed-down search experience. These portals usually cater to a niche need like finding a job, property to rent or buy, searching for a life partner, or even finding a social cause to support. The most popular portals in this segment are job, real estate, and matrimonial portals—also referred to as online classifieds. They all began in a directory-listing manner that had a basic search facility that allowed users to register themselves and sift through the other entries listed. Simple search facilities were developed that helped the users filter out listings on basic criterias. Over time, these portals have graduated to developing sophisticated tools to organize data lying in the huge databases that are listed with them. The search engines have given way to matching tools that match the requirements of the one who is searching with the one who is being searched. The massive size of database provides the pull for potential new users on one hand and necessary parameters for research on the other.

Freemiun, also called the Google model, is a common revenue model used by community-based businesses where a part of the services offered are free and the others can be accessed for a fee. There are two sub-models within this model as well. The first one lets the users access the basic product for free but for any meaningful service they need to pay. For example, on property or matrimonial portals, users can see the matching requirements, they can search and look at the profiles that suit their requirements, but to be able to contact them they need to pay a premium service fees. The second model is where users can register for free and can use all the services offered by the portal for them free of cost. Here the revenue comes from businesses that pay for an access to these users of the portal. This model leverages the collective strength of communities to attract and negotiate with businesses. This payment can be in the form of advertising on the portal or as targeted marketing by brands—either online or offline. For example travel companies selling honeymoon packages would find matrimonial portals a perfect place to advertise online, while a builder launching a new property project might want to do a road show in a locality by reaching out to its users through a property management portal they use.

As these portals involve large numbers of active users engaging in interactions and transactions, a database of user behaviour, their choices, and preferences is built in the process. Most of the companies are using analytics to fine-tune their products and offerings to their consumer base today and for building new features. They are using the data to iron out any issues that may be making it difficult for their customers to use their products and for bringing new customers on board. Sometime down the line, this could lead to mass aggregation of data lying in different servers. I see a much bigger role of analytics emerging in the coming years as databases build up, and cross-linking and aggregation takes place. We would exist as much in the virtual world as in the real one with every click of ours noted to record details like location, device etc.

At one end, it is thrilling to think that one would literally be able to recreate or replay their life based on what they did, but on the other hand it is chilling, as human memory becomes redundant and privacy, as we know it today, would cease to exist anymore. As a first step towards this, most portals encourage their users to link their social media co-ordinates with their profiles.

The choices to pick from in this segment were many and far apart, both in terms of verticals and the models that they employ. My challenge was to look for representative cases so that the spectrum is covered to a large extent from the perspective of domains that have been really impacted by digital enterprises and the way they engage user communities in an economically beneficial manner.

Shaadi.com is the oldest company featured in this book, having been around for sixteen years. Having the perfect name for the portal, gives added strength to this formidable brand. Started as a fun experiment in the late nineties, this portal has become the de-facto choice for people looking for life partners for themselves or for someone in their family. The journey of connecting life partners is quite fascinating. They have picked up a concept that is quintessentially Indian or, at least, South Asian, and successfully tailored it to the digital space in a way that it has opened up the world for its users. As a cascading impact, this phenomenon has now spun an industry around matrimonial services. Now we see so many portals offering similar or slightly different services. Shaadi.com has come a long way from the time it worked like an online classified to actually playing a matchmaker by suggesting matches to users based on their profiles and their partner preferences. The product is constantly evolving to offer better experience to its ever-growing user base that gets a favourable advantage from the current demographic spread of India and Indians. I was keen on understanding how they manage the fake profiles and malpractices around weddings. It was heartening to hear that they are exploring technology to bring these down.

Among the property portals, I chose CommonFloor.com as they had a different approach than most other portals that operate on the classified mode. It is a company that I have personally observed and used since its nascent days. They started by organizing the communities of property users and building a platform for them to interact and manage community affairs. Gradually they included the various service providers, property dealers, and finally construction companies in the game. Today, with a base of property users who come to their portal for their day-to-day needs, they have an attractive proposition for all kinds of property players. With a vision to become the go-to-place for any kind of property-based requirement, they are an organization to look out for. With their community-based approach, they have been able to keep a sustained interest in the portal as compared to other portals where people come only when they have a need and as we know properties are not bought and sold, or even rented every day. However, they had been very Bangalore-focussed and mostly limited to residential properties till now; how they move out of these comfort zones is what will define their future. To me their business model was of real interest.

Rang De is an organization easy to fall in love with. It is a microfinance company which works on peer-to-peer lending format using a technology platform. They act as connectors between those who can afford to lend small amounts of money and those who need them. In an offline world, these two sets of people have no way to find each other. Even if they were do find each other, it is nearly impossible to transact across geographies in a transparent way on a regular basis. By using technology, Rang De not only connects these two diverse set of communities but has also achieved it on a scale that is making India more inclusive by allowing 'those who have' to help 'those who do not have' directly. This is also a beautiful example of how technology can be leveraged for social change and how, with the right intention, you can get people to join your movement. As a business, I especially liked the way they have leveraged social media and their own community to spread their wings and raise funds for the communities they work for.

IndiBlogger is a unique community as well as a product. They bring together bloggers—a species that owes its very existence to the Internet, on a single active platform. As a product, they study blogs across the spectrum, collect their various rankings, and combine them to give each blog a collective score that is refurbished regularly. They work with the businesses who like to engage bloggers to spread the word about their products and services, or run promotional campaigns for their product launches. Their format typically includes physically bringing together the online warriors through their meets and leveraging a feeling of community. At this point in time they are one of the smaller businesses featured here, involving on one end a small but influential community of bloggers in India and on the other hand a handful of brands. I chose them for the uniqueness of the business that is like is a layer on top of Internet content creators and the potential that their product holds for a global rollout if they are able to scale it up to the next level.

I wanted to pick a portal in job search as they cater to one of the basic needs of the young Indians. After a bit of research, I realized that most of job-related activities have shifted to Linkedin, with candidates managing their profiles online along with features like endorsements and references from colleagues and ex-colleagues. Having said that, another set of job portals are emerging which are trying to organize the unorganized job markets by connecting unskilled workers or manual labourers with the people who are looking for them. This includes people like drivers, housemaids, cooks, office boys, nurses, security guards, and construction labourers. There are quite a few portals coming up but they need some more time before they can be studied and documented. However, they are truly bringing the power of Internet to the bottom of the pyramid and as Dr C.K. Prahalad would have said, there is a lot of wealth there.

Another space I wanted to study was education. I spoke to a few entrepreneurs and studied many portals in this space, but could not get anyone with a strong sense of direction and vision. In the education space, the models are still evolving and the space that seems to be doing reasonably well is the communities around competitive exam preparation. The challenge here is that people come and join these communities for a purpose and move on once the purpose is achieved so the binding glue wears out after a while. There are portals providing information on various types of exams and running discussion forums to discuss the same. Basically the support industry in education has moved online to an extent. I could not find many that were working with a vision to leverage the potential of Internet to either make education more accessible or more effective. The same is more or less true for health portals. Most of them are still in the nascent stages and still experimenting with what will work and what won't.

I hope that the diverse models and domains covered in this section inspire you to think of some new ideas for creating communities online.

SHAADI

The Digital Cupid

ARRANGED MARRIAGES ARE A quintessentially Indian concept. It is only in India that families find a match for their eligible sons and daughters based on a number of criterias that can range right from community and caste to astrology. Getting a good match can be a lifetime goal for many parents. Someone who gives them vast choices of prospects from across the globe is bound to get rewarded in the process. Well, this is how Shaadi.com became one of India's best-known Internet brands. With the sheer numbers and spread of Indians across the globe, they also make Shaadi.com the world's largest matrimonial service.

Shaadi.com pioneered online matrimonial services when it was started way back in 1996 as Sagai.com. Growing from strength to strength, today it is the de-facto leader in its category. Anupam Mittal, the founder of Shaadi.com, nostalgically recalls how this idea occured to him when an uncle approached him with a bunch of resumes of prospective brides for him. This gave him the idea of putting up resumes of people looking to get married online and letting them find a match for themselves. The idea was born and experimentation continued for the next 5-6 years on the sidelines. They would fiddle with the look and feel of the site or play around with some features. Slowly traffic began to grow. Around 2000, they looked at the data, and the huge traffic on the portal indicated interest in the concept. From that point on, it became a serious business that has never looked back. Anupam says, they are trying to solve a problem for humanity by providing them as best as possible an experience of finding their life partners.

Looking at the matrimonial domain, they have created a kind of phenomenon with many more players that have come up in all these years and that can now be called competition. This includes niche ventures that are coming up in this space like elite wedding portals that combine online data with manual matching, portals for second marriages, portals based on communities or special cases. All these players who are thriving in the matrimony space indicate that the market is strong for the services provided. This has also put a lot of organization into a space that was not only small and extremely fragmented but also gave a very limited choice to people. Incidentally the advent of online portals is also coupled with the fact that families are now spread across geographies and hence the search for partners has also gone global.

The objective of a matchmaking website is simple to state—it provides a superior matchmaking experience to eligible Indians all over the world. The devil as always lies in the detail. The biggest impact that online matchmaking services have

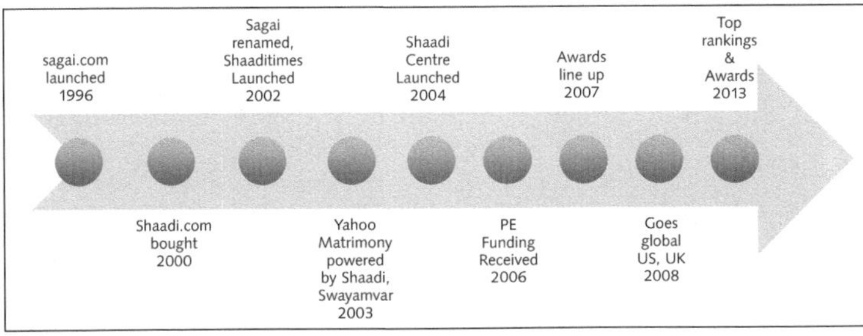

Fig 1: Journey of Shaadi.com

had is the removal of geographical or spatial constraints for finding a life partner. Thereby, exponentially increasing the probability of finding a more suitable match.

MATCHMAKING—BEHIND THE SCENES

In one line, the business process of running a matrimonial portal involves getting as many eligible people as possible to list their profiles on the site. Index this data on as many relevant parameters as possible based on the candidate's own data and their partner preferences. Use this data to match profiles and suggest them to users or let members search and sort results as per their preferences. This is extended to providing a platform for them to interact in a safe and secure way, in exchange of a listing fee for premium services offered.

Creating a profile on Shaadi.com is as simple as filling a form and giving all possible details about the member and their preferences in a potential partner. Members have an option to add their pictures and control visibility of the pictures. Once the data is uploaded, members can start looking for potential partners using basic search on parameters like age, height, marital status, location, and religion. Advanced search lets them add parameters like education, profession, etc to narrow down options. They can additionally look for members who are online and at the same time, new members who have joined since last login. They can also search for members based on when they last logged in to restrict search to active members only. There are bound to be quite a few passive profiles on the portal and this takes care of not showing those profiles again and again to you. There is also an option to block certain profiles from contacting you, for eg., if you are very sure that you do not want to look for anyone outside your religion. Often repeated tasks on the portal like search criteria and shortlisted profiles can be saved for future reference. A simple accept and decline feature is the beginning of communication between two potentially interested candidates.

Basic membership comes free and allows members to list their profiles, do basic search, and express interest to other members. Premium membership has two levels categorized as Gold, Gold+, Diamond, Diamond+, Platinum, and Platinum+, and it can be taken for 3, 6, or 12 months. Different packages give different access like enabling members to send messages to other members, permitting the e-matchmaker tool for better matching, getting a bold or highlighted listing, a classified ad in newspaper in addition to online listing etc. Then more personalized services come into the picture where a relationship manager helps the member with exclusive matchmaking service—essentially do the searching, sorting, and initial contact on behalf of the user.

E-matchmaker is the flagship tool that matches profiles among the millions listed on the portal. It provides matches based on 4 primary matching criteria:

- Preferred matches: Members who exactly match members' Partner Preferences.
- Broader matches: Members who match some of member's Partner Preferences and are slightly outside some other Preferences.
- Reverse matches: These Members have set Partner Preferences that match member's Profile information.
- 2-way matches: Both of you match each other's Partner Preferences.

They have also started suggesting 5 matching profiles everyday based on best 2-way matches which helps save a lot of search time and members can quickly accept or reject the profile. Match Guarantee is a feature that guarantees money-back if as a premium member you have expressed interest to at least 10 members and not received a single acceptance within 30 days. This is a kind of hidden feature, not prominently advertised on the portal, so I wondered if it was really used. Anupam told me that they do end up refunding money for a small set of people every month if the guarantee is breached.

Shaadi.com and most other matrimonial portals follow a freemium model. Members can get listed for free, they can also look at other profiles for free, but to move ahead and contact other members, they need to pay. There are other services like bold listing and relationship manager that again come for an additional fee. About 20 percent of the listed members at

Shaadi are paid members. They tried advertising as a revenue stream but found that it was distracting for their users and was coming in the way of non-intrusive browsing, so they decided to do away with it. More or less, all their revenue comes from the paid listings where the members get extra privileges based on the plan they have chosen.

Shaadi rewards is the affiliate programme of Shaadi that lets website owners put a Shaadi widget on their sites and earn a share of revenue that they generate for Shaadi. The payouts are as big as 75 percent of the revenue earned and above a certain number of paid subscriptions that come through a website, payouts can be 100 percent as well. To me this appeared to be an indication of how difficult it is to get a paid profile on the website, but Anupam clarified that this payout is only on the first payment; any renewal revenue remains with the company. This is a foolproof way of reaching out to the intended audience by establishing your presence on other websites and sharing revenue only when it is generated. It is common strategy through which many digital companies are leveraging the power of networks. Even if revenue ticking is limited, brand visibility gets a massive boost when your brand is visibly placed on popular websites and blogs.

Research at Shaadi has established the 6 Cs of a successful marriage: Compatibility, Chemistry, Commitment, Community, Communication, and Compassion. The catch though lies in the fact that everyone has personal preferences so the weights on these parameters are as personal as they can get. Some people are looking for someone exactly like themselves, while others are looking for exact opposites, and most are looking for something in between. Some people know exactly what they are looking for and would only be interested in interacting with those who fit their criteria to the T, while others want to explore and hope to find someone whom they can fall in love with. Anupam described the journey of the portal from being a database of potential brides and grooms to a platform which connects people. In the beginning, it was a searchable database where people browsed through the profiles, selected some profiles, met offline, and if everything went well, got married. In its next stage, it became a discovery platform where you could discover people instead of just names and resumes, people who were like or unlike you, the kind of people you would look forward to spending your life with. This was done through enhanced options in search and filters in profiles and partner preferences. At this stage, it is about connecting people through matchmaking services that can help you shortlist the profiles you interact with based on as many criteria as possible and as much as technology can enable.

In their network of sites, they have two other portals—ShaadiLive and ShaadiTimes. ShaadiLive is a blog that shares tid-bits about the company and its achievements, product updates, a selection of inspiring success stories, trends in matchmaking, and tips for Shaadi members. In its 'Ask an Expert' section, they get renowned counsellors to answer readers' queries. It's a forum for Shaadi to talk about what they are doing, and to seek feedback from the users. ShaadiTimes is a relationship and wedding portal to provide information, expert advice, and services for members to manage all aspects of their wedding experience and relationships better.

Business-wise, it works as a testing ground for potential new complimentary ideas. It also provides an insight into what users are looking for beyond just finding a partner or after they have found one.

Geek Cupid

Shaadi management has a basic belief that technology can do all that is replicable. So while technology is integral part of their product, it is not a big differentiator in the long-run as anyone can replicate what they do. What makes Shaadi stand out is their ability to understand the user and what they are looking for and then create a product to suit those needs.

You would appreciate their use of technology if you study the evolution of their product. As mentioned earlier, in the beginning it was more like newspaper classified ads in an online format with limited search facility. As technology evolved, Shaadi kept adding features like e-matchmaking, interactivity, privacy, and security. Profiles are far more detailed, with pictures and a messaging system that lets prospects interact in real time. An embedded messenger allows chatting without any need to share other co-ordinates on the Internet while also keeping a record of the conversations. In the last three years, their effort has been on using technology to improve the matchmaking process and reduce misuse of the portal in any way. They are also working on crowdsourcing a lot of information by integration of data with social media profiles of the members. This ensures that people are not providing conflicting information about themselves for eg., their photographs can be matched to ensure that profile pictures are not very dated.

Maintaining a mobile application is also their current focus as 10-15 percent of traffic to portals now comes from mobiles. They feel they are way ahead of competition in this space but they fear it may just be a temporary advantage as everyone is coming up with mobile apps and sooner or later are bound to catch up.

ATTRACTING THE PROSPECTS

Being a pioneer and very early starters, they have the advantage of numbers and in the digital world numbers attract numbers. At 20 million profiles, one wonders if everyone available in the marriage market is already there. Each successful marriage through the portal is a marketing campaign for it as everyone present at the wedding finds out about the role of the portal, and the fact that real marriages are happening through it. You can just imagine the hope this presents to all the mummies at these weddings who are looking for suitable matches for their children.

Anupam says that for them Television has worked very well as a marketing channel. Way back in 2004, he himself appeared in their first TV commercial and that has built a kind of trust that, he thinks, cannot be replicated by competition. They had also partnered with a TV channel for a programme called *Shubh Vivah* that had Madhuri Dixit as its anchor. It was supposed to be a reality show where Shaadi.com came as content partners but the show did not take off and the idea died a natural death. Their current TV commercial with the tagline 'Love, arranged by Shaadi.com' features Chetan Bhagat as the brand ambassador. They feel he has the right resonance with the brand as Chetan's stories are mostly based on real life stories and Shaadi.com is all about real people and their real stories. The idea is to have a brand appeal that is youth-oriented and brings in a feeling of fresh love, without alienating the families, as they are an integral part of any Indian's life. I feel Shaadi as a brand is building a focus on youth finding a partner for themselves which to me is a looking ahead. Their closest competition on the other hand focuses on the families finding partners for their eligible sons and daughters, the way it happens or rather happened traditionally.

As part of its social responsibility, Shaadi is associated with Pranay Milan Sammelan for the Hearing Impaired, an initiative by Delhi Society for Deaf Women to help deaf women find suitable partners. Shaadi.com supports this initiative by promoting it online as well as on ground; thereby helping these women reach out to a larger audience.

Making Shaadi Social

Of all the digital businesses that I studied, Shaadi.com uses the social media most effectively to engage its users and potential users. They have 1.5 million Facebook fans and about 10 percent of them are actively engaged on a daily basis. This makes them an active forum for people to interact on topics around Shaadi and has led to achievements like 'The World's Most Engaging Brand on Facebook'. On Twitter, they are active but not as aggressively. A characteristic that helps their popularity on social networks is the fact that weddings are synonymous with fun and happiness. Marriage probably provides most fodder to humour that is universally relatable. You see a lot of tips and humour being shared on their platform along with beautiful pictures which can be quite touching.

Unfortunately, marriages in India come with their own set of social issues like dowry, child marriages, and domestic violence. Social media is the perfect platform for Shaadi.com to raise awareness about these issues. In 2012, they ran a successful campaign to bring awareness about the issue of dowry through a game called Angry Brides, inspired of course by Angry Birds.

Angry Brides Game: Dowry is illegal in India since 1961 but every year thousands of young women die and many more suffer physical and mental violence due to dowry issues. This campaign aimed to bring awareness about the menace of dowry through an online game on Facebook that had three levels where the player deals with three potential grooms with heavy dowry price tags. The player strikes the dodging grooms with a weapon of their choice. The weapons include household items like rolling pins, sandals, utensils, books, computers, and brooms. Each hit decreases the price of the groom, and adds the saved money to a fictional 'anti-dowry fund'. Players can publish their contribution to the anti-dowry fund on their Facebook wall or tweet about it. The game was conceived, designed, and developed in-house by the Shaadi.com team and engaged about 5,00,000 players across 35 countries. It won the IAMAI award for 'Best Usc of Internet for Social and Economic Development', and 'Innovative Digital Marketing Solutions' Award at the 4th International Award in New York for highlighting the practice of dowry demands in marriages.

It is very difficult to measure social media engagement and its contribution to business but it sure helps to keep the brand alive in the memory of all those who are engaged. For a brand like Shaadi that can work very well with referrals, every person they engage on social media can lead to more customers. It also provides them with insights into their customer mindset, as there are real life conversations on social media. An infographic by SocialSamosa rates them as world's most engaging brand on Facebook.

With millions of engaged users on their social media channels, they have the potential to become a media channel by themselves. Think of the potential if they figure out a way to open it up to other brands that would want to target this user base. Take an example, if they let wedding planners or honeymoon planners use their platform to either advertise or co-promote, there is a huge business potential waiting to be tapped. In fact I am surprised that they have not done this already.

NEW TWISTS FOR THE OLDEST GAME

Going Offline with Shaadi Centres

Shaadi centres are a company-owned network of retail outlets across India that offer matrimonial-related services, from matchmaking to wedding planning. First launched in 2004, these centres are now present in 87 cities in India with 100+ centres. The first international centre came up in 2010 in Ontario, Canada. Their current plan is to roll out 250 such centres in India and abroad. It is a first of its kind retail chain ever that attempts to organize the otherwise unstructured and fragmented 60,000 crore matrimonial industry in India. For their customers, it works at two levels—one it provides a face to the online company and two, it provides help to the families who are not yet very comfortable with computers or may have limited access to them.

Analytics

Over 16+ years of existence, Shaadi has built a strong database of eligible population, some of whom may be happily married now, covering what people are looking for in their partners. Since this data is tagged with many socio-economic parameters like religion, caste, financial status, education, age groups etc, the analysis of data can be quite insightful. I got to read a few of their data sheets and some of the data they had shared with the media. As of now they are using the insights as a material for public relations or as marketing tool. Sometimes they have shared data for good causes like analytics for profiles that have a physical diability and how they can find better matches for themselves. Tomorrow they can give deep insights into social change over the years and by throwing light on some evil practices may help bring them down. Take an example, in a conversation with a visually challenged young man, it was noted that one of the key challenges he had was not being able to find a life partner. Now when I look at the data sheet of physically-challenged people from Shaadi, I find that differently-abled people as a community are scattered across locations and may be willing to let go of other social criterias like caste and location when choosing a life partner. There are tonnes of similar personal data that they are sitting on that can be aggregated to generate quite a few statistical trends besides insights that help them improve the core product on a continuous basis.

Analysis throws light on some amusing trends such as the demand for PSU-employed grooms goes up every time the economy goes down. There are city-based preferences in terms of how many people give importance to the education of their partner, and for how many it is not a criteria at all. Put together, this analysis can give serious insights into our collective psyche and our changing preferences given the other environmental factors.

DEVILS TO DEAL WITH

For the purpose of marriage, people share some of their most personal information on the portal and keeping this information secure is the greatest challenge that needs to be addressed in order to secure customer confidence. At the organization level, Shaadi is certified from both TRUSTe—privacy seal for safety and confidentiality of user data, and VeriSign—secure site seal for security of payments and credit card information. It has also received ISO 9001:2000 certification to ensure that quality systems and processes are in place that listen to customers, understand their requirements, and address them. Let us look at some of the domain-specific challenges.

Confidentiality, Privacy, and Security

Marriages attract a lot of fraud as people try to provide false information to get married. This happens in traditional setups and it is bound to happen in online systems too. The challenge is to see if technology can help bring down this menace and bring authenticity to new relationships created through it. At Shaadi, the check for authentic profiles begins with the CRM team screening every profile before it is visible on the portal. Over the years, their data and their experience has provided enough check points that indicate if the profile is good to go live, should be validated before it goes live, or must be stopped at the verification stage. This includes small data indications like time taken to create the profile, number of profiles created from a single IP at a given time, the order in which the options are chosen from the drop down lists, the location of the profile creation etc. Anupam says they have spent the last 3 years bringing down the number of fake and duplicate profiles on the system. He says that even if such profiles get through the system, they are trying to devise ways so that they do not remain in the system for too long, and this could mean no longer than a few hours. This could be a big innovation if they are able to crack it, as this will take their credibility through the roof and people would definitely be willing to pay a premium for it.

Screening Photos

Photographs are the starting point of interest in an arranged matrimonial alliance. Though it is not mandatory to upload a picture on the profile, they encourage members to upload pictures for better response. Controls have been provided so that members can choose who can see their pictures—they can even password protect them so that only those who have the password can see the pictures. They can also set general rules like only verified members or only members accepted by them can see their pictures. All photographs uploaded are screened to ensure that they are genuine and do not violate socially accepted norms. Images are watermarked and cannot be downloaded by other users. Similarly, only verified phone numbers are displayed and members control the visibility of their contact details. In case of any misuse or misconduct by a member, there is an abuse control button which alerts the Shaadi team at the click of a button, and then it's the team's responsibility to resolve the issue.

The future is bright for Shaadi.com as every year more and more Indians across the globe move into the marriageable age bracket, and as more and more people enter into matrimony more than once. Besides their core matchmaking services, I can see a lot of complimentary businesses that they can branch into like a niche travel service for honeymooners and the obvious ones like wedding planning and event management. With the kind of user base and brand visibility they enjoy, I wonder why they have not already diversified into complimentary services.

eFarmDirect

Chennai-based eFarmDirect is an information exchange portal that is doing matchmaking of another kind between buyers of agricultural produce and farmers. eFarmDirect is empowering the farmers by connecting them to a wide variety of buyers and giving them the choice of choosing who they sell to. Since this segment is not really technology savvy, they have built a phone-based interface to provide information. Just like Shaadi, they are adding buyers and suppliers constantly to build a strong, verified database that can be searched on various parameters like geography, price, availability, yield, rating, organic certification etc. Sellers provide information on produce, expected yield, and price. They also have access to information on demand of their product and can adjust the price accordingly. Sellers get to deal directly with the farmers, eliminating the middlemen and the benefits are shared by both parties. Overall the wastage goes down as the demand is more efficiently fulfilled with the supply. Unlike Shaadi, the profiles here do not get passive once they have met their match and once on-board, they would remain on the portal as long as they see the benefit of being a part of it. A rating system where buyers and sellers rate each other is being put in place in response to some bad deals between those who met through the portal.

As a B2B portal, it deals with bulk buyers like hotels, restaurants, caterers, food processors, exporters, local traders, and retail supermarkets. At the time of writing, they had more than 5000 agricultural products listed on their exchange, across categories like fruit, vegetables, cereals, pulses, flowers, and plantation crops and the varieties thereof. Farm-based products like dairy products, honey, poultry products, and meat are also included. Revenue for the site comes from the subscription fee that both buyers and sellers pay on an annual basis. In future, they can attract companies that need to market their products to farmers in remote corners and it can emerge as a big revenue stream for them.

REFERENCES

Information provided by the company and its website

Conversation with Anupam Mittal of Shaadi.com

Conversation with Srivalli Krishnan of eFarm and information provided by her

http://economictimes.indiatimes.com/tech/internet/matrimony-portals-making-serious-efforts-to-counter-rising-tide-of-divorces-ensure-lasting-unions/articleshow/20768944.cms

http://www.authorstream.com/Presentation/ramagrawal-1192525-matrimonial-market-analysis/

http://www.SocialSamosa.com/2012/10/shaadi-com-most-engaging-brand-on-facebook-infographic/

http://newsfeed.time.com/2012/01/18/angry-brides-game-attacks-indias-illegal-dowry-tradition/

http://www.afaqs.com/news/story/32786_Shaadi.com-launches-Angry-Brides

http://www.hindustantimes.com/photos-news/Photos-Brunch/angrybirdsripoffs/Article4-844084.aspx

shaadi.com

The World's Largest Matrimonial Service

Name of the company:	People Interactive (I) Pvt Ltd
Website:	www.shaadi.com
Year of incorporation:	1997
Founder:	Anupam Mittal
Headquarters:	Mumbai
No. of offices:	7 in India and 4 abroad
No. of employees:	1400
Cities present in:	38
No. of members:	20 million
No. of views per month:	350 million
Succesful marriages to date:	2 million

RANG DE

Change for the People by the People

MANY OF US WHO are socially privileged have often wondered if we can do something to bring down the poverty levels in the country. Every time we see a documentary or a new item highlighting their plight, we have an urge make a difference. With the best of our intentions, we do not know how to help them in a way that empowers them. Can Internet-based communities be extended to connect socially diverse groups of people and, in the process, help bridge various divides that exist between them to make the society more equitable? Can those who have money, lend to those who do not have any, and become a catalyst in making their dreams come true? We know the first set of people exist on the Internet and the other probably have no clue about what it is and what it can do for them. So how do you leverage the power of Internet to connect these two groups? How do you keep track of small disbursements made to micro-ventures across the nook and corners of the country? Ramakrishna N.K.'s (Ram) Rang De does exactly this by leveraging the power of the Internet to reach out to potential social investors and the power of NGOs who work in the fields at grassroots level.

Rang De is an online social venture that provides low-cost microcredit to rural entrepreneurs with an aim to create a positive and sustainable impact on their lives. Its vision is to make the model of microcredit sustainable in such a way that no entrepreneur—big or small—should be denied a loan to improve his or her business. With this in mind, their platform orchestrates peer-to-peer lending where one set of individuals fund the needs of the other set in India through what they call 'social investment'. Technically speaking, they are providing microfinance or micro-credit through the funds that are crowdsourced using Internet as the platform. Ram was one of the first entrepreneurs I spoke to and the first question that I asked him was whether he would have managed this without the Internet as a platform and his answer was a clear no. Rang De, as much as it is being a catalyst in social change by way of poverty alleviation that is its primary objective, it is one of the finest examples of leveraging the power of Internet.

The First Steps

The husband-wife team of Ram and Swati came up with this idea after being inspired by the work of Dr Mohamed Yunus of Gramin bank. They looked at the model that the leading microfinance company Kiva uses to fund the small finance needs of the poor in the world. They combined the inspiration with a proven model and came up with Rang De.

Ram devotedly says it is the volatile passion of Dr Yunus that inspires him the most and meeting him every time has only recharged him about this work.

Microfinance involves providing small loans to people with low incomes who do not have access to organized finance that requires lot of collateral before giving a loan. These micro-loans typically come at a very high interest rate to off set the potential defaults in the absence of collaterals. Rang De is an attempt to bring down the cost of microcredit by enabling peer-to-peer lending of small sums of money through an online portal. The main difference between Rang De and traditional microfinance is Rang De's focus to lower the interest rate and its fundraising model. By raising social investments from individuals, Rang De is able to bring down the cost of microcredit and offer loans to people at reduced and hence affordable rates. The objective is to bring down the cost of capital for small borrowers and make this a key driver for poverty alleviation. They observed that there were a few similar microfinance initiatives on the ground but they could not scale up because of limited reach. So they decided to use the Internet as a medium to reach out to larger masses. This was also a tool that could bring in complete transparency by providing updated information on borrowers and their credit history. Their first big support came in the form of funding from the ICICI Foundation as a grant to support the operations and for facilitating low-cost loans to beneficiaries across India. The grant helped Rang De build the technology platform, which forms the core of the organization. It helped them build a dedicated team of

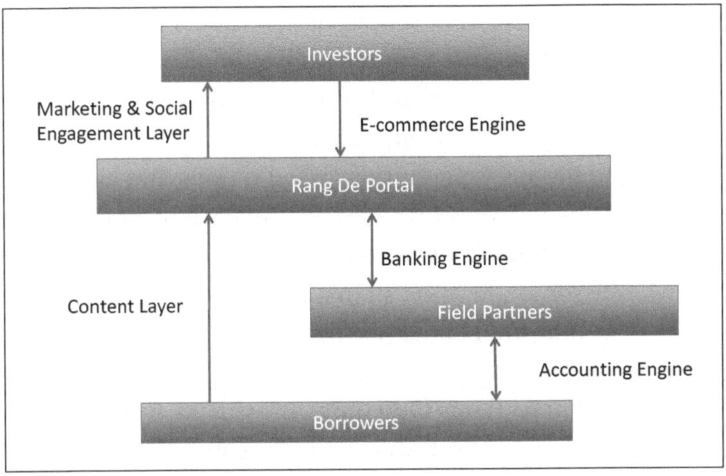

Fig 1: Rang De Business Model

professionals and form a robust organizational structure. It also formed a part of its working capital.

Ram likes to say that he is in the business of impact, and a lot of it can come from mere documentation of the impact, an aspect that is ignored by many social entrepreneurs. A look at the website demonstrates this belief of his as you look at the profiles of the borrowers, complete with their pictures, stories, credit needs, credit history, and the impact of Rang De on their lives.

CREATING IMPACT WAVES

There are many aspects of microfinance that one needs to understand before setting up a business around it. If you want to help a poor person in setting up a business that can more appropriately be called a source of livelihood, you can either give money in charity or lend your spare money to them. For people looking to make a difference by lending, the challenges are finding those who genuinely need money, tracking if the money is actually impacting lives, and finally following up with repayments. Many of us would be happy to outsource these activities to someone who can manage it professionally, while keeping us informed of the positive change that the money is bringing about.

This is where Rang De comes in with its web portal to connect lenders and borrowers. Lenders can invest easily from the comfort of their homes or offices. The process is extremely simple for a computer literate person—browse through the profiles of identified borrowers, read about them, understand their needs and fund requirement, and choose the person to lend to. Lenders can also choose to lend by region, by the field partner NGOs, by amount required, by category of intended use of funds, or the type of investment. In case they do not want to spend time in choosing, they can always leave it to the Rang De team to decide on their behalf. Once the borrower repays lender has the choice to recycle the funds to another borrower or withdraw it from their account.

At the ground level, Rang De works with the NGOs whom they refer to as field partners. These NGOs act as the front-end for loan disbursement. They identify and screen the borrowers, make the actual loan payment, and track the progress of work for which loan was taken and repayments. They also act as the agents to measure the impact through these micro loans on the families of borrowers. The documentation they create helps the borrowers get the next level of loan.

Crowdsourcing of funds typically falls into three categories:

- Charity or Donation: Money paid is not expected back by the contributor and is added to the working capital of fund managing entity i.e. Rang De.
- Lending with zero interest: Borrowers only expect the principal amount that they have lent to be returned, and the interest received is added to the corpus of Rang De.
- Lending with some nominal interest: Lenders treat funding as investment but at lower or nominal rates of interest.

Rang De lets the lender choose how they want to help the lesser-priviledged and treats them all as social investors. Worldwide, most crowdsourcing takes place as charity.

Irrespective of the mode chosen by the social investor, Rang De has a standard model of disbursing the loan at a fixed rate of interest. This helps in maintaining simplicity, standardization, and transparency at the borrower end.

NUMBER CRUNCHING

Microcredit refers to small size loans that are collateral free and are lent to low-income households to meet their working capital needs. Typically, the loan size lies between ₹5,000 and ₹15,000. These loans are usually utilized for income generation activities. The borrower has to repay the loan according to a preset repayment plan. Rang De charges its borrowers a flat rate of interest at 8.5 percent that works out to about 15.3 percent APR. This rate is standard and, at this point in time, comes with no extra costs like processing fee or disbursement charges. This standardization removes any scope of manipulation or malpractice by the field partners. This is a reasonable rate compared to the average of about 26 percent charged by established microfinance companies. The interest income generated is divided in the following manner:

- 5 percent to the field partner for their effort in managing the funds.
- 1percent to Rang De.
- 2 percent goes to the lender as a return on their investment.
- 0.5 percent to a contingency fund.

In the first glance, the 1 percent return on funds invested looks bleak, but if you look at the volumes they are targeting, it seems viable. The potential, however, to create impact through such a venture, as the cliché goes, is priceless.

Besides microcredit, Rang De also has options of micro-venture and education loans. Micro-ventures refer to bigger loans and are typically lent to artisans when they have a job order and require greater capital to execute the order. The role of the field partner here enables to create market linkages to first procure these work orders. In such cases, the borrower group pays a higher rate of interest and social investors earn a higher rate of return as well. Rang De also provides loans for educational purposes to individuals referred by the field partners. The rate of interest paid by the borrower is 5 percent of which 4 percent goes to the field partner and 1 percent to Rang De contingency fund. The borrower lends money as a goodwill gesture without expecting returns from such a loan.

At the time of writing, Rang De's repayment rate stands at a sturdy 96 percent. A high repayment rate empowers the overall microcredit system by building trust among the borrowers and in turn enables them to aspire to expand their business. Based on their repayment history, borrowers can apply for a higher amount of loan from Rang De or other financing agencies. As a byproduct, a credit history is getting built for the small borrowers that can in the long run help them as financing agencies who till now have had no way of assessing credibility of the small borrowers with no financial records.

Interest rate breakup of borrower repayments in flat rates for Rang De's loan products:

Loan Product	Field Partner	Rang De	Social Investor	Contingency	Total (flat)	Total (APR)*
Business	5.00%	1.00%	2.00%	0.50%	8.50%	15.33%
Education	4.00%	1.00%	–	–	5.00%	9.02%
Micro-venture	3.00%	2.00%	4.00%	1.00%	10.00%	17.97%
*APR interest rates are calculated on a monthly repayment schedule.						

Interest rate breakup of the yield to each stakeholder in APY for Rang De's loan products:

Loan Product	Field Partner	Rang De	Social Investor	Contingency	Total (APY)*
Business	9.02%	1.80%	3.61%	0.90%	15.33%
Education	7.27%	1.82%	-	-	9.02%
Micro-venture	5.39%	3.59%	7.19%	1.80%	17.97%

*APY interest rates are calculated on a monthly repayment schedule.

Sample Monthly Report Card

24,874 BORROWERS IMPACTED	**5,173** SOCIAL INVESTORS	**94.19%** REPAYMENT RATE
Rs. 115.2 million SOCIAL INVESTMENTS REPAID	**Rs. 52.6 million** OUTSANDING PORTFOLIO	**Rs. 174.5 million** SOCIAL INVESTMENTS RAISED

CHECKS AND BALANCES

Rang De's field partners are small to medium-sized NGOs and microfinance institutions. They are Rang De's gateway to the borrowers. Selecting the right field partners is crucial to the whole model of Rand De, as they are the ones who work with the beneficiaries directly. Their credibility, integrity, efficiency, and productivity can be the weakest or the strongest link in the whole chain. Rang De has consciously worked towards defining a robust process for the selection of field partners as well as for working with them.

Here is a snippet of due diligence process that Rang De follows for selecting its field partners:

- All interested organizations can apply for partnership through a simple form on the portal.
- Rang De verifies that the applicant meets the base criteria of being an NGO and has a minimum of 1-year experience in microfinance. Once verified, a Partnership Profile document is sent to them to be completed and information is screened through a telephonic conversation.
- The applicant is then required to submit documentation that includes certificate of registration, copy of latest annual report, copy of audited statements for last 3 years, along with a nominal application fees of ₹500.
- If the documents are all in order, the Rang De team makes a field visit to meet the prospective partner, their borrowers, staff, etc. After the field trip, observations are shared with the entire Rang De team and partners are finalized based on overall findings of the visiting team.
- The shortlisted organization then signs an Agency agreement and a Field Partner Mandate document.
- The field partner is trained for using the online application. For the first 3 months, Rang De limits the number of transactions with the new partner to:
    - Maximum of 20 applications per month.
    - Maximum of 1 lakh per month in disbursement.
    - Performance Review is done after 3 months and a decision is taken for increasing the limits.

Similarly, Rang De has well-defined policies in place for defaults by the borrowers. A small portion of all returns from the investments go to a contingency fund that can be used to take care of any defaults. If a borrower defaults on a loan due to genuine reasons like casualty, natural calamity, or death, a part of the principal amount will be recovered from Rang De's contingency fund and the remaining portion will be borne by the social investor. In case of process violations by Rang De or a field partner, the responsible party will meet the defaults in full as the case may be. They are in the process of implementing the Sig Sigma framework to bring in efficiencies in the system both for their internal and field partner interface processes. At the time of writing, there are about 40 NGOs associated with Rang De, of which about 18 are active. They also organize annual meets where their field partners can exchange ideas and best practices.

Rang De has funded more than 250 unique businesses till now, making funds available to anyone who needs them, but their preferred focus area is education. With their presence in about 13 states of India, right from Kerala to Manipur, they have a Pan India presence. Ram says they are open to working with field partners anywhere in India as long as they work with the underserved communities that can benefit from microcredit.

About 96 percent of the social investors at Rang De are individual contributors. 40 percent of their investors donate the interest component to Rang De, which goes to show the trusting relationship they share with the investors.

LEVERAGING TECHNOLOGY FOR THE GREATER GOOD

On the face of it, Rang De's website looks simple, but Ram told me that behind this simplicity is a sturdy architecture that is designed to handle both complexity and scale. The core technology engine was one of the first investments Rang De made in the business. They roped in the core team from a leading IT company to design an architecture that is robust and scalable. Ram proudly related that they may have faced many issues in the journey of Rang De, but never one on the technology or architectural front.

From an investor's perspective, Rang De works like an e-commerce platform with an integrated payment gateway through which investors can make payments to Rang De for investment. Between Rang De and their borrowers, portal works like a bank that keeps track of disbursements, interest calculations, repayments, and consolidates all these accounts into the corporate account for Rang De. Third part of portal is the content where subjective and objective data about each borrower is maintained and a blog that works as a platform for sharing information, communicate with the investors, potential investors, media, and anyone in general. There are other parts of the portal that allow communication with field partners online.

On the portal, there is an Investor Dashboard which helps in maintaining complete transparency between investors and borrowers. Transparency is key to Rang De's success; after all it is a non-profit peer-to-peer lending platform. Social investors can track their investments at the click of a button just like they can invest at the click of a button. Each social investor has access to a personal dashboard on the portal that provides comprehensive reports of investments, repayments, number of borrowers impacted along with their individual details, state and sector-wise break-up of investment, withdrawals by the investor, and donations, if any.

Technology is managed in-house by a small team of 4 persons. Rang De also went through a season of outsourcing but design issues, loss of time during the requests that needed urgent attention, and absence of agility led them to bring technology in-house. Since Rang De is not a usual business, the domain knowledge was not readily available in the market and they had to invest in building it in-house. This was difficult with an outsourced vendor, as teams are not directly under your control. In-house teams sense the requirements in the environment as they are a part of the same larger team and hence are able to appreciate the problem or opportunity at hand much better. Hence, they are able to come out with better technology solutions for the company's requirement. An interesting point that came out during my conversations with Rang De and other startups is that outsourcing vendors tend to put their best resources for big projects of their bigger clients, leaving the trainees for the smaller projects or startup clients.

Tapping into the Positive Energy of Social Investors

Rang De is one of the few companies in the book which has leveraged social media in a big way. Their marketing and promotions are pivoted around their social investors and the impact, thereof, on the borrowers.

Social Media

Rang De very intelligently uses social media platforms to run campaigns and generate funds through fun-filled contests. Out of the many campaigns that I learnt about, three really stood out. These campaigns show their creativity in coming out with campaigns and the breadth of potential investors they cover with these campaigns by tapping into various human emotions. Rang De World Cup Fever is their most successful and highly visibile campaign that struck a chord with the cricket-crazed denizens of India. Their Mother's Day campaign carried the message of their mission through a very personal emotion. Corporate campaigns reach out to corporate citizens, each of whom have the potential to be a social investor as individuals or as a group.

Rang De World Cup Fever

What better platform than the Cricket World Cup in India to raise awareness about a social initiative and also raise funds for the cause in a fun-filled way at no extra cost! As I was reading about this campaign, I realized that they had very smartly used all channels of communication at their disposal for making the best use of this once-in-every-four-year opportunity. India of course won, and the excitement, and in turn effectiveness of this campaign, went straight through the roof.

The idea was to leverage India's cricket mania that peaks around the World Cup to create awareness about Rang De and its cause of low-cost microcredit by encouraging people to pledge funds based on some quirky and funny criterias. They

www.rangde.org/world-cup-fever-2011

Semifinal - India v Pakistan - 30 Mar - 31 Pledges raised Rs. 290,300 in Social Investments

Name	Pledge	Value	Fulfilled
Vivek Joshi	Rs 1000 for every run over 300 of india's total. Rs 1 lakh extra if india wins	Rs.100000	
Srinivasa Adepalli	100,000 if India wins	Rs.100000	
Ramki	Rs.1000 for every boundary made by Indian batsmen	Rs.30000	
Nagesh Kukunoor	If India beat Pakistan, for @RangDe World Cup Fever, I will invest Rs.10k	Rs.10000	
Kiran Challapalli	Rs.25 for every run Sachin scored in semis and Rs.2500 if India wins	Rs.5000	
Ram	# of runs Sachin scores * 25 & Rs. 2500 if India wins!	Rs.5000	
Nitin Paranjpe	If the match ends in a result i pledge to invest 5000 / -	Rs.5000	
Pranav Shah	If India enters the Finals, I will invest Rs.5000. Period.	Rs.5000	
Kiran C	25*Tendulkar's runs + 2500 if India wins	Rs.5000	
Ninad	I will invest Rs 50 for every run scored by Sachin Tendulkar	Rs 4300	
Karishma Kiri	For every boundry, we'll donate Rs 100!	Rs 3000	

Fig 1: Rang De Cricket World Cup Fever Pledges

started by announcing this campaign on their blog and reached out to a small group of people who follow their blogs, mainly their investors, who would then in turn talk about this to their social circles. The criterion was simple; you make a pledge based on some outcome of the match and once that criterion is met, you invest that amount at Rang De, and they will update your details for others to see and be inspired. There was a small prize at end of the day if you make a real whacky pledge and by doing so they allowed people to be as creative in pledging as possible—adding to the fun of watching cricket rather than view it as charity. Other rules were simple. You could invest any amount in the multiples of ₹100 and you could pledge as many times as you wanted in a match or across matches.

A Facebook event page was created for announcements and for sharing the pledges made by the people—the same were also updated on Twitter. On Twitter, they used the big pledges as talking points about the campaign and to share the excitement about the pledges that were being met as the matches progressed. Linkedin was used to reach out to businesses and high networth individuals. The Rang De team managed the whole online campaign in-house, with support from their chapter members, volunteers, and social investors. They started slow and built up the momentum as the tournament progressed and people got more and more involved in the game. They had to set up a dedicated campaign team by the time India reached the quarter-finals. The wackiness factor was maintained through the campaign and the wackiest pledges like '₹100 for every T and A in the two finalist country names' were shared across social media platforms. On Twitter they designed a campaign poster to be used as their display picture and everyone who participated was encouraged to use this as their display picture too.

The intended impact of the campaign was to create awareness about Rang De and its work, but it also ended up raising funds to the tune of ₹10 lakh. The popularity of the campaigns attracted prominent print publications who wrote about this campaign in particular and Rang De in general, and that brought in more awareness and more investors. This campaign has now become a popular case study for zero-investment social media campaigns.

What a wonderful way to drive your team through a cricket World Cup by promising them that they wouldn't miss a ball.

Rang De Mother's Day Campaign

Mother's day is one of the more popular days to celebrate, after may be Valentine's Day, in India. We are an emotional lot when it comes to our mothers. The Rang De team decided to give its own twist to the Mother's day in 2012, pursuing their mission of raising funds. They invited individuals to invest Rs 1,000 or more for Rang De Moms—mothers in their borrower community who needed money for the education of their children. As a reward, the Rang De team would send a handwritten Mother's day greeting card to your mother, mentioning the good work you are doing by supporting those who are in need.

This 12-day campaign raised ₹1,50,000 as new investments by 60 social investors. This campaign was also run across all their social media channels like e-mail, blog, Facebook, Twitter, and Linkedin. All the creative work for the campaign was done in-house making it another 'no additional cost' campaign.

95 percent of Rang De borrowers are women
750+ of these have taken loans to educate their children

Run for Rang De at Mumbai Marathon

In January 2011, 65 Axis Bank employees ran for Rang De in Standard Chartered Mumbai Marathon. They contributed their Marathon bib cost money at the rate of ₹5000 per bib to Rang De that in all raised ₹3,25,000 as fresh funds. Most of them ran the half marathon or dream run as it was called, but the idea was to come together for a cause and raise awareness about it. Marathoners carried 'India helps India' posters and banners that announced a fight against poverty by saying 'Small Loans Big Impact'. They created awareness about the cause and reinforced the fact that every individual can help another. A small amount for many of us can have a life-changing impact on another person's life. This event was managed by their Mumbai chapter volunteers, again driving on the power of the network of Rang De social investors.

If you notice, in all the campaigns, they leverage the positive energy in their social investor community to reach out to more and more investors. The campaigns are also designed with a dual purpose of raising awareness and raising funds. With every campaign, Rang De is widening its net by encouraging new social investors to join and at the same time inviting fresh investments from existing investors. Most of their investors are active on social media and Rang De lets them brag about the investments they have made at Rang De. Some investors who are also active bloggers have run campaigns on their respective blogs to raise funds for Rang De.

They have started the concept of Rang De Box Office with a tagline Discover India, Discover Yourself. Under this umbrella, the city chapter members organize film screenings followed by a discussion on films which highlight the problems plaguing India like poverty, malnutrition, or lack of education. The idea is to make members brainstorm about what they can do to alleviate these problems.

An On-going Journey

A constant challenge for Rang De is to maintain credibility with the partners at both ends of their value chain. Investors need to know that their funds are being used with integrity, and for the purpose they have been borrowed. This means a vigilant eye on the field partners and ensuring transparency through processes and checkpoints. Rang De team regularly goes for field visits to meet their borrowers and field partners and they also encourage social investors to join in. Each borrower has a complete profile on the website along with the purpose they need funds for and the amount required. The repayment details make for their credit history. Rang De also documents the impact beyond numbers by talking about the impact the loan has made on the borrower and their family. They send regular updates to investors with Rang De's latest data and the status of individual investments.

Though they did not face any specific challenges, but I think, maintaining the momentum and keeping it clean and transparent is going to be a constant challenge. This is what would keep them in business.

References

Interaction with Ram NK and other Rang De team members

Data provided by the company

Company Website & Blog

http://blog.rangde.org/2011/03/the-rang-de-world-cup-fever/

http://india.ashoka.org/fellow/ramakrishna-nk

Name of the company:	Rang De
Website:	www.rangde.org
Year of incorporation:	2008
Founders:	Ramakrishna NK, Smita Ram
Headquarters:	Bangalore
No. of offices:	1
No. of employees:	17 (currently)
States present in:	16
No. of registered users:	15,682
No. of views per month:	100,000+
No. of borrowers:	26,000+

COMMONFLOOR

Meet Your New Neighbours

INDIA IS GETTING MORE urban by the day. Indian cities are getting bigger and denser. People from rural areas are moving to urban areas, and every movement brings with it a need for a house to live in and that translates into an opportunity to connect those who own the properties and those who want to live in them. New residential areas are coming up in clusters in the form of apartment complexes or gated communities where ownership of the property is individual but the ownership of common areas and facilities is shared, calling for a common management of the same that is usually managed by Resident Welfare Associations (RWAs) using the common pool of funds.

These communities of residents have quite a few common needs that are serviced by a spectrum of service providers ranging from a plumber to a security agency to property agents. Put together, these RWAs are a market for these service providers. Since they buy in large numbers for the communities that they represent, they have the power to negotiate with the vendors. As most residents in a society hail from different parts of the country, or the globe, there is a need to connect and socialize in the neighbourhood, whether for common interest or common need. RWAs need to manage their funds, communicate with residents, locate and work with vendors and ensure the overall welfare of the society. At the other end of the spectrum is the community of suppliers that supplies the core ingredient to these communities to manage—houses. Yes, the property builders, followed by the related product like CCTV Cameras and service providers like interior designers. Construction companies need to connect with potential buyers, who may be currently living in rented houses, looking to buy another house for investment purposes, or looking to upgrade their current residence. Most properties in their lifetime go through a series of transactions, i.e. they are bought and sold a few times or rented many times, creating a constant need for the buyers and sellers to reach out to each other.

There was a white space for a platform to connect all the players in a way that they can reach out, interact, and transact with each other easily. Most of the residents in gated communities are upwardly mobile and use Internet as a preferred medium to seek information and interact—this lays bare a natural need for an online platform. This is where CommonFloor.com stepped in by creating an online portal that connects all the players related to housing and housing needs at one place. Vikas Malpani, Sumit Jain, and Lalit Mangal founded CommonFloor in 2007 as India's first real estate portal dedicated to apartments and gated communities. Today, it claims to be the fastest growing real estate portal in India and a one-stop shop for home seekers, residents, association members, and service providers with a vision to be the go to place for any property-related need in the country.

> A McKinsey Global Institute report predicts that by 2030, 70 percent of new jobs in India are likely to be created in cities, where the population will soar to 590 million from 340 million in 2008, indicating the scope of solutions like CommonFloor.

CHASING THE HOME CYCLE

Three key players in the CommonFloor model are registered property owners who may be part of the one or more communities, service providers i.e. vendors for these communities, and the real estate industry that is looking to connect with people who come to the platform for property related needs—specially buying/selling and renting in/out.

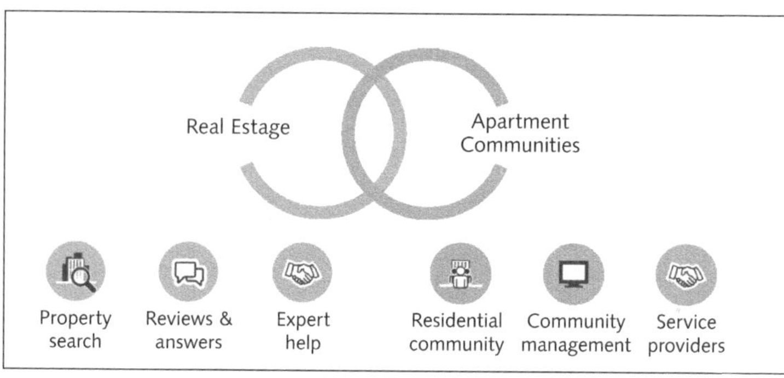

Fig 1: CommonFloor Landscape

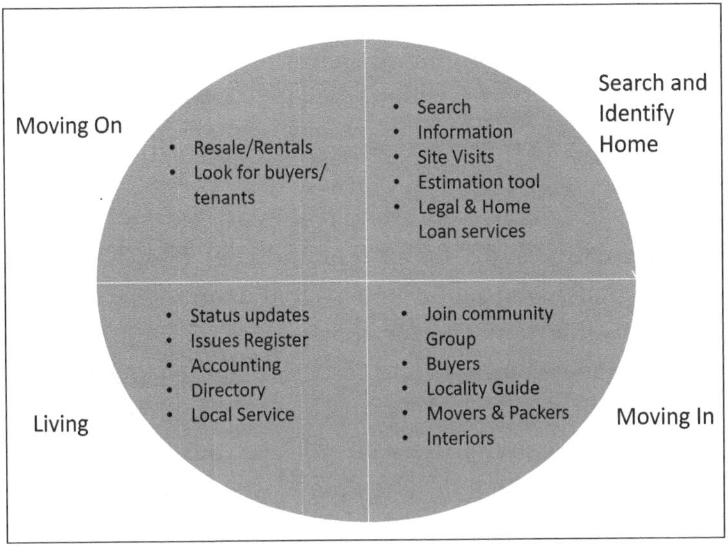

Fig 2: Homeowner Lifecycle

Let us look at the lifecycle of a home seeker—it begins with the search for a suitable home, either to buy or to rent. At this stage, they need information about the available properties and this includes both existing and upcoming properties. They need to be able to shortlist a few properties based on their budget and other preferences like locality, layout, facilities etc. Once they have a shortlist, they need to visit the properties and choose one. From here they move on to looking for finance options and other legal or regulatory requirements—like registering the property or paying taxes. Once they are ready to move in, they require services like packers and movers, interior designers etc. Once they have moved into the property, they would want to socialize with the neighbours, take membership of RWA, and may be manage it too. At some point, they may decide to move out of this property and the property would be up for rent or sale again.

There are many established real estate portals that have huge property listings up for rent and sale. They have built strong brands in the online property market and at the moment have a clear advantage over players like CommonFloor, in terms of sheer volumes. The catch is that they engage their users only at stage 1 and 4 of the lifecycle, which on a time scale are far apart so users do not visit their portals on a regular basis, making the shelf life of users very limited and hence offer no loyalty for the other stakeholders. Resident communities have been using online groups like Yahoo or Google groups to communicate within their communities for some time now, but these groups come with some limitations like communication is either one to one or one to all, leading to too many unnecessary e-mails in the mailbox.

CommonFloor takes a lifecycle approach and provides some services or tools for each stage of home needs. This creates enormous customer loyalty. Users once on CommonFloor tend to stay there, using different sets of services depending on the lifecycle stage they are in. At the time of writing, they have a strong community of more than 5 million property owners or users and this is their biggest strength vis-à-vis competition. These users are visiting the site regularly and their loyalty is what makes CommonFloor a viable choice for vendors and service providers who are trying to cater to these users. Advertising, listing fee, qualified leads become potent sources of revenue for the portal.

As per CommonFloor research, about 40 percent properties in a community are up for renting at any point in time and this constant churn implies that property seekers, owners, and dealers are always pursuing each other. This in turn, ensures perpetual traffic for the portal, making it attractive for relevant advertisers. The presence of homeowners on the portal also makes it an excellent channel for direct rentals bypassing middlemen. Though Sumit Jain, CEO of CommonFloor, says that property dealers are pretty much a part of the ecosystem and they are in no way trying to replace them or make them redundant. He, in fact, quotes a few examples where being a part of the CommonFloor ecosystem has benefitted the property dealers. He explains that the profile of dealers is definitely changing with online portals, from being holders of prized information about properties to being service providers who understand needs of the customer and helps them with properties that match their requirements, and then provide services like legal documentation, cleaning, painting etc. So from property dealers, their roles are evolving to those of consultants or service providers. Before builders came on board, rentals were their key area of focus; but they soon realized that transaction value for rentals is small compared to potential revenue that new property projects offer by way of advertisements or for lead generation. Property companies launching new projects also have huge marketing budgets and a fair share of that is dedicated to online marketing.

CommonFloor follows the freemium, or more commonly called as Google model, for revenue generation that we have discussed in earlier chapters. This means that the platform is free to use for end users—community members and managers—while businesses pay for access to them. Businesses pay CommonFloor either for providing services to communities listed with them or for talking about their products to them through listing of their services on the portal or advertising. Typical cost elements for CommonFloor are the operational cost, a huge percentage of which is salaries, followed by cost of technology and the cost of reaching out to new markets. Revenue streams include paid customers and advertisements. It rents out electronic real estate on its website for advertisements and gets a commission from any deals via those advertisements. Like Zomato, they also have a hyper localization advantage. They can precisely customize the advertisement for a locality i.e. either customers coming from a certain locality or seeking out properties in a certain locality. Sumit quoted a study that indicates that roughly 20 perecnt of a household's income is spent on rentals or EMIs and about 70 percent of the income is spent within 5 km radius of their homes, thus indicating the importance of hyper-local reach. Though given the rise of e-commerce, these figures may alter quickly enough.

CommonFloor team likes to say that they are in the matchmaking business as they provide access to interested buyers, much like a matrimonial portal that lets you access the single and ready to mingle partners.

Typical Revenue Streams for CommonFloor

1. Paid Customers
    a. Property Dealers
        i. Pay per lead generated
        ii. Paid basic listing
        iii. Paid premium listing
    b. Builders
        i. Paid listing
        ii. Paid promotion
        iii. Qualified potential buyer list
2. Vendors
    a. Listing fee
    b. Access to quotation requests from associations
3. Advertising

The fact that online marketing budgets of real estate companies are on an upswing helps their cause. The market is kind of recession resistant, as when the sale or purchase of properties goes down, the rentals go up and vice versa. Home, of course is one of man's most basic needs. A validation of CommonFloor's business model comes from the trust that leading VCs have shown in them. They have managed to raise three rounds of funding so far. Series A funding came from Accel India in 2009; Series B was raised from both Accel and Tiger Global in 2012; and in 2014 they have raised a Series C funding from Accel and Tiger Global again.

Building Brick by Brick

Most first-time products go through many iterations before they take a mature shape. Each iteration improves the product by incorporating the learnings and insights gained in the journey so far, by responding to changes in the environment, and by expanding to include the complimentary offerings and CommonFloor as a product is no different. When its young founders began their journey in 2007, all they wanted to create was a product that would help apartment owners manage their property better by interacting with their neighbours on a day-to-day basis. Somewhere, it aimed at allowing the neighbours to know and socialize with each other. Before this, the team had already experimented with a few ideas like a product to stop the menace of telemarketers or a deal search engine etc. The learning from these experiments took them literally to the doorsteps of residents of apartment complexes in Bangalore. Sumit and Vikas fondly remember that they would visit societies through the day and would sit and code at night. They managed to get 70 societies on board in about two months. During this time, at an informal, coffee shop entrepreneur event, they met and formed a bond with Sameer Guglani of The Morpheus, who helped them with brainstorming and acted as their sounding board. By April of 2008, they had three reputed VCs approaching them. Of these, they joined hands with Accel Partners and moved out of their proverbial garage and by the end of the year, they were ready to hire employees to form a team.

They started by using local businesses as their pivots.

First, the experiment was to print discount coupons for them and distribute. But they soon figured out that it was neither scalable nor cost-effective as printing coupons cost a lot of money. So they focussed their energies on building the Apartment Management Software, a mini ERP for the apartment managers that allowed them to have a directory listing of residents, send messages to them via e-mails or SMSs, and do basic accounting. Over the years, this software product has matured and now offers facilities like various modes of communication, member management, resources management, issues management, social networking, and of course accounting with integrated payment gateways. Except for some premium features like payment gateway and a domain name, everything else comes free for the societies and their members. This piece of software remains at the core of Comonfloor and it would not be an exaggeration to call it the heart of the system. It does not generate any revenue per se, but it is the strength of this part to hold the users together that pumps blood for the rest of the system, as it keeps bringing the users back to the portal on an every day basis.

By 2009, data indicated that a lot of visitors to the CommonFloor portal were looking for properties, along with the fact that roughly 30–40 percent of the properties belonged to non-residing owners. The company had an option to list the properties for sale or rent, but the visibility was limited to community members. Based on the data, CommonFloor opened up the listing to the rest of the visitors and this opened a world of possibilities for them. Brokers came looking for the data, for this was a gold mine for them and they were willing to pay for the access. Since the community had both buyers and sellers, owners and tenants, the brokers saw an opportunity in adding to the listings for a fee and the response they got was encouraging. This led to the CommonFloor team working closely with the brokers, as they wanted to keep the above mentioned apartment management software free for the communities.

Sometime in 2011, CommonFloor experimented by bringing a builder on board and the response from the users was again overwhelming. This was the beginning of their association with the builders and today, they are an important building block in the CommonFloor ecosystem. This also completed the lifecycle mentioned above, with an engagement point at every step of the journey of a home seeker to a home owner. Now, you can see all the upcoming property projects on the portal in the city you login from. Each new project has a buyer forum that facilitates interactions between the buyers, potential buyers, and builders. They have started offering facilities like site visit to help the users choose properties as part of their going offline in bringing two parties closer.

CommonFloor's mobile application is now a key alternate platform, as origin of Internet traffic slowly shifts there. It extends the functionalities of their website to the mobile platform, like search, sorting based on parameters like price, size, relevance etc., and the ability to save and share search results. The added advantage comes from a map-based search that gets you properties within 2-3 km range from where you are. They have experimented with an augmented reality that allows you to view properties around you using a phone and its camera by showing all the properties listed in the direction pointed by camera. They see an increase in the percentage of traffic coming from mobiles, though one would assume that property is not really something that you hunt for on the go. You sit back, research, examine, and then pick a property.

Most Used Features on Apartment Management System

- Discussion forums
- Money manager
- Personal messaging

Most Used Facilities Listed on the CommonFloor Portal

- Home loans
- Movers and packers
- Interior designers
- Security agencies
- Maintenance requirements

BUILDING BLOCKS

Technology is the backbone of all digital platforms. Co-founder and CTO, Lalit Mangal, says that the philosophy behind developing the technology platform is to find out what is the right thing to do and then go ahead and do it in the best possible way. So they have small releases of features on their portal almost every week and the ones that work are improved upon and others discarded. He mentions that on digital platforms, five years equal a generation, and the users' expectations change accordingly. Today's tech-savvy users seek instant answers and that is what any agile platform should throw up. CommonFloor uses open source with an ability to add layers and scale up. Lalit shared some examples of how they responded to the user needs like fine-tuning the system based on city-based user preferences, for eg., in Delhi people prefer to communicate via SMS while in Bangalore via e-mails. Some other users indicated they wanted to have discussions forums on mobile just like the web.

The game plan is to be a data-centric company that is the information backbone of the real estate industry in India. Besides aggregation of data and making it easily searchable, their goal is to give every property in India an identity on CommonFloor with information collated from all possible sources. Some sources of information that they spoke about include geo-spatial layer of information like information about the water table, demographic information with a projection into the future. Given that property has a long and deep association with people's lives, projection of traffic growth, water condition, or even expected price movements can be useful information for investors or buyers.

Apartment Management System (AMS) works as a source of direct data for CommonFloor, as the users both consume and generate data. At one end, it tells CommonFloor what kind of data about the properties is being consumed by users; on the other hand users generate data every time they interact using

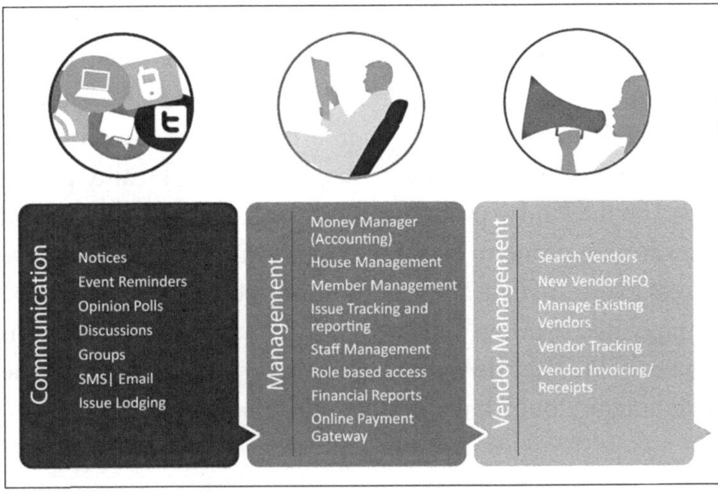

Fig 3: Apartment Management

the platform highlighting gaps in data. Viewed through this lens, AMS appears even more fundamental to their model than just attracting the advertisers. The user research team regularly meets users and invites them to office to gather feedback and ideas from them, as digital analysis still needs to be verified in the real world.

I liked the way Lalit referred to his Map Based Search feature as an intelligence of proximity, that leverages the geo tagging to make location-based searches and recommendations of properties. Now, map based search is in no way a differentiator for a real estate company, as nearly every other portal offers it. The real differentiator here would come from the sheer number of properties that are listed on CommonFloor, and more the number, better is the relevance of any search.

As of now, they do some basic information crunching like property price movements, price trends, and property profile of localities that can be aggregated at any level of hierarchy. They have tried to bring in some intelligence by providing information on the localities like, what is the locality profile based on the kind of properties it has, kind of facilities it has, and the running property prices. Going forward, they would have access to piles of data about community behaviours that can be extrapolated to urban behaviours, and would be some precious data to hold. They do want to use advances in technology to be able to figure out what a customer is looking for.

Building the Numbers

The company's single-minded goal has been of getting more and more communities on board. Greater the number of communities, more attractive it is for paying customers that include builders, brands, and service providers. CommonFloor did not really have a marketing strategy in place for a long time except the standard online strategies that every online entity follows. Since they got VC funding also quite early in life, they did not have to create any branding to get money on the table either. They got their first communities outside their home ground of Bangalore too, through requests by existing members who moved to new cities. Word of mouth worked wonderfully for them and took them all over the country. However, after the company achieves a certain size, marketing cannot be avoided. So, let me take you through a couple of examples of their marketing and brand building efforts.

Campaigns like Property ki Home Delivery: Inspired by the home delivery of Pizzas, they created a campaign that essentially attempts at delivering properties at your doorstep. A kind of reverse property show was planned for this. Instead of buyers going to an event, the event came to their compounds. A team of experts were taken to events set in communities giving residents access to all the information, guidance, and advice on all aspects of property like legal advice, vaastu expertise, home loan options, interior designers, and builders. Spread over two months, this initiative reached out to more than 7 lakh people across 120 odd gated communities in Bangalore. It helped the company drive the highest ever daily traffic to the portal that had a cascading effect, and the portal saw many more communities join in. I see this move as an effort to connect in the real world, an impact that most digital companies cannot really choose to ignore. They look at this as a part of their matchmaking effort and call it an event to connect, driven by knowledge. This was one big, branded campaign, but they have been conducting smaller, single brand events also in the communities, primarily in Bangalore. Another interesting example they shared was the Apartment Cricket League and other sports-based events that they conduct on a regular basis.

Right Step Conclave: This is CommonFloor's offline event that they have recently started in all the major cities where they are present. It brings together players from across the board to share common concerns and potential solutions on the five elements of nature, i.e. earth (prithvi), air (vayu), water (jal), sky (aakash), and fire (agni) for healthy and safe living. The people they have roped in include politicians, civic authorities, subject matter experts, administrative bodies, and RWAs. First Right Step Conclave was organized simultaneously across Chennai, Pune, Gurgaon, Bangalore, and Hyderabad in the run up to the Earth Day. Topics like air pollution, waste management, mobile tower radiations, safety measures for societies, and fresh water conservation were discussed with the intent to bring awareness and to share solutions. The event also highlights community management as a field in itself. My assessment is that these kinds of initiatives will help them build a brand that is focussed around the welfare of the communities.

Topical Campaigns: In 2013, when the state of Uttarakhand was hit by floods and thousands of people lost their homes in the disaster, CommonFloor launched 'Finding Hope a New Home' initiative to provide financial assistance to build/rebuild homes and provide permanent shelter to the calamity-struck residents of Uttarakhand. They reached out to its huge user base of visitors and communities across the country appealing for monetary contributions in tandem with SEEDS India, a non-profit organization that works to protect the lives and livelihoods of people exposed to natural disasters. I thought this was a good synergistic campaign that was in line with CommonFloor's strong branding around homes while it helped the people impacted by the tragedy.

CommonFloor is active on social media but they see it more as a platform for content consumption rather than marketing. Buying homes or even renting is a serious decision for people where they like to research with very specific needs—like locality, facilities, and budget—in mind. It is quite unlikely that social media can influence or spur their decisions. Moreover, CommonFloor's community discussions are a niche in social media itself. For the offline marketing, they have used radio to some extent, as it has good local reach. Their events in communities remain their biggest marketing and connecting vehicle.

Enriching Community Living

Ecosystem Approach: The biggest innovation of CommonFloor lies within its model that spotted an emerging white space of needs of gated communities. They identified all the key stakeholders in this space like residents, property dealers, construction companies, and service providers and created a platform to connect all of them in such a way that each one of them gained from being on the platform. In the process it delivered business value for the platform, which is essentially the business of CommonFloor. Communities lure in the real estate players, and their presence, in turn, makes the platform more consumable for communities and its members. They feed on each other's presence and hence give a reason to the other for being there. This also spreads their footprint beyond just the pure real estate players and includes the ancillary industries, as well as other ecosystem players like banks. Multiple revenue streams give CommonFloor insulation against any downturns as it is highly unlikely that all things will go down simultaneously. For example, if the property market is down and not many new projects are coming up, the rentals market will still have steam, people would still need to maintain their premises and would still need service providers.

Knowledge Management: An awful lot of laws and regulations apply to properties. There are one time activities associated with buying and registering the property and there are recurring requirements like paying property tax periodically. They differ from state to state, sometimes within the state too, depending on the type and size of property. These laws and regulations change from time to time. On CommonFloor, communities can create their own knowledge base of documents and processes relevant to them for the reference of the whole community and can be of big help to new joinees to the community. Various forms can be made available online, and work can be divided and handled by groups of people so that time and effort is saved. Discussion forums let members discuss issues and seek help from each other. For communities this is a ready-to-refer database, a dependable asset, and for the portal it means more customer loyalty.

Facility Management Academy: Most communities hire managers to manage the common facilities in their premises. CommonFloor realized that this is an emerging breed of professionals who have no training facilities. So it started an academy that trains facility managers with the intent to give a career path by equipping them with the necessary tools and processes to manage their work. They give them basic computer training including how to operate their software. This would in time give trained manpower to both the communities and the industry.

I see two logical extensions to their current businesses—one is going global i.e. listing properties from outside India. There may be some localization required, but property markets are not drastically different in most parts of the world. Second, logical extension can be stepping into the commercial property space in India that is a giant in itself. CommonFloor, at the moment though, is focussed on home market in India and if they feel they can crack it completely—become de-facto place for any property-related need of Indian homes—then they would like to think of taking the product to the next market.

CommonFloor has managed to establish a lead in the home base of Bangalore, but is yet to capture the eyeballs in other major property markets. There are other players coming up in the same space like ApnaComplex, ApartmentAdda, JustMyNeighbour who, in a similar fashion, would establish a lead in their home cities. Some of them are charging for the apartment management software and some continue to use the freemium model. How this space pans out and how well is CommonFloor able to sustain itself, only time will tell. What they would always have to their credit is bringing the different stakeholders on a common floor or platform.

References

Conversations with Lalit Mangal, Sumit Jain, and Vikas Malpani of CommonFloor

Information provided by the company

http://www.CommonFloor.com/
http://www.mckinsey.com/insights/urbanization/urban_awakening_in_india

commonfloor.com

Name of the company:	MaxHeap Technologies Pvt Ltd
Website:	www.commonfloor.com
Year of incorporation:	2008
Founders:	Sumit Jain, Lalit Mangal, and Vikas Malpani
Headquarters:	Bangalore
Offices:	Bangalore, Gurgaon, Noida, Pune, Hyderabad, Mumbai and Chennai.
No. of employees:	500
Cities present in:	120+
No. of registered users:	1 million+
No. of views per month:	5 million+
No. of communities:	75,000+
No. of active properties listed on commonfloor.com:	Nearly 2,00,000
No. of paying customers:	Nearly 10,000

INDIBLOGGER

United States of Indian Bloggers

BLOGGING IS AN INTERNET era phenomenon that empowers every individual to express himself through his own webpage. Blogs come in all sizes and shapes. There are blogs with written words, with pictures, with videos and now, even audio and music blogs. Blogs make every blogger a media in themselves. Blogging is a purely online activity, for blogs are authored and shared online with people who read them online. The thoughts and expressions that are shared through them, of course, come from both the real time offline world and the virtual world. There was no equivalent of blogs in the pre-Internet era. Today, after more than a decade of the existence of blogs, there are many, who have become famous by blogging and many famous people have taken to blogging. With more and more people taking to blogging and some of them even taking it up professionally, there is a need to organize the blogging community so that they can be discovered easily and can network with each other. This is where IndiBlogger steps in.

IndiBlogger is a common platform for all Indian bloggers and goes with the tagline *Indian by Birth, Blogger by Choice*. It is a platform where all bloggers meet, share their thoughts, learn, and bond with each other. IndiBlogger's story is straight out of a movie. Four friends set out on a journey, not knowing where it would take them, but with faith and hope that something exciting is in store for them. So they kept moving ahead at a swift pace, bringing as many like-minded people as they could on the way. The company was born in August 2007, when four young friends, Renie Ravin, Anoop Johnson, Vineet Rajan, and Karthik DR, all of them still in their early 20s, were brainstorming on ways to voice and share their opinions. Incidentally, they were all bloggers and concluded that blogs are excellent platforms for people to express themselves, share their opinions, their joys and sorrows, or just about anything. Blogs are a medium which has no middlemen, like editors in traditional publications, so the communication is pure and direct. They saw that if different voices and opinions of bloggers could be brought together on a single platform, it could be a formidable force of expression. This is how the idea of a blog directory bringing together all Indian bloggers to one place took root.

Laying Down the Rules of the Game

Blogging is about creating content that is original and comes from a blogger's personal experience. As a new medium, content is yet to be created on the online platforms. As more and more people get online and require information, views, reviews, and perspectives, online content is bound to gain importance. People tend to equate social media platforms like Facebook, Twitter etc with blogs. Social media platforms are for sharing and instant communication while blogs are content holding platforms with a distinct voice. Between social media and blogging, blogs have an edge though they may get beaten down in the instant gratification mode. Social media are closed networks, technically searchable but are hardly searched. Do you ever remember going to Facebook or Twitter to search for some information. Blogs on the other hand are indexed and are easily searchable by search engines. Content once created on a blog can be referred to at any later point in time. A blogger is a one-person publishing giant—they write their own content, publish it themselves, and market it themselves. As per IndiBlogger data, the number of bloggers in India is increasing exponentially and so is content writing. Take travel writing for example, earlier the only sources of information on travel destinations were travel guides, the odd article in print publications, and information provided by tourism organizations. Today, most of us look up travel blogs to get first-hand accounts from bloggers whose personal portrayals are more accurate—and hence helpful—than marketing brochures.

Building an Active Community

IndiBlogger started as a plain directory of bloggers. Their first observation was that many people—as the case usually is with most new projects—start blogging with enthusiasm, but are not able to sustain it for long. Sometimes, it is the lack of persistent effort on their part and sometimes other work commitments keep them away from their blogs. IndiBlogger recognized a need to maintain a list of active blogs so that users are engaged with active content. So they put together some basic functional criteria in place for the blogs to be listed with them. This ensured that active bloggers got a platform to mingle and that the space was not cluttered with all the blogs that are not updated.

They also sensed an opportunity in bringing together this community of bloggers to meet in person once in a while and put faces to names and opinions. So, the next step of the portal was to organize offline meets and become a meeting platform for bloggers. At the same time, the portal was also given a direction to become a live platform that gave users live interactivity. Eventually, IndiBlogger, as we know it today, emerged as a niche social network for bloggers in India. Today, it is a buzzing community with thousands of blog posts every month that get shared across social media channels of its user base. It helps bloggers get more readers and gain much-needed visibility for their work. In fact, visibility is what prompts people to come for the offline meets too. As a logical response, businesses and brands are interested in engaging with this community as they are influential voices that are heard and trusted.

IndiBlogger has crystal clear focus on two things, and both are pretty much embedded in their name—being Indian and being a blogger—and so far this has worked well for them. You can have million social media followers, but if you do not have a regularly maintained blog, you are not a part of this community. At the same time, if you maintain a blog but have no following on social media channels, you are welcome to be a part of the community. They are also discreet that bloggers have to apply to be a part of the community and unless they apply, their blog will not be a part of IndiBlogger directory. This essentially means that bloggers are willingly joining and participating in the community. This is an approach unlike aggregators where listings are made on certain criteria like influencing index, number of followers, or based on their own intuition. Aggregators also pick up blogs to list on their own without an explicit intent by the blogger. At IndiBlogger, a manual check is done before accepting the listing. Typical checks are, is the content of the blog authentic, has it existed for some time, does it have substantial content to be called a blog, there is no plagiarized content, and if posts are archived. There is no judgement made on the content or opinion expressed in the blogs except the obvious exceptions of objectionable content like pornography. Though there are rules, moderators always use their instinct to take the final call on whether to list or not list the blog in the IndiBlogger directory. Blogs are interactive and features like comments allow readers and bloggers to interact, while most websites are one-way communication portals for the readers. At IndiBlogger, websites have also been kept out of the purview—it is blogs and only blogs for them.

Earned Media

As per Nielsen's Global Trust in Advertising report 2012, 92 percent of consumers around the world say they trust earned media, such as recommendations from friends and family, above all other forms of advertising. Online consumer reviews are the second most trusted source of brand information and messaging, with 70 percent of global consumers indicating they trust messages on this platform.

Menu on Top

Directory

This is the core and central feature of IndiBlogger. It allows anyone to find Indian bloggers by subject, name, or location. So if you are looking for food bloggers, Delhi-based bloggers, or cricket bloggers—you can get a list of them sorted by their ranks, in a way that you see the top bloggers first. Blogs are tagged by their owners and get classified accordingly. This directory can be used by anyone who wants to access blogs and interact with the bloggers.

IndiVine

This is the most happening and lively section of IndiBlogger where most recent and most popular blog posts are listed. You can browse through them as they are listed on the site or you can browse according to your interest, like say Lifestyle, Nation & Politics, Science, or Business. Categories are an evolving entity; new categories get added to the list as and when there is enough focus on them. For example, social causes are highlighted when some events in the world bring focus to them.

IndiRank

This is a proprietary algorithm-based relative ranking system for the bloggers. It is a unique scoring methodology for bloggers that takes into account various established blogging-related metrics like mozRank, Alexa rank, and page rank along with considerations like frequency of blogging, last update, and external links that link to the blog. IndiRank is a good measure of how influential a blogger is compared to the rest of the bloggers. The graphic below explains, in typical IndiBlogger tongue-in-cheek style, how a blog is ranked. Ranking is refreshed roughly every month and the last ranking has no bearing on the new ranking. While the team wants to keep the actual algorithm under wraps, as it obviously is their competitive advantage, they pretty much share what all contributes to ranking, giving bloggers a clear indication of what they need to work on. They are quite open in acknowledging that the various algorithms were openly discussed in online discussion forums on IndiBlogger and a lot of ideas came from there. They also feel that the ranking system has huge credibility with users because people understand what parameters have gone into the ranking. The scoring is inspired from cricket, so blogs get ranked on a scale

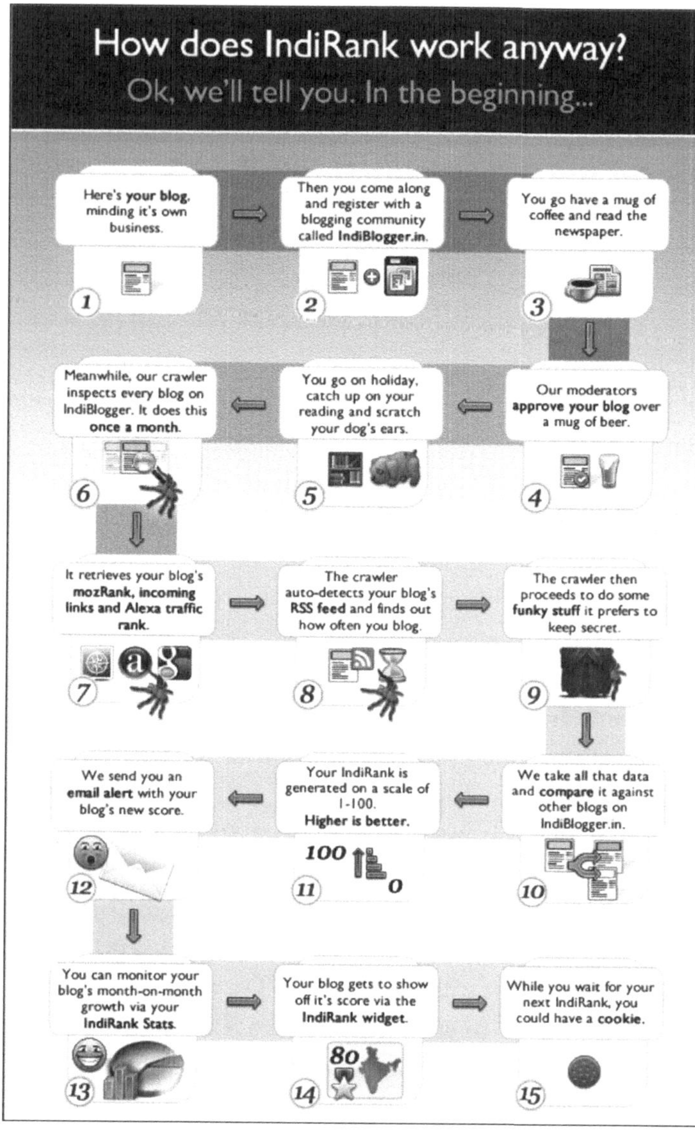
How does IndiRank work anyway?
Ok, we'll tell you. In the beginning...
Here's your blog, minding it's own business.
Then you come along and register with a blogging community called IndiBlogger.in.
You go have a mug of coffee and read the newspaper.
Our moderators approve your blog over a mug of beer.
You go on holiday, catch up on your reading and scratch your dog's ears.
Meanwhile, our crawler inspects every blog on IndiBlogger. It does this once a month.
It retrieves your blog's mozRank, incoming links and Alexa traffic rank.
The crawler auto-detects your blog's RSS feed and finds out how often you blog.
The crawler then proceeds to do some funky stuff it prefers to keep secret.
We take all that data and compare it against other blogs on IndiBlogger.in.
Your IndiRank is generated on a scale of 1-100. Higher is better.
100
0
We send you an email alert with your blog's new score.
You can monitor your blog's month-on-month growth via your IndiRank Stats.
Your blog gets to show off it's score via the IndiRank widget.
80
While you wait for your next IndiRank, you could have a cookie.

of 1-100, the higher the score, more influential and more active the blog is. This is the only ranking system for bloggers in India till now. They let bloggers brag about their ranks by giving them a small widget that they can put on their blogs that automatically displays their ranking.

Forum

This is a space for bloggers to discuss the various aspects of blogging, exchange ideas, share tips, and ask queries related to blogging. Many features at IndiBlogger have germinated in the discussion forums here.

Meets

Meaningful offline meetings were a part of the original thought process of IndiBlogger. They had their first meet way back in Febuary 2008 and the blogger turnout was better than expected—giving them confidence that this is what bloggers are looking for. Over a period of time, big brands have come to recognize the potential and influence of bloggers and these meets. Now IndiBlogger's clients, who want to interact with this powerful community, sponsor most of the meets. The format of the meets is still kept very informal, with no formal presentations or any set agenda. The focus is on letting bloggers network with each other and letting the agenda, if any, evolve. It is a community event and bloggers must be made to feel comfortable. They also make it a point to collect feedback after every meeting and this helps them design their next meeting formats. Anoop, the marketing director, says that most people come with no expectations, some expect some knowledge to be imparted, some are looking for inspiration for their blogs but almost everyone is happy interacting with other bloggers. To feel the collective energy of the meets, all you need to do is read up a few blog posts talking about them. Most meets are managed by the IndiBlogger team itself or with their trusted partners like event managers, who have worked with them for some time now. IndiBlogger feels that not many people understand the difference between a brand event and a community event and they want to keep all their meets as community events. On the portal, Meets is just a small feature where bloggers can get information about the upcoming meets, register for them, talk to other bloggers about the same, and post their reviews.

IndiBlogger 'Spices' up the Delhi Blogging Community

IndiBlogger in association with Spice Mobiles, hosted the Spice Mobiles IndiBlogger Meet on 10 June, 2012 in New Delhi. The meet was a part of a launch campaign for the Spice Stellar Mobile with an aim to create awareness about mobile security. Spice Mobiles chose to engage with bloggers directly to spread the importance about total protection against virus/data loss/theft/financial security on an android device for its customers.

Tech guru Rajiv Makhni led a discussion on the myths and facts of mobile security, as well as a fun quiz. More than 250 bloggers from Delhi/NCR attended the meet.

Drives

This section houses various contests and engagements designed for connecting bloggers and businesses. This usually involves inviting bloggers to write about or around a brand with some prizes to be won in the end.

The Shopper's Stop Perfect Look Contest

Pick your favourite apparel and accessories from www.shoppersstop.com and put together an ensemble that's the perfect look for this festive season. The most stylish look stands a chance to win some exciting prizes!

The campaign reach statistics comprises of three components:

- Blog Readers
- Reach via IndiBlogger.in website
- Twitter Impressions and Reach

Medium	Users Reached
Blogger participation	207
Blog Readers (A)	32,20,334
IndiBlogger.in Contest Page (B)	5,92,763
Twitter Reach (C)	5,00,109
Twitter Impressions	9,72,201
Total Reach	43,13,206 (A + B + C)

A detailed analysis of the campaign is provided to the client giving breakups on various parameters like gender-wise participation, city-wise breakup, Indirank wise participation, day-wise traffic driver, Twitter mentions, type of bloggers engaged etc.

A campaign for HP Laserjet Printers

Take Flight With Colours

Think about something that's Black & White—it could be an old movie, old pictures, a zebra, your headlights, your wedding gown, your monochrome tattoo or anything that pops up in your head. Now imagine it in colour and blog about it!

More than 100 bloggers participated in this contest.

IndiStream

This is a combined live stream of the IndiForum, IndiTalk, and all the Twitter activity involving IndiBlogger and its drives.

Indichange

It is a social change initiative that works as an independent portal with the tagline 'Blogging against Evil'. Bloggers can be agents of change by lending their voices to the social causes that need attention by writing about them, and bringing awareness about the causes and the remedies. This vertical of IndiBlogger brings together people who are working for these causes—say NGOs and bloggers who believe in those causes. In a way, this helps bloggers fulfil their self-actualization needs. IndiBlogger has been associated with 'Bell Bajao' or 'Ring the Bell' initiative in the past. At the time of writing this book, about 800 bloggers from across India had blogged for IndiChange.

While all these features are independent modules, they are also interconnected, and feed into each other. At the back-end, together they all form one unified solution

In true sense of the word, the product IndiBlogger, as it stands today, can be called a crowdsourced product. The ideas kept pouring in from the bloggers and the team kept developing them, experimenting with them, and then launching features that worked. They kept making refinements as feedback emerged from more and more bloggers who used them and as the requirements changed.

I asked Renie and Anoop about their journey of developing a product which doesn't have a precedent, at least not in India. I had assumed that they would have experimented with many things, of which some would have succeeded and some not, but to my surprise they said they never had to take off any key feature that they had launched. This sounded too good to be true to me, but what they told me did have some logic to it. They said that as most of the new feature ideas come from their forum, they are discussed and debated—sometimes, even at the algorithm level—before they are developed and launched as part of the product. This means that there is already a demand for the feature when it is launched in the community. Of course, refinements keep happening over a period of time.

Everything Online

Each blogger listed on IndiBlogger is an individual marketing channel for the company. Most bloggers are active on social media and share their posts and their affiliation with IndiBlogger there. Each meet conducted across the country, and one even outside the country, becomes a channel to create awareness around the brand IndiBlogger. Most meets get heavily plugged in social media, through live updates on popular social media sites like Facebook and Twitter, and it creates a substantial value for IndiBlogger.

Anoop and Renie claim that they have attended every single meet organized under the banner of IndiBlogger. Their aim is to meet as many bloggers as possible and reach out to them personally, as far as possible, and establish a relationship with them. It helps build a bond between IndiBlogger and bloggers that contributes to the association that is still evolving. Both the parties are trying to understand each other and how they can grow with each other. Ravin says that after every meet they come back recharged and more focussed on the product. They go to the extent of saying that without these meets, IndiBlogger as a business may not have seen this day.

I Googled IndiBlogger and got precisely three links under the News section—something that is very unusual when most news businesses try to get media coverage. This indicates the sheer online focus that IndiBlogger has. To an extent it makes sense as both the bloggers and the consumers of blogs are online. From another perspective, it appears to be a total disconnect from the offline world to the extent that no one in mainstream media is talking about you even when you are doing something unique in the new media.

They do market themselves to the potential customers i.e. businesses who may want to leverage the power of bloggers to get a word around for their products and services. This is where their revenues come from. They organize events for businesses where they can directly connect with bloggers. Another strong revenue stream is online contests that are relatively inexpensive for the clients but create an online buzz around their brands. They help brands design the campaign with a punch in terms of creativity and invite bloggers to be as creative as they can get. With the blogging community spread across the big and small towns of the country, brands can reach far and wide through these bloggers who are influencers for their readers and social media followers. Some of their engagements have also involved sampling for customer's products by sending them across to interested bloggers for their opinion. This helps businesses test their products with select users and get initial feedback.

The IndiBlogger team has a clear focus on the kind of brands they want to be associated with. They work with brands and campaigns where bloggers can be most effective. At this point in time, this can also mean high-end products and brands has most bloggers. Demographically, bloggers belong to a segment that has access to Internet and is savvy with technology and they tend to influence a similar segment of people. Some of the brands they have worked with include Samsung, HP, Tata Motors, Stayfree, Lakme, Nokia, Vodafone, Expedia, and Shopper's Stop.

Typical competition for IndiBlogger would be PR agencies, but whether these agencies really have a finger on the pulse of new media like blogging and the psyche of bloggers is anybody's guess. Most PR agencies tend to treat bloggers the same way as mainstream media or journalists to whom they pitch the story angles through press releases or press conferences. Bloggers need to be engaged differently as most of them blog for passion rather than for a living. They are committed to their readers more than anything else and work hard towards building a strong bond with their readers. So, a part of IndiBlogger's task involves educating businesses on the characteristics of blogging and bloggers, its potential, and its impact. One of their big challenges when they started was to convince the businesses about the value that bloggers bring to the table; but with each new meet and online campaign, this is getting easier as it showcases potential brands new and creative ways to explore the world of blogging. They see emergence of social media agencies,that are the equivalent of online PR agencies as an affirmation of the fact that the market is opening up to digital influencers.

They have not yet started using the data generated on their website to gain insights into Indian blogosphere. Based on their experience, they say that to bloggers, independence of opinion and freedom of expression is the most important thing. Content on blogs has to be pure and not driven by any agenda. The dilemma though, at the moment, lies in generating revenues from the blog while keeping the content totally independent. In this spirit, they make sure that when they act as bridge between the brands and the blogs, there is no pressure whatsoever on the bloggers to write in any particular way. They are encouraged to voice their genuine experience and opinion, which also helps businesses that are seeking genuine feedback.

While I was writing this, IndiBlogger announced India's first blogging awards, honouring the best blogs in various categories. I would expect them to graduate to host something like a blogging conference soon enough. They may also become a platform where full-time professional bloggers would be able to generate sustainable income through blogging. As of today, barring a handful of technology bloggers, not many bloggers are earning substantial money through blogging. Most bloggers start blogging as a hobby, but now we do see some bloggers taking it up as a full-time profession.

The quirkiness that is maintained on the website makes it a fun place to be. It seems to be a natural style of the community, given the fact that most bloggers are young and vibrant. For example, while the system is checking the authenticity of a blogger's post, the message says—'checking for your grammatical mistakes or your criminal records' in all good humour. Team IndiBlogger likes keeping it this way—fun and easy going.

Staying true to the spirit of Internet companies, all the four founders of IndiBlogger are based out of different cities. Renie Ravin, Managing Director and Web Architect, operates out of Chennai, Anoop Johnson, Director Marketing, operates out of Bangalore, D.R. Karthik, Director Sales and Business Development, operates out of Delhi/NCR, and Vineet Rajan, Director Presales and Consulting, operates out of Mumbai. While Ravin was always based out of Chennai, others have all moved from Bangalore to spread themselves across major cities to be closer to their community and the businesses they wanted to target. They face no problems in operating as a dispersed team; in fact they feel they are far more productive and focussed in their respective works. The fact that they have been buddies and their comfort with use of technology to communicate also act as huge factors in their working styles.

In terms of financial numbers, they are still a very small company. The product they are developing by taking along their community member is one of its kind in the world. As our lives move more and more online, the relevance of the product will increase exponentially. Today, they may be just focussed on building an Indian blogging community but tomorrow, they can always take this product to the rest of the world and build thriving blogger communities across the world. To me that day is not far.

References

Conversations with Anoop Johnson and Renie Ravin of IndiBlogger

Information provided by the company

http://www.nielsen.com/us/en/newswire/2012/consumer-trust-in-online-social-and-mobile-advertising-grows.html

IndiBlogger.in

We Blog, Therefore We Are

Name of the company:	Scissor Paper Stone Web Solutions Pvt Ltd
Website:	www.indiblogger.in
Year of incorporation:	2007
Founders:	Renie Ravin, Anoop Johnson, Karthik DR, and Vineet Rajan
Headquarters:	Chennai
Offices:	4
No. of employees:	10
Cities present in:	4
No. of blogs listed:	35,000+
No. of categories:	75+
Average no. of blogger meets per month:	2
Blogs from non-metros:	20 percent
Regional language blogs:	15 percent

ECOSYSTEM

The Support Economy

EVERYTHING IN THIS WORLD is interdependent, strung together by a network of people and ideas. Sometimes we can see the dependence very clearly and sometimes it is not so obvious. This new breed of digital entrepreneurs is also bound to impact the environment as with their new ways of working come the new needs that need to be fulfilled. They would also impact some of the old ways of working. We see an emergence of support industry around these new business models. I spoke to some of the players in support economy to see how traditional industries are reshaping themselves to suit the needs of the new generation enterprises and how niche players are emerging to cater to specific needs of a digital channel. This ecosystem will keep evolving in tune with the industry, but let's discuss how it looks today.

LOGISTICS – DELIVERING AT EVERY ADDRESS

Logistics is a big need of all the e-commerce players dealing in physical goods. In fact it is a game changer for them vis-à-vis a brick and mortar store. In a brick and mortar store what matters the most is managing the inventory and its placement on the store shelves, the store location, and the flow of customers into the store. In an online store, inventory is more or less managed automatically and so are store operations. What needs to be managed by the company is the logistics—making sure that customers' orders are delivered at their doorsteps in the right condition and within the committed time. All other things being more or less equal as far as ordering through the website is concerned, it is how the order is fulfilled that makes a difference to the customer experience and directly impacts customer retention. The customer base in India is scattered across its massive length and breadth. Even though orders may come from urban clusters, the small percentage of orders from remote corners also needs to be delivered with the same efficiency.

When it come to logistics, it is a build versus buy decision for e-tailers. Many big online retailers have invested in building their own logistics arm, but it is not really feasible for small startups. Even if they build this division, it is near impossible to have reach across the entire country. The obvious solution is to tie up with existing logistics players who have substantial reach—and that is what many of them do. This, however, comes with its own set of problems as the process involves multiple parties including the complexity of Cash on Delivery (CoD).

Cash on Delivery (CoD)

CoD is not a new concept. In fact, before stamps were introduced, in the postal services, the receiver had to pay for the post on delivery. Our good old post offices always had the facility under the name of Value Payable Post(VPP). Some of us may remember the delivery of books via VPP, but then very few VPP orders were placed in a year. CoD has been a key success factor for Indian e-commerce. However. it brings its own issues like cash reconciliations and management of rejected orders after delivery. E-tailers have already started profiling customers and geographies where they do restricted CoD due to high rejection rates. I see *swipe on delivery* as the next wave that can be a preferred option for the vendors and the customers replacing a large part of CoD orders. We also see emergence of independent cash collection agencies that work in tandem with logistics companies. These independent cash collection agencies send executives to go and collect cash after the orders have been delivered. I see a multi-point interaction at the customer end for a single order as not very welcome. From the e-commerce vendor's perspective, Nitin Pamnani of iTokri.com, a niche e-tailer based in a Tier II city was very happy with the separate channels to deliver the order and collect cash as he felt both are efficient in doing what they do individually. How these players will co-exist or compete will emerge in time.

CoD Pros	CoD Cons
Increases customer confidence	High rejection rates–low buyer commitment
No dependence on payment gateways/credit card availability	Necessitates reverse logistics
Risk moves from customer to supplier	Cost high per transaction for collection services

This presented an opportunity for the traditional logistics companies to look at e-commerce as a potential business opportunity and design an organization geared towards providing services to them and gain through economies of scale. I spoke to Sanjiv Kathuria, co-founder and CEO of DotZot—the e-tail logistics specialist arm of DTDC. He obviously sees opportunity in this space that is expected to grow exponentially in the future. He spoke about how traditional logistics companies like DTDC or BlueDart were not designed to handle the bulk amount of packages to be delivered at home addresses. Most of them were designed for handling documents to be delivered to office addresses that are usually located in business districts. Businesses can receive any consignments at any point in time within their office working hours. In a traditional setup, 80 percent of the consignments are documents and 20 percent parcels. For e-tailers, parcels constitute 100 percent of the consignments and, of these, 90 percent have to be delivered at home addresses that are scattered across the city. Then, there are high-value, delicate, and odd-sized items which need special handling.

Build Vs Buy

	Build	Buy
Reach	Low	High
Time taken per order	Medium	High
Cost	Low incremental cost, high setup cost	Low for metros, high for semi-urban, rural areas
CoD	Low incremental cost	Additional per transaction cost
Returns cost	Low incremental cost	Additional per transaction cost
Customer complaints	Greater control	Multi-party communication involved

*It is ironical that Indian postal services with their widest network and lowest cost is missing out on this huge opportunity to cater to e-tailers

An e-tailing specialist company uses a drop-shipping model that picks up parcels from various vendors across locations in different countries and delivers it to customers across locations. Sellers and buyers can exist across online platforms. These specialist companies have an in-built mechanism for CoD that takes care of automated cash management and periodic reconciliation with e-commerce companies. There are API integrations i.e. integration between the software layers of the two companies and the information flow is between the triangle of customers, e-commerce company, and logistics partner. The CRM team of e-commerce vendor handles customer queries including any order cancellations. Queries related to

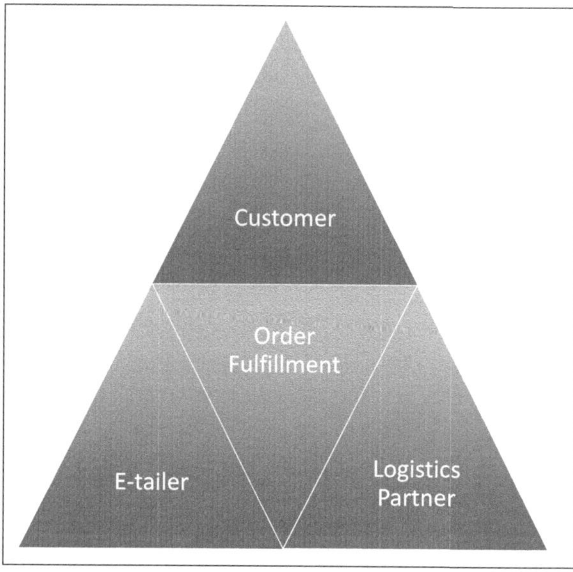

Fig 1: DOTZOT

any delays in shipment are also routed through the same CRM team that then needs to interact with the logistics partner in real time. Delivery tracking has to be available in real time to all the parties in this triangle.

The Order Returns feature offered by many e-commerce vendors demands a complete reverse logistics process to be enabled. This is nearly non-existent in traditional logistics setups. Returns could be because of non-acceptance of orders when they reach the doorstep, exchange offers run by e-tailers, or defects in order delivered. Non-acceptance is high in CoD orders as people have no obligation to accept the order as they have not yet paid. However, it is the other rejects that add additional complexity, as people want the returns to be picked at their convenience from the location of their choice. These returns also require proper packing to be shipped back to the supplier and of course the reversal of the whole transaction for all parties involved.

These specialized logistics arms remove a key entry barrier for new players in an e-commerce space, who need not stress about the logistics and can start as soon as their supplier side is sorted. From a costing perspective, if partnering with someone like DotZot will be more efficient as they have scale to bring down the overall cost or doing it in-house would be better as you remove a player from the process will depend on the volumes. The overall pricing will go down as the volumes go up but location spread will play its role as cost of delivery in rural areas is way higher than that in metro cities while the product pricing remains constant for customers across regions.

Payment Processing—Enabling Smooth Flow of Money

A commercial transaction is completed when payment is received for the product sold or service provided. In online businesses, when transactions are happening via technology, money also needs to move via technology from customer's account to vendor's account. In developed economies where credit cards are all pervasive and customers are absolutely comfortable with swiping them for their purchases, they work as the primary instruments for transactions. This means, all a merchant needs to have is a facility to accept credit cards and they are all set to receive payments for their products and services. In India, first of all, credit card penetration is extremely low at less than one percentage of the population, and the trust associated with using credit cards online is even lower. This could have been the biggest limiting factor for e-commerce but for CoD and payment gateway solutions. Payment gateways provide the option of processing various types of e-payment options through a single interface. This includes payments through credit cards, debit cards, net banking, cash cards, mobile payments, and even Integrated Voice Response System (IVRS) payments over phone. They also bring various players in each of these segments together so that users can choose to pay through any of these options seamlessly and individual e-commerce companies do not have to tie up with banks and credit card networks individually. They bring in strong validation processes that may include additional layer of one-time passwords, personal information validation through calls to ensure safe transactions and minimize fraud.

PayPal—a commonly used system in west to receive payments via e-mail is restricted by regulation in India. There is a need to have a parallel India-based PayPal like service e.g China has built its own AliPay. It is arguably the easiest way to transact online.

Success rate of online payments still hovers around 70 percent and this means about 30 percent transactions fail, which is a huge number. Failures have been attributed to issues like long checkout processes that require customers to go through multiple pages before completing the transaction. As technology companies are trying to crunch this process, the government has added a layer of One Time Password—another layer of security—adding one more page to navigate. This reminds of Amazon's one-click checkout process that allows customers to checkout in one click after they have selected items to buy. This is a key success factor for Amazon as customers do not have to worry about failed payments. Then, there can be environmental reasons like slow servers or power outages that lead to many interrupted and, hence, failed transactions.

For integrating a payment gateway on the e-commerce portal, typical operational parameters that need to be evaluated are setup time and ease of setup, settlement processes, transparent and live reporting, range of payment products covered, and support provided. Security and fraud management have to be integral to the payment solution for them to be effective. Pricing varies across players and from time to time. It can be a key-deciding factor but over a period, the trustworthiness of the systems and processes is what the merchants would be willing to pay a premium for.

CCAvenue has been a pioneer and leader in the payment gateway space in India since 2001. Their corporate presentation says more than 80 percent merchants in India use their gateway and they clocked more than 100 million transactions in FY13. They have built systems like FRISK (Fraud and Risk Identification Systems and Knowledge Base) that leverages a combination of technology and smart analytics to bring down fraud. As a byproduct of this system, they are building a kind of credit rating for their users. SNIP or Social Networks InStream Payments is another small innovation that leads to social commerce. This technology allows customers to convert the leads from social networks into sales by directly taking customers to a payments page from social page. Basically it just cuts the navigation from social media page to merchant site and increases the conversion rates from leads to sales. Same process applies to Quick Response or QR codes as well. Other prominent player in this space are Times Group's Direcpay, EBS, and PayU. Flipkart has just launched its solution called PayZippy and coming from an experienced merchant, I expect this would be a more sturdy solution.

The Government of India has stepped in by setting up National Payments Corporation of India (NPCI) in 2008 with 10 core promoter banks, with an objective to consolidate and integrate multiple payment systems into a nation-wide uniform and standard business process for all retail payment systems. They have launched RuPay—an e-commerce friendly domestic card payment network that would work just like Visa or Mastercard. This is a part of RBI's vision to offer an Indian system that allows Indian banks to participate in the e-payments. They started by offering Debit card/ATM card payments through this network and plan to issue credit cards by 2014. 3 million RuPay cards are already in circulation and by the end of FY14 they aim to take this figure to 10 million. Most of these cards are in Tier I and Tier II cities. Smaller banks are being brought into the network with an aim to bring Tier III and Tier IV cities customers closer to e-commerce. Processing charges for RuPay are lower than market rates and that would mean that banks and merchants would prefer to use them.

Payment processing is a work in progress space, there have been many developments and there will be a need for more especially with respect to security and fraud. New solutions that would provide wider coverage to the customer as well as bank will always be welcome. Costs per transaction will always have the scope to go down and new models would always be on testing table. On a lighter note, I worked on this chapter towards the end of my writing journey for this book. I should have just looked at the client list of CCAvenue and other payment gateways to have my initial long list of companies to research, since almost everyone is using their services and is on their client list.

SECURITY SERVICES—OUR ONLINE SECURITY GUARDS

Customers share their personal confidential data with e-commerce companies and their partners like payment gateways or banks. Security of this data travelling and residing across various channels and servers becomes paramount for preventing malpractices like fraud. This directly impacts businesses, as they need to maintain the customer confidence to transact online with ease and safety.

Primarily, the aim of the security services and products is to ensure the safety of two types of data—cardholder's credit or debit card data and customer's personal data. Since the former contains financial information, and is more prone to direct fraud, a lot of current focus is on ensuring that wherever this data resides, it is safe and secure. Most digital companies avail the services of the payment gateways or banks to process

Key Security Checkpoints for Digital Companies, Especially E-commerce Companies

1. Data centre operations
2. Network components—firewall, switch, router
3. Web-based payment applications
4. System components including server and user desktop
5. Web hosting provider
6. Third party inline frames
7. Third party hosted payment page
8. Payment gateway

payments and do not keep any data in their own servers. In fact, their payment processing page takes you to the gateway or bank website and brings you back to their portal after payment is processed. Some leading players though have started storing credit card information for two primary reasons—one to make the process of payment faster and simpler for users and second to run loyalty programmes based on credit card used. This requires them to build an additional security layer and get a certification that their systems are safe enough to store cardholder data.

The second set of data, which is non-financial but may still have key identity information like PAN card number, driving license number, address, phone number, and e-mail address is not a big focus for security at the moment. The onus lies on the digital companies to maintain it in a safe way and ensure there is no leakage of data to anyone who is not authorized to use this data. Not many guidelines exist for this data as of now. In the future, a policy framework may define the responsibilities of the companies that hold this data in their servers and the way they can use or cannot use this data.

I spoke to Nitin Bhatnagar of SISA, a Bangalore-based security services company to understand what they do to ensure that we can transact without worrying about the security of our data. As a leading player in Information Security Governance Risk and Compliance space, they provide two primary security-related certifications. PCI-DSS (Payment Card Industry Data Security Standard) certification endorses safety of the cardholder's data and reinforces the trust that customers have in digital merchant's network and technology infrastructure. ISO-27001 [Information Security Management System] formally specifies that management system brings information security under explicit management control.

Industry Association—Coming Together for Common Pain and Gain

IAMAI is a professional industry body that represents the digital industry in India. It is an industry association established in 2004, under the Societies Act with more than 130 member companies, to address the challenges faced by the digital and online industry. This association works as a bridge between the industry and the policy makers. At one end it works with the IT and Telecom Ministry and attempts to convey the potential impact of digital economy on the overall economy and how to leverage it. On the other hand, it helps industry by lending a helping hand to startups in online and mobile space.

Its members include the biggest names in the digital world like Google and Yahoo along with small startups across the country. Since it is an association, everyone is a stakeholder. Nilotpal Chakravarti of IAMAI walked me through the key activities of IAMAI.

Events

IAMAI organizes industry events that bring members together to discuss common issues and share ideas. These events act as knowledge management forums where different players can learn from each other's experience. There are regular conferences on different subjects where the relevant organizations come together to share ideas and professionals network for common good. Roundtables are small events focussing on niche areas that provide business development opportunities to its members. Their flagship event is India Digital Summit that is held every year and it brings together business leaders of Internet and mobile industry, government officials, NGOs, and evangelists on a single platform. IAMAI is more prominently known for the awards that it gives to digital companies in various categories like Digital Advertising Awards, Website Awards, Mobile VAS Awards, Digital Payments Awards, and Digital Social and Economic Empowerment Awards.

Research

IAMAI engages in primary research for Internet and mobile companies. There are three types of researches that they undertake. First is market research that is primary research to publish key numbers that indicate the evolution of digital economy and its various segments. They have partnered with market research organizations like IMRB to conduct this research. Leading member companies of IAMAI also contribute data on periodic basis to contribute to research. They publish monthly data on certain trends like the number of resumes uploaded on job sites or number of profiles uploaded on matrimonial sites or ticket booking data on IRCTC or growth of e-commerce in designer labels or growth in classified space. Their research reports are a reference material for a lot of secondary research implying the significance they hold for industry and analysts. Second is a set of vision documents that they publish where they look at the future with respect to digital industry and what kind of impetus is required. These documents can act as roadmaps for niche spaces within the Internet and mobile economy like the need for local language websites etc. Third is custom research that is commissioned by the clients, depending on the their specific needs.

Working with Policy Makers

IAMAI actively works with various government agencies that device various policies that directly or indirectly impact the players in the digital space. This would mean being a part of various committees under the IT and Telecom Ministry and providing them inputs for various policy parameters. They would also be representing industry to the government and in a way influencing them to keep their interests in mind when devising policies. So far they have contributed to policies like IT Act, Copyright Act, prevention of child pornography, and dealing with SMS Spam etc. Through their vision documents, they also try to project the impact of providing a push to the digital entrepreneurs on total economy. Looking at the future and the data in the various reports that they publish, they can argue the potential of Internet and mobile to create employment and cascading impact on the economy specially in rural areas. I see them as a link between the industry data and policy makers.

Awareness Creation

Media plays a big role in disseminating information and creating awareness, so IAMAI actively engages with them for spreading out various messages. They have run campaigns like Safe Surfing that educates students in schools and colleges on how to surf the Internet in a safe and secure manner. This involves giving them simple tips like logging out every time after you are done with your work or to understand various signs on the screen to know if the website is safe to browse. They are associated with digital educators who provide courses on various requirements of digital companies like digital marketing, social media management, search engine marketing, and various certifications like IPv6 etc. They have worked with police departments to help them understand the nature of cyber crimes. Their monthly magazine 'Thinking Aloud' works as mouthpiece of the industry and aims to be a knowledge-sharing platform for the industry and by the industry.

Social media agencies are appearing as an alternative to traditional PR agencies in the digital universe. They provide digital PR to brands that can be offline or online. I spoke to Windchimes, a Mumbai-based social media agency and they spoke about technology-enabled Online Reputation Management that includes managing or monitoring the reputation of a brand or a personality in the digital world. They highlighted how managing social media involves live engagement with the community vis-à-vis passive one-way reach out in the traditional media. Digital brand management also requires a good knowledge of technology as well as an understanding of social media platforms. This needs to be coupled with good design sense and an ability to adapt to any new development in technologies on the go. This requires an on-going investment in training for the social media professionals and investment in technology. Most of the cases mentioned in this book do not use an external social media agency and manage their social media pages on their own. They still fit into the scheme of social media agencies as they do partner with offline brands for co-promotions. Flipkart gift vouchers are fast becoming the default giveaway for online contests. This is emerging as a space for managing brands in the digital space and using the social media channels to reach out to potential customers. As of today, this is one of the services that digital specialists offer, but going forward other services may emerge to bring a better synchronization between the online and offline brand personalities.

There are many other services that are emerging or will

emerge as the digital enterprises gain prominence. There would be another time and space to study them.

REFERENCES

Conversation with Sanjiv Kathuria, Co-Founder and CEO of DotZot
Conversation with Nitin K. Pamnani, founder of iTokri.com
Conversation with Nitin Bhatnagar of SISA Information Security
Conversation with Nilotpal Chakravarti of IAMAI
Conversation with Nimesh Shah of Windchimes
http://www.delhivery.com
http://www.gharpay.com
http://www.windchimes.co.in
http://www.ccavenue.com/
http://www.npci.org.in/
http://www.nextbigwhat.com/comparison-payment-gateways-in-india-297/
http://www.sisainfosec.com/
http://www.iamai.in/

CONCLUSION

I SPOKE TO MANY big and small entrepreneurs across the digital map. Towards the end when I look back at their journeys, dreams, and thoughts, there are some common insights that come out from the transition that is taking place in the business and social landscape as a result of the digital revolution currently underway. In this section, I bring out the collective insights from all of them, including the ones who could not make it to the book. Put together, these observations point in the general direction that digital enterprises, in India, are taking towards what is working for them and what is not. What are their collective learnings of creating digital customers and clients in the country and what can next generation of entrepreneurs learn from them.

Evolving Digital Avatars of Users

Google's Eric Schmidt and Jared Cohen in their book *New Digital Age* talk about the future of citizens, states, revolutions etc in a completely connected world. They discuss the role of technology companies that will have to devise their own policy frameworks like governments because of the amount of data in their servers about all those who uses their platform and that may include almost everyone. While they are talking primarily about hardcore technology companies that own servers and platforms used by people across the world, this may not be entirely irrelevant for online businesses as well. Let me take the example of my online grocery store. They know exactly what I consume from apples to potatoes and from junk food to medicines, they know how much of what I consume, they know what time I am home, where I live, my phone number, e-mail id, and credit card details. On one hand, they can make life easier for me by crunching all these numbers to make product recommendations to me, but on the other they can aggregate consumption data and sell it for right or wrong reasons. They can also sell my private data to other agencies that may want to use it to reach me, to breach by privacy for financial gains, or to hurt me for other reasons. The responsibility will eventually lie with the company to safeguard the information and be very transparent about the possible uses that they may put the data to. They would need to maintain their own credibility to keep their customer base intact and to avoid any legal actions that may result from the breach.

THE ONLINE-OFFLINE MIX

Last decade saw the digital marketing spending of brick and mortar businesses go up from zero to a substantial number.

Every business worth its salt has created an online presence through at least a web page, if not more. A good number of offline businesses also established parallel online channels to sell and market themselves. The coming decade will see online players making their presence felt through offline channels. The first indication of this comes in the form of advertising through traditional mediums like print, radio, and television. It is not unusual to get to know of an online sale through a newspaper ad, an outdoor hoarding, a radio jingle, or even a television commercial. New product launches are well advertised on television. Many online ventures are setting up pop out stores in the physical world along with offline campaigns to be closer to the customer and to show that they are for real and have an existence beyond the website too. The trend has already begun with stores like CaratLane's Experience Lounges where customers can touch, feel, and try their products. Shaadi.com's Shaadi Centres have been around for a while and provide personalized service to walk-in customers using the same database. MakeMyTrip has offline offices that both create a brand presence besides generating sales. Offline events like the ones CommonFloor organizes for its communities are another way digital businesses are connecting with their users and customers in the real world. A kind of osmosis is happening where pure offline players are trying to understand the digital world and use its reach, while the pure online players respect the need of physical presence for the customer and connecting beyond the screen.

Ecosystem Advantage

Most of the digital ventures are centred in Bangalore, and even those which are technically not registered in Bangalore have their technology and digital marketing teams in Bangalore, followed by Delhi/NCR. Mumbai is a distant third in this aspect with any other city hardly making a mark. As soon as this observation dawned on me, I made it a point to ask some of them why Bangalore is their chosen destination for digital enterprises. What's interesting is that the founders do not necessarily belong to the city, which implies that the city is able to attract, nourish, and, hence, retain entrepreneurial talent. While this can be a subject of exploration in itself, some of the top reasons shared for choosing to start up a venture in Bangalore are:

- Most digital ventures have technology as a core component of their business and Bangalore has the right talent pool for that. It primarily comes out of large IT organizations based here with relevant experience and exposure.
- The mentoring ecosystem in Bangalore provides the much-needed direction to young entrepreneurs. They can always go to seniors for help, guidance, and advice. Bangalore has a culture of discussing new ideas over coffee across the city.
- After a threshold level, entrepreneurs themselves became a part of the ecosystem supporting each other and helping others with resources and insights.
- The city accepts entrepreneurs. They are not looked upon as a wayward lot who could not get any jobs elsewhere.

Glass Ceiling of Digital World

Of all the founders that I spoke to, including the ones that are not featured in the book, only 3 are women. Out of these, two had content-based enterprises and this seems like the space which has some women presence. Are women better at generating and managing content—especially when it is softer or right-brain content? In this book, Lakshmi Rebecca of Chai with Lakshmi and Smitha Ram, co-founder of Rang De are the only two women entrepreneurs, though there was no dearth of women employees in any of these organizations. It is a skew that is difficult to explain but what did come out during the interactions was the difference between where the focus lies for men and women. Most men spoke in detail about the work they are doing and made sure they highlighted their achievements. Most women were extremely focussed on doing what they are doing and somewhere undermined the importance of a getting a word out about their businesses or themselves. Could that be a reason why we haven't heard much about woman entrepreneurs? I do not have an answer, but these are questions these interactions left me with.

Technology Close to my Heart

Across the board, technology is a component that is completely in-house for all online businesses profiled in this book. Of course, we understand that domain and technology are two equal components of a digital business. What is interesting is that some of the companies did try to outsource all or some parts of technology but had to eventually bring it in-house. Primary reasons for not outsourcing technology are:

- Technology is a core part of the business and not an enabling function like for brick and mortar businesses.
- Speed/agility is lost when technology is outsourced—the change process goes through many layers and contractual bindings and many opportunities are lost in the process.
- Accuracy of data may not be dependable when it is outside your control.
- Vendor teams do not understand the business and are not connected to the dynamics of the business and hence have low motivation levels compared to in-house teams. In-house teams have better understanding of business and have better domain knowledge.

The challenge for digital companies in the initial days is the ability to attract best talent needed to build a good product. In later days it is to keep the technology team updated on latest technology all the time through constant training. Most of the companies now control the architecture and design of their technology pieces and when required, outsource the small parts of application development or independent pieces like mobile application development.

As many founders hail from a technology background, their companies are also rolling out technology products that could serve as independent lines of businesses for them. The idea is to test the products on their own portal, make them generic enough, and roll them out for other players to use them. For example PayZippy by Flipkart is a payment gateway that comes from their experience of running an e-commerce portal and has now been rolled out for others to use. IndiBlogger's product engine, that is a first of its kind in the world, can be easily licensed out to other geographies unless they choose to expand globally like Zomato. redBus, as I already mentioned in my introduction to the e-commerce section, has an ERP product for bus operators.

SOCIAL MEDIA IS FOR SOCIALIZING

Surprisingly, not many companies think that social media drives any sales at the moment. In fact, some of them even go so far as to say it is a deterrent at times. Having said that, all of them do have well-founded presence on social media channels like Facebook and Twitter. They almost unanimously said that they use these channels to interact with the customers and get first hand insights into their behaviour. Sometimes they also launch new campaigns or features and test the acceptability through these channels. They make themselves available for any issues or feedback that customers might have. It is not unusual to see the CXOs of these companies being tagged on Twitter for brickbats and bouquets. Similarly, brand-building exercises are always on the social media channels especially when something new, like a new collection or a new feature, is launched. Though, none of them blatantly said so, but my guess is that they are tracking customer interactions and waiting for substantial volumes to build before they look at social networking sites as a viable sales channel. An interesting insight I gained is that a lot of these businesses are using social media to recruit people and some of them find it the most effective way to find new people for the company. If you follow these companies on Facebbok and Twitter, you will invariable see the job positions that are open. Some of them said they are more inclined to pick up candidates who have been following them and hence, know the business from the other side of the table and have some pre-built affiliation with the brand.

The Human Touch

One of the most profound insights that I received was that no matter what the level of automation is, human intelligence just couldn't be ignored. While the interface is via a machine and big data in the servers along with live click streams are being analysed to understand the buyer/visitor behaviour, none of these companies are undermining the value of human intuition. Sandeep Maheshwari, the CEO of ImagesBazaar himself chooses the top pictures to be displayed from a shoot on the homepage. Zomato still collects the core information first hand by visiting all the restaurants listed on its portal while it can be easily automated. Flipkart still makes lots of decisions manually when data throws up exceptions. Rang De takes its social investors along on field visits to verify the right use of investments. BigBasket still uses its ground team's intuition to pick up best produce. So, we see that across categories and verticals, in businesses driven completely by technology, the ultimate decision that makes the difference still lies with humans who are behind those big screens. All of these companies put a very high-value on the word of mouth publicity. In fact, the whole initial impetus for companies like Flipkart, Shaadi, and MakeMyTrip came from word of mouth.

Piggybacking on Each Other

A long time back I heard an entrepreneur say that, 'Best source of help of any kind for a budding entrepreneur is other entrepreneurs. They have gone through or are still going through the same pains as you, so they understand your pain and can potentially offer you the best solutions'. As I was looking at the linkages between some of these players, I figured out that subtly they are all helping each other. A lot of times these businesses are piggybacking on the traffic that each of them generates and the other can potentially use. For example, MakeMyTrip plugs in the data from TripAdvisor and Zomato, while Zomato has an exclusive tie-up with Flipkart for distributing its food guides. In the process, they are expanding the overall size of their vertical in the industry while also leveraging the fact that a customer who buys one thing online is more likely to buy another too.

Making Users a Part of the System

Customers or users of digital enterprises are a part of the system more intimately and interactively than they are in offline businesses. They interact by way of providing feedback, writing reviews, rating facilities or features besides users spreading a word about businesses by talking about their association with it. So, at Flipkart, it would be product review; at MakeMyTrip, it would be feedback; and at CommonFloor, it would be vendor rating. At Zomato, the whole engine gains credibility because of the layer of user-generated reviews. In essence, this is making users a part of the enterprise in a way that they can impact the future business of the enterprise or those doing business through them.

While this interlink is reasonably understood, there is a reverse rating also taking place simultaneously. Since these digital enterprises can track each and every action of the users online and also link it to their offline behaviour wherever there is an offline interface, they are also rating and classifying their users. For example, at Flipkart, if you are a trusted user coming from a trusted locality, there is no check done for you when you place cash on delivery orders. This trust can come from your personal history of paying and accepting orders earlier and it can come from the aggregate data of your profile and locality that puts you in a safe category. Similarly, users at Zomato get classified according to the number of reviews they write and the kind of engagement that their reviews generate. Tomorrow, if the company wants to test a new line of business or even a new feature, these people would be their first choice to engage. IndiBlogger is in the business of rating and categorizing bloggers in way that brings complementing bloggers and brands together. A lot of digital identities across these platforms are getting connected though a common Facebook or a Twitter login. Shaadi.com uses this effectively to wean out fake profiles and ensure that candidates put their recent pictures on their profiles. Eventually, even primary e-mail and phone number can become a single identity linking all other identities. So it is a matter of time, or should I say an idea, that our data across these platforms gets aggregated and creates our digital profile that would have inputs on our credibility.

Data analytics are done by all businesses but right now, it is limited to understanding visitor behaviour and using this to serve the customer better. This usually takes the form of a recommendation engine that suggests users other products and offerings from the portfolio or profiling users to make the systems more efficient and secure. As these companies collect more and more data, they would be able to get insights on their community as a whole and this would be a good input for policy makers, policy implementers, and for those who make big plans for the future for the society as a whole. To a limited extent, Shaadi.com has started publishing some insights from their data like data on the preferences of differently-abled persons or the professions that are in demand based on the current state of economy. Today, these serve as PR and CSR material for the company but tomorrow this may lead to major campaign for dealing with prevailing social evils around marriages in India. Similarly, our consumption patterns across product and service categories will generate insights. This may take some time but eventually we might have policies based on real hard transactional data recorded in real time.

NEW AGE MIDDLEMEN

A lot of digital businesses started with an objective to bring the customer and the vendor together on a platform enabled by technology, with the intent of doing away with remove the so-called middlemen. In the process, it looks like they have all become in their own ways the new age middlemen. And, this middleman is different, it is powered by technology, and it tells you more than most middlemen ever would. It educates you in case you need to know like the knowledge on Diamond Selection at CaratLane. It lets you compare and contrast and at the moment it listens to you as well, but they are all middlemen nonetheless. How this class evolves over a period of time remains to be seen. Will they bring in their own practices to the system, will they be also thrive on the power of brand or will they be trusted across the board is something we need to wait and watch. At the end of this research, the brightest spot that I found was the amazing transparency that these businesses are bringing into the system. Since everything can be tracked, compared, and experiences broadcasted on social media—being completely transparent is not really an option for the digital businesses. It gives me hope that this will lead to reduction in corrupt practices either real or perceived.

LIVING LABORATORIES

Experimentation would be one word to describe all these young enterprises. They are experimenting constantly, keeping the ideas that work, and quickly discarding the ones that do not. They did not have any precedence, and wherever they went ahead and experimented, there were limitations of culture and local requirements. So, they are all building first generation businesses based on constant experimentation. They build features and offerings on a regular basis, throw it open to their users and customers, observe deeply, and based on the response, either strengthen it further or discard it. Each of them narrated lots of failed experiments that took place on the way. Some of them made their way in their respective chapters while others stayed in my notebook. If I synthesize the information across businesses, they all are in persistent experimentation mode. To me, this is because of an entirely new way of interaction between businesses and their users and customers. Both the businesses and users are learning and adapting to each other, through each other, and for each other. These experiments are new experiences for users too and they figure out their own reaction only after they have tried and tested it. So somewhere companies and users are experimenting together, learning together, and discovering new ways for communicating and consuming through the ubiquitous screens connecting them. Eventually the experiments and data would drive digital companies to serve individual customers as per their personal choices and not as part of a mass consumer. There is limited personalization at the moment, but the trends overall are moving in that direction.

Internet penetration that stands at roughly 15 percent in India at the moment remains a major limitation for all the businesses. For digital companies, the base size of the market available for targetting is directly proportional to the people having access to the Internet. In terms of sheer numbers, the market size is good enough for a business to flourish, but in terms of potential opportunity that can be tapped there is a big pie out there that would slowly open up as Internet access makes its way through. Mobile phones are fast becoming an alternate channel for Internet access and companies are losing no time in making sure that their offerings are available on small screens in an optimized way. All of them have a mobile application. On an average roughly 10-15 percent of the total traffic is coming through mobile screens. Even MakeMyTrip has substantial transactions coming through mobile, indicating that even in the mobile space travel as a vertical maintains its lead. BookMyShow is another company with a big percentage of mobile-based transactions. My gut feel says that slow penetration of the Internet is actually giving lead time to these businesses to prepare themselves to deal with large population, have the processes fine-tuned, supply chains established and ecosystems prepared. It is giving them an opportunity to scale along with the increasing market size and diversity.

In my opinion, the next big leap will come from the adoption of vernacular languages. Digital businesses are yet to take their first steps in this direction. India is a unique market when it comes to languages. English works well and the percentage of population that can make do with English is substantial. So far most Internet users could use English as the working language. This gave an initial impetus to the businesses, as they had to make no efforts on languages front to begin with. To go beyond the segments of society that speak English they would have to get into vernacular languages otherwise the upper ceiling would be hit soon enough. This is where the challenge begins for these entrepreneurs—how many languages to cater to? There is no one language that dominates the country and a lot of them come with their own script. Quite a few languages like Hindi, Bengali, and south Indian languages have their own sizeable market. This calls for fresh innovations in technologies that can be plug and play for entrepreneurs to convert their content and their interface into various languages without the need of a repeat effort. There are unsolved issues related to regional language fonts and translations. Online search today is still pretty much restricted to English. The only vernacular content that exists today is in multimedia format. I looked at the consumption patterns of print and electronic media content. The number of vernacular newspapers and regional television channels and their respective readership and viewership numbers are staggering compared to English. Assuming that the same population is the consumer for web-based businesses, the need for vernacular reach would be difficult to ignore.

The year 2007 seems to be a marquee year for digital India. Many of the organizations listed here either began in that year or took a leap around that time. It may be because of the substantial number of Internet connections which by this time were large enough to act as the proverbial tipping point for the industry. Many companies that were launched before this could not gain momentum due to very small numbers of users online and lack of facilities like payment gateway solutions. For example, the BigBasket team had launched an online grocery store before dot com bubble but had to convert it into an offline business, but this time they are doing very well as an online grocer. You observe a streak of patriotism when you see companies being launched on 26 January and 15 August, even though technically they are both national holidays. IndiBlogger was launched on 15 August and the name Rang De is inspired from a famous song from the freedom struggle days.

My biggest return on writing this book has been my conversations with all these young entrepreneurs and their teams. I would always cherish them and I hope you enjoyed reading them as much as I enjoyed writing about them.

Reference

New Digital Age by Eric Smidt and Jared Cohen

ACKNOWLEDGEMENTS

IN ONE SENTENCE—THANKS to that every speck of dust that turned the winds in such a way that this work came successfully through my hands. An author's work is a culmination of his or her experiences and some universal forces sending the right support their way by way of people who meet them at the crossroads. There are innumerable people who would have helped shape my interests, my thoughts, and even my expressions. Some have contributed directly and many more indirectly. I am not sure if there is a way to say thank you to all of them, but here are a few who directly contributed to the book. All the entrepreneurs featured in this book deserve a big thank you for sparing time and effort to talk to me and share information with me. Your enthusiasm and your passion will always stay with me. I wish I could feature some more of you, and hope there would be another time to do that.

Some people without whom this book may have remained only an idea—Hrradyash Deshpande, Director DYPDC who first approached me for India Innovates Series published by CII, and connected me with Seema Gupta and Jibak Dasgupta of CII with whom this idea was first shared and shaped. Thank you IAMAI for letting me use your research reports for the book.

I want to thank my management mentor Ramesh S—someone I really respect for his way with people and organizations. Jatin Desai—my favourite innovation consultant and a very dear friend was my sounding board for the idea; unfortunately he left this world before this book could be out.

Thanks to Kiruba Shankar and Lakshmi Rebecca for connecting me to many entrepreneur friends of theirs. Thanks to my young entrepreneur friends Santosh S. Kumar and Inder Sen for listening to my ideas, for suggesting names, and for asking why are you not featuring us. Some day.

A spouse is a co-author of the book in more than one ways and it is very awkward to say thanks to them publicly—but thanks Shashi for all your patience and for letting me have that time and space that I needed to write this book.

Thanks Rukun for connecting me to team Random House—Radhika Marwah, Milee Ashwarya, and Caroline Newbury. It was a pleasure working with you and learning a bit about the world of publishing.

A NOTE ON THE AUTHOR

Anuradha Goyal wears many hats to pursue her three prime passions—innovation, travel, and books. She studies business innovation, especially business models, and blogs about them. She has earlier co-authored the India Innovates Series published by CII showcasing innovations from across the country. She was a jury member for *Economic Times* Power of Ideas Contest in 2010. Her papers on business innovation have appeared in various journals and forums.

She is one of India's leading travel bloggers, writing a popular travel blog for a decade now. Her travel story has been published as part of an anthology 'Celebrating India' and her paper on 'in-city travel' appeared in travel journal *Earth*. Her stories regularly appear in various print and online publications. She has close to 400 book reviews to her credit on her book reviews blog. She is a keen student of Indian art history. She regularly speaks on these topics at various conferences and institutes.

In her earlier avatar she worked in the IT industry for over a decade. She studied computer applications for her master's degree and physics for her graduate degree at Panjab University.

She currently lives in Goa.